LAW OF THE YUKON

TO

RON

From PAUL & Tara
THALHOFER

We felt you really appreciate
this book

Paul Lara

Dedication

To my dear friend and partner, Rob Ingram, who provided inspiration, encouragement, editing, childcare, cooking and humour during the writing of this book.

LAW OF THE YUKON

A Pictorial History of the Mounted Police in the Yukon

by Helene Dobrowolsky

Royal Northwest Mounted Police and women of the Imperial Order of the Daughters of the Empire in front of the Commissioner's Residence, Dawson City, 1915. At this ceremony, they unveiled the monument commemorating the members of the Lost Patrol.

LOST MOOSE

THE YUKON PUBLISHERS

1995

Published by Lost Moose, the Yukon Publishers
58 Kluane Crescent, Whitehorse, Yukon, Canada Y1A 3G7
phone 403-668-5076, 403-668-3441, fax 403-668-6223

Canadian Cataloguing in Publication Data
Dobrowolsky, Helene.
Law of the Yukon

Includes bibliographical references and index.
ISBN 0-9694612-6-7 (bound) -- ISBN 0-9694612-8-3 (pbk.)

1. Royal Canadian Mounted Police--History. 2. Royal Canadian Mounted Police--History--Pictorial works. 3. Police--Yukon Territory-History. 4. Police--Yukon Territory--History--Pictorial works. I. Title.
FC3216.2.D62 1995   971 9'102   C95-910263-9
F1093.D62 1995

Maps by Tanya Handley
Design by Mike Rice
Production by K-L Services, Whitehorse
The title for this book was inspired by the Robert Service poem, "The Law of the Yukon."

Printed and bound in Canada

Glenora on the Stikine River, B.C., 1898. *From this settlement, the Yukon Field Force blazed a trail overland to Teslin Lake in the Yukon. Watercolour by YFF soldier John Tinck.*

Front cover photographs, clockwise from upper left: **Maj. Gen. Sam Steele; Andrew Kunizzi—former police guide; Kate Ryan; Cst. Frenchy Chartrand and his lead dog; Transfer of Command Parade, Whitehorse, 1992; Cst. Karen Olito; Sgt. Engel and members at Fort Constantine, ca. 1896; S/Cst. John Moses with his son.**
Back cover photograph: **Cst. Joe Kessler at Forty Mile.**

FOREWORD

The story of the Mounted Police presence in the Yukon is interesting and compelling. One hundred years ago the discovery of rich fields of gold in the Klondike precipitated a flood of avaricious men and women to the northern territory. Suddenly, this pristine northern frontier was threatened with conflict and disorder. The presence of large numbers of Americans also called into question Canada's sovereignty in the area. Experienced by two decades of enforcing the law on the western frontier the North-West Mounted Police were called upon to meet the challenge of the Yukon.

The accomplishments of the Mounted Police in this northern setting have long stirred the imagination of Canadians and indeed, of much of the world. Popular accounts of the deeds of these Mounties helped establish the force as a national icon. However, until this book by Helene Dobrowolsky no pictorial history has been devoted to explaining and illustrating the force's role in the development of the territory. It is fitting that this void is now filled as part of the commemoration of the 100th anniversary of the Royal Canadian Mounted Police in the Yukon.

I am very pleased to recommend *Law of the Yukon* to all those interested in this fascinating subject. Helene Dobrowolsky recognised that the history of the force in the Yukon can be told at two levels. First, the story of how the Mounted Police performed its arduous duties must be recounted in detail.

But second, the readers must be made to appreciate that the members of the force were not alone in facing the challenges of the frontier. Right by their side were the native people, the women and the other members of the community. It was only by action in common that so much was accomplished. This book explains and richly illustrates all of this.

Dr. William Beahen
Force Historian
Royal Canadian Mounted Police

In "Centennial Patrol," Yukon artist Chris Caldwell looks at the past and present of the Yukon Mounties from her unique perspective.

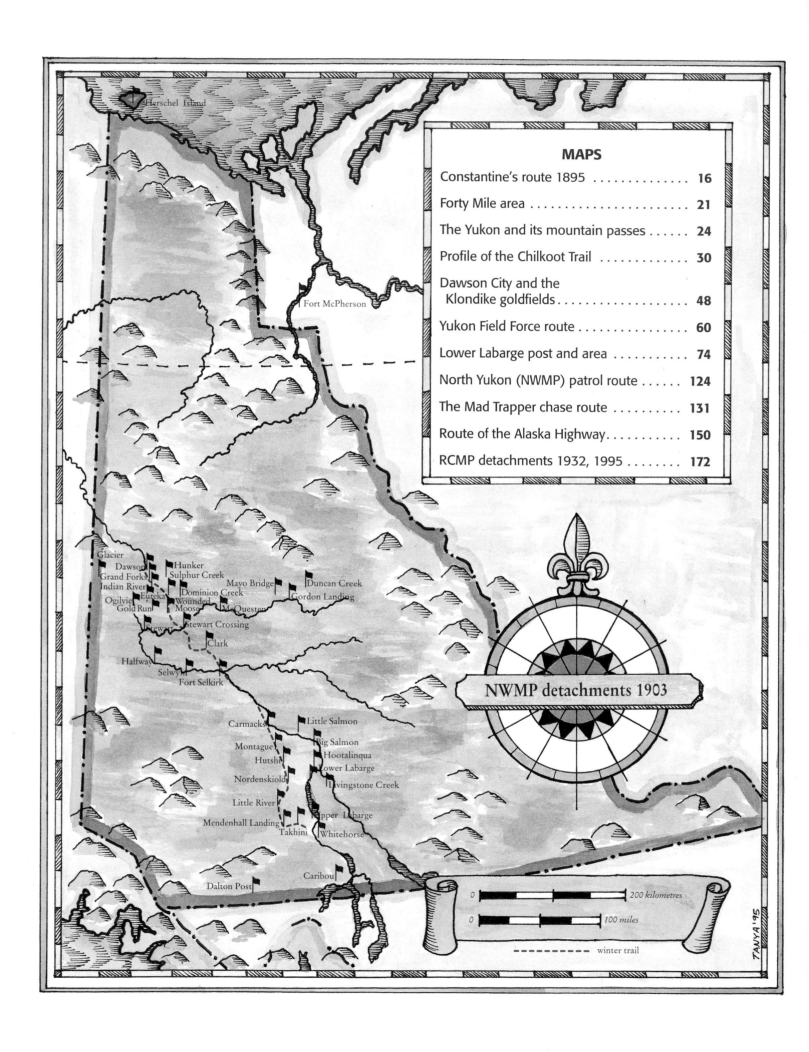

Herschel Island

Fort McPherson

MAPS

Constantine's route 1895 . . . . **16**

Forty Mile area **21**

The Yukon and its mountain passes **24**

Profile of the Chilkoot Trail **30**

Dawson City and the
　Klondike goldfields **48**

Yukon Field Force route **60**

Lower Labarge post and area **74**

North Yukon (NWMP) patrol route **124**

The Mad Trapper chase route **131**

Route of the Alaska Highway **150**

RCMP detachments 1932, 1995 . . . . **172**

Glacier
Dawson
Grand Forks
Indian River
Ogilvie
Gold Run
Eureka
Hunker
Sulphur Creek
Dominion Creek
Wounded
Moose
Mayo Bridge
Duncan Creek
Gordon Landing
McQuesten
Stewart
Stewart Crossing
Clark
Halfway
Selwyn
Fort Selkirk

Carmacks
Montague
Hutshi
Nordenskiold
Little River
Mendenhall Landing
Takhini
Little Salmon
Big Salmon
Hootalinqua
Lower Labarge
Livingstone Creek
Upper Labarge
Whitehorse
Caribou
Dalton Post

NWMP detachments 1903

0   200 kilometres

0   100 miles

- - - - - - - - winter trail

TANYA '95

ACKNOWLEDGEMENTS

This book could not have been written without the assistance and support of many individuals and institutions. Max Fraser of Lost Moose Publishing approached me with the idea of preparing a pictorial history of the Mounties' 100 years in the Yukon, then coaxed me through the many stages of getting it researched and written. Most of the travel and research for this project was funded by the Heritage Studies Program of the Yukon government's Heritage Branch. The MacBride Museum in Whitehorse gave me access to their Mounted Police research material as well as funding part of my research at the RCMP Museum in Regina and the Glenbow Museum and Archives in Calgary. A grant from the Yukon Foundation's Hougen Family Fund purchased reproductions of most of the photographs shown in this book. I appreciate the support and assistance of "M" Division members: Superintendent Hank Moorlag, Inspector Russ Juby, Sergeant Bob MacAdam, Corporal Dave Edwards, Sergeant Al Hubley and Corporal Ron Bocock.

Adeline Charlie of Old Crow interviewed Charlie Peter Charlie and Andrew Tizya, who shared their memories of working with the police in the Northern Yukon. Buffy Genier helped liaise with Mr. Charlie and Mr. Tizya. Clara May spoke of her experiences as a nurse at Fort Yukon and police wife at Old Crow. Over the years, retired Corporal G.I. Cameron has generously assisted many historians and researchers, including myself. I am grateful to Mr. Cameron and Dr. William Beahen for permission to quote from their recorded interview. Retired member Dennis Levy spoke to me about the formation of "M" Division. Former Constable Derek Parkes let me use his wonderful pictures and shared interesting anecdotes about his time at Herschel Island. He is but one of the many Mounted Police whose writings and photographs have fleshed out the bones of this history. The following people also shared family photographs, documents and stories: Olga Anderson, Roger S. Brown, Richard A. Dickson, Mabel Johnson, Katherine McKernan, Nancy Pope, Bill Pringle, Nick Veres and Eloise Watt. The Inuvialuit Social Development Corporation gave me permission to use interview excerpts with Inuvialuit elders documented in the *Yukon North Slope Inuvialuit Oral History*. The painting on page 175 is reproduced with permission from the artist, Jim Robb, and the owner, former member Nick Veres. The Chris Caldwell centennial poster is reproduced with permission of the artist and the RCMP.

Dr. William Beahen, Glenn Wright and Glen Gordon of the RCMP Public Affairs Directorate in Ottawa were most patient and helpful with my many inquiries. Bill MacKay, curator of the RCMP Museum at Regina, provided much help during my short but fruitful visit to the museum. Normand Fortier, the RCMP Archivist at the National Archives of Canada, facilitated access to everything I needed while I was in Ottawa, while the NAC reading room staff helped me work my way through many stacks of file boxes. The staff at the Glenbow Archives in Calgary were equally cooperative. The Vancouver Museum kindly gave me permission to use the E.B. Brown drawings. Parks Canada in Whitehorse gave me access to their research collection. Sharon Uno at the RCMP Library was most helpful. I continue to be indebted to the staff at Yukon Archives for all their help on this, the latest of many projects that have relied on this excellent facility. Thanks also to the *Yukon News* and *Whitehorse Star* for additional photographs and research material.

Louise Profeit-LeBlanc offered valuable assistance with the First Nations chapter. Patricia Halladay shared her Yukon Field Force research material. Meteorologist Herb Wahl explained weather patterns on the mountain summits. Al Alcock fielded some out-of-the-blue questions about military rank and procedure. Historian and author Dick North was a great help with the patrol chapter. Dave Neufeld, Yukon and Western Arctic Historian of Parks Canada, improved the manuscript with his rigorous editing. Others who reviewed this manuscript in part or in whole include Flo Whyard, Brent Slobodin, Patricia Halladay, Emily Krangle-Long and Julie Cruikshank. Once again, I enjoyed working with the crew from Lost Moose—Mike Rice, Alison Reid, Max Fraser, Arnold Hedstrom, Wynne Krangle and Peter Long—on the design and editing portion of this project.

My deepest thanks to you all. The opinions expressed in this book are mine alone, as are any factual errors.

Helene Dobrowolsky
Whitehorse, 1995

The Officers' and Sergeants' mess of A Battery, Yukon Field Force at Dawson City, 1898. Watercolour by Yukon Field Force soldier John Tinck.

PREFACE

The Mountie, standing tall in red serge tunic and stetson, is one of the most potent and recognizable Canadian symbols. The Yukon Mounted Police evoke images of Hollywood's Sergeant Preston and his dog, Yukon King, fighting a blinding snowstorm to track a fugitive or rescue a lost soul. There is scant truth to the fictional version but behind the myth are real people and true stories that require no embroidery to enthral the reader.

The Yukon was never a lawless frontier, although it certainly had all the makings. In the waning years of the nineteenth century, the Yukon was home to First Nations people who had lived here for thousands of years with their own systems of government and justice. A few prospectors began to trickle into the country but even they had a rough, but workable, system of self-government. Richer gold discoveries swelled the number of miners and others looking for a more direct path to riches. Their simple democracy threatened to collapse into chaos and violence. Enter the Mounted Police.

When thousands of gold-crazed stampeders poured into the Yukon during the Klondike gold rush of 1897-98, the Mounties were there to meet them. In the years that followed, a small force patrolled thousands of square miles of wilderness to maintain order, represent the Crown, and perhaps most importantly, look after the welfare of isolated miners, trappers, traders and First Nations people. The story of the RCMP in the Yukon is closely-bound to the founding and development of the Territory as a political entity. But it is also the story of the Mounties themselves, their lives and their work.

The legend of the forthright Mountie from the Yukon still appeals to the viewing public. The popular television program, "Due South," features an RCMP constable from the Yukon transplanted to Chicago. Canadian actor Paul Gross plays the hero, Benton Fraser. His dog Diefenbaker, part wolf and completely deaf, joins him on his American adventures.

The Mounties did not stand alone in keeping peace in the Yukon. They relied on the skills of First Nations special constables, interpreters, guides and artisans. These able people led the Mounted Police through the land they knew so well, hunted and fished for the police and their dogs, and introduced them to their culture and languages. Women worked for the police as prison matrons, gold inspectors and tailors. Mountie wives were the unofficial partners who ran the isolated detachments during their husbands' absence on lengthy patrols.

I review the major situations and events of the force's history in the Yukon so the reader can appreciate the milieu in which the police were expected to perform and the national importance of what they did. More particularly, however, I look at individuals, both outstanding and ordinary. Here are the well-known leaders like Sam Steele and Charles Constantine; I also portray the people in the field who were the heart blood of the force. Many fascinating stories were found outside the official record in photographs, diaries, letters and oral history interviews. I have quoted excerpts from these journals and correspondence using the original spelling, capitalization and punctuation. Although the writers may not always have had a firm grasp of current grammar, nonetheless they expressed themselves forcefully and with eloquence. These glimpses into the lives of wives, First Nations guides and special constables, and the staff of small detachments provide an insight into the daily life and conditions of the times. No history can ever be comprehensive, however, and many stories remain to be told.

During this centennial of the first Mounted Police detachment in the Yukon, it is most appropriate to look back at the force's contributions to Yukon history. For me, however, it is just as important to bring to light the lives and endeavours of the real people who played such an important role in building the Yukon. Their stories are better than Hollywood any day.

Many radio and television fans of the 1940s and 1950s only knew of the Yukon as the home of Sergeant Preston and his faithful companions, Rex the horse and that remarkable dog, Yukon King.

Drilling on horseback in NWMP compound at Whitehorse, ca. 1902.

INTRODUCTION 12

CHAPTER 1   THE FIRST POST – FORT CONSTANTINE 16

CHAPTER 2   THE KLONDIKE GOLD RUSH 24

CHAPTER 3   REINFORCEMENTS MEET THE GREAT STAMPEDE 48

CHAPTER 4   AFTER THE RUSH 64

CHAPTER 5   FIRST NATIONS PEOPLE AND THE POLICE 82

CHAPTER 6   CRIME, CONSPIRACY AND COURT 94

CHAPTER 7   WOMEN AND THE FORCE 104

CHAPTER 8   PATROLLING THE YUKON 120

CHAPTER 9   AT EASE 140

CHAPTER 10   WARTIME AND ALASKA HIGHWAY CONSTRUCTION 150

CHAPTER 11   DOG STORIES.. 162

CHAPTER 12   POLICING TODAY 172

HONOUR ROLL   184

REFERENCE   ENDNOTES 186

             SELECTED BIBLIOGRAPHY 188

             ILLUSTRATIONS 189

             INDEX 191

The formation of the force

… the most important matter of the future is the preservation of order in the Northwest and little as Canada may like it she has to stable her elephant.

— Alexander Morris, Lieutenant Governor of Manitoba and Northwest Territories, 1872[1]

In 1869, Canada purchased the huge area known as Rupert's Land from the Hudson's Bay Company. Dubbed the Northwest Territories, it included what later became the prairie provinces and northern territories. Canada's first prime minister, Sir John A. Macdonald, determined that Canada's westward expansion and settlement should be orderly and peaceable. He was also mindful of the presence of American settlers at the southern border and the possibility of U.S. encroachment. Over the next few years, problems came from American whiskey traders who set up their deadly trade near the Canadian border.[2]

Colonel P. Robertson-Ross, Adjutant-General of the Canadian militia, suggested a police force be formed to safeguard the west. He also recommended adopting the famous red tunic for its associations with British authority.[3] The year 1873 marked the formation of the North-West Mounted Police. The force was based on two models: the Royal Irish Constabulary, and the units of mounted rifles used by the Northern Army during the American Civil War. At its inception, this was essentially a colonial force representing the central government in Ottawa. The Mounted Police were given many federal responsibilities, including customs collection and judicial duties.[4]

Most of its first officers had a military background. Recruits had to be "of a sound constitution, able to ride, active and able-bodied, of good character, and between the ages of eighteen and forty." They also had to be literate in either English or French.[5] For the next 20 years, the Mounted Police rode the plains from their stockaded forts to enforce treaties, maintain order and establish Canadian authority. This was the force charged with bringing law and order to the Yukon.

The Yukon situation

In the 1880s, the land now known as Canada's Yukon Territory was an uncharted blank on the North American map. This so-called frontier was the ancestral homeland to northern First Nations people[6] who travelled the country on their seasonal round of fishing, hunting, trapping and gathering. From the 1840s, these people and the rich furs they harvested attracted the Hudson's Bay Company and other fur traders. Missionaries followed the traders, seeking new converts.

First Nations people in birchbark canoes on the Yukon River at Fort Selkirk, 1883.

Later still, prospectors travelled north from the goldfields of California and British Columbia to explore the Yukon River watershed in Canada and Alaska. Enough paydirt was found to attract others. The traders began carrying mining supplies as well as trade goods for furs.

The increased activity drew official interest to the area. Both the United States and Canada sponsored exploratory expeditions to the region in the 1880s. The reports from Frederick Schwatka's 1883 military expedition for the American government, and the Canadian expedition, led by George Dawson in 1887, proved to be valuable sources of information during the Klondike gold rush a decade later.

The first major gold strike came in September 1886 when two miners found

Placer mining on Miller Creek, 1894.

coarse gold 23 miles above the mouth of the Fortymile River, close to the Alaskan border.[7] Word spread and by the summer of 1887, 300 miners had extracted $75,000 worth of gold from the Fortymile area. Alaska Commercial Company trader Jack McQuesten soon set up a post and, within a few years, Forty Mile was the largest settlement on the Yukon River.[8]

This new northern metropolis was a hodgepodge of simply-built log cabins with pole and dirt roofs and doors made from roughly-sawn slabs. Glass was a rarity and the crude windows might be made of scraped, untanned hide, a piece of white cotton canvas, or bottles laid on end then chinked with moss. Miners built simple furniture from poles and chunks of log. Few owned metal stoves; most did their heating and cooking with simple rock fireplaces.

Early self-government was equally crude, home-made and functional. The mainly

American populace introduced the miners' meeting or miners' committee, an import from the California goldfields. Members of the mining camp gathered to settle disputes. More formal gatherings elected a chairman and recording secretary. After both sides presented their cases, there was a general discussion followed by a vote. The judgment of the majority was accepted as law. The loser might be fined, or in extreme cases, banished. In small camps, all accepted the fairness of this rough justice.

As the population of the Fortymile area grew, however, the decisions became erratic. More meetings were held in saloons and decisions tended to favour the most free-spending disputant. Fines were often levied for trivial causes in order to buy drinks for the house.

The prevalence of liquor and its effect on the local population alarmed Anglican Bishop

William Bompas. In August 1892, he had established a mission for the local First Nations people. He campaigned against those who illegally sold liquor to the native people or taught them to brew their own "hootch," a lethal variety of home-brewed alcohol. Bompas wrote government officials, demanding that police be dispatched to the area to stop the illegal liquor trade.

The bishop was backed by C.H. Hamilton, the assistant manager of the North American Trading and Transportation Company (NATT). The American trader drew attention to whiskey-smuggling and distillation of hootch, and requested police protection. His employer, John J. Healy, also lobbied to bring law and order to the frontier. One of his letters went to an influential acquaintance, Superintendent Samuel B. Steele of the North-West Mounted Police.[9]

After neglecting the region for years, Canadian officials finally awoke to the fact that a potentially profitable corner of the country was being occupied by American miners and traders. Forty Mile was close to the Alaskan border and many were unaware that they were actually mining Canadian ground.[10] Until 1895, the community's post office was an American operation, with mail collected and sent downriver via Alaska.

William Ogilvie was a former member of George Dawson's 1887 Yukon expedition and Canadian representative on the international boundary commission. He advised Ottawa to show the flag in the Fortymile area. In April 1894, the government turned to the North-West Mounted Police, instructing them to send an experienced officer on a fact-finding mission. The job went to Inspector Charles Constantine, who requested Staff Sergeant Charles Brown as his companion.[11]

Mounties to the Yukon

In May 1894, Constantine reported to Ottawa for briefing. His orders were to check into the liquor trade, establish customs collection and look into the situation of the First Nations people—but not to commit the government to any action on their behalf. Finally, he had to determine how best to police the region.

In June, Constantine and Brown steamed up the west coast to Dyea on the Alaska panhandle, then negotiated with people of the Chilkat First Nation to pack their gear over the Chilkoot Pass. From there the Mounties hiked to the Yukon's headwater lakes, where Constantine hired a few miners to help them build a rough boat, then followed the lakes and Yukon River down to Forty Mile. The

entire trip took 53 days. Within a few years, thousands of goldseekers would follow this same arduous route into the country.

Constantine kept a diary describing his trip, the surrounding countryside, the people he met, trading posts he visited, and any mining news. Below are a few excerpts.[12]

Friday 29th June Left on S.S. Chilkat [from Juneau] at 3 a.m. for Dar Yea (Chilkoot), 9 persons going on to "40 Mile" including 2 women and boy. Arrived at Wilson & Healy's at 4 p.m. Cost $10.00 to get selves and goods from steamer, distance about 12 miles.

Friday 13th July River rising. Cold rain & wind. 2 miners came along about 11 a.m. will make boat and help us through. Made a bargain. Have to go as far as way down Lake Bennett to get timber. Will take 6 days to saw lumber & make boat. This is a God-send to us as there was no knowing when we would have got here but for this. Brown sick with neuralgia…

Saturday 4th August…Arrived at Ogilvie, Hooper & LeDuc's [Harper & Ladue's] trading post at 9 p.m. and camped for night. Bought a few groceries. 60 Mile Creek comes into the Yukon opposite this trading post. Millar Creek runs into 60 Mile about 60 miles up and is said to be very rich…40 Mile is, I hear, being deserted by all except Whiskey men. The decent miners

Forty Mile settlement, ca. 1895. Fort Cudahy is in the foreground on the west side of the Fortymile River.

are wintering at other places. People are wanting force to stop this business.

Tuesday 7th August...*Arrived at 40 Mile at 11.20... Am glad trip so far is done. Was well tired & sick of the everlasting river. Had just enough grub to see us through, getting here with about enough for another day...*

Constantine stayed in Forty Mile for a month gathering information. He interviewed miners, traders and, with the aid of Bishop Bompas, some First Nations people. He checked out the extent of the mining activity, the miners' nationalities, confirmed reports of

the illegal liquor trade and, despite some resistance, instituted customs collection.

In early September, he caught the season's last steamer, travelling downriver to St. Michael, Alaska. Brown remained behind to collect customs over the winter. By this time, the heyday of Forty Mile was nearly at an end. Many miners were moving further downriver to new strikes at Circle, Alaska, while others chose to stay on their claims and avoid the saloons of Forty Mile.

In his subsequent report, Constantine described his trip and the situation at Forty

Mile. He recommended that a force of 40 be sent to the Yukon, stating that:

> *The miners are very jealous of what they consider their rights, and from what I can see and learn, any enforcement of the different laws will have to be backed up with a strong force at least for a time.*[13]

The Canadian government's other Yukon expert, William Ogilvie, disagreed. He felt that ten members should be more than adequate. The government compromised, deciding to send 20 North-West Mounted Police north the following year. From these beginnings, the Mounted Police began its hundred-year association with the Yukon Territory.[14]

Move to unhorse Mounties

The Yukon assignment came at a crucial point in North-West Mounted Police history. The force was fighting for its life. The NWMP had served 15 of its 20 years under a Conservative government. While in opposition, the Liberals had questioned the existence of the force on constitutional and economic grounds. They opposed using a federal agency to police the settled west, feeling this should be a local responsibility. They also saw the police as a great expense and a long-standing instrument of Conservative patronage. When the Liberals formed the government in 1896, many felt an excellent way to cut costs was to eliminate an organization supposedly staffed by loyal Conservatives.

The force proved to be too valuable to be discarded, however. The Mounties demonstrated their value during the Klondike gold rush by keeping order as well as asserting Canadian sovereignty and administrative control. The Liberals also began to exercise their own patronage powers, directing the force to use suppliers friendly to the government. After NWMP Commissioner Laurence William Herchmer retired in 1900, the government appointed Aylesworth Bowen Perry, a Liberal supporter, to the commissioner's job and allowed the NWMP to continue.[15]

Inspector Charles Constantine.

15

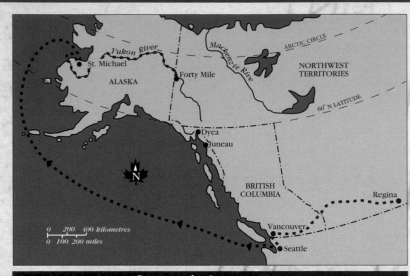

CHAPTER 1

Constantine's route 1895

Off to the Yukon. Mounted Police aboard the steamer Excelsior, which would carry them from Seattle to St. Michael, Alaska. Inspector Constantine's son, Francis, stands by the life belt.

"Alone in the country"

The force sent in …should be of not less than two years' service and from twenty-two to thirty years of age, of large and powerful build,—men who do not drink. It is to be remembered that they are alone in the country, to all intents and purposes shut out from the outer world for eight months in the year.

—Inspector Charles Constantine, 1894[1]

The Yukon's first North-West Mounted Police detachment left Regina by train on June 1, 1895. Four days later, they boarded the steamer *Excelsior* at Seattle. Their mission—to extend Canadian government authority and law enforcement to this most northerly corner of the British Empire. Two women and a child accompanied the expedition—Mrs. Henrietta Armstrong Constantine, Inspector D'Arcy Strickland's wife Tannis, and the Constantines' son, Francis.

This time, Constantine avoided the gruelling trip over the Chilkoot Pass and down the Yukon River. Instead, he and his small force steamed up the west coast, around the Alaskan coastline, then inland up the Yukon River from its mouth at St. Michael, Alaska. It was a less strenuous trip but longer—much longer. By the time they reached the endless flats of the lower Yukon River, all were weary of monotonous scenery, voracious mosquitoes, unbearable heat and one another. A few years later, Staff Sergeant Hayne described his own misgivings and depression at this time:

…in the deadly monotony of our surroundings on that first day on the river, with idle hands and the eternal daylight, it was impossible not to feel low-spirited… And at the end of it—what? To be landed for two years in a miners' camp, with no accommodation prepared for us, none of the daily pleasures and varieties to which we had been accustomed, and no certainty of any fresh meat during the whole of the time; not knowing how our presence there would be regarded, nor even how far our jurisdiction extended. Verily as bad an attack of the "blues" as one can ever wish to have…[2]

The journey improved further upriver. The scenery became more varied and moose were spotted, providing sport and a welcome change of diet. On July 24, the party reached Fort Cudahy, the North American Trading and Transportation Company trading post, across the river from Forty Mile. The NATT post consisted of a few log store buildings and a sawmill.

The first Yukon contingent at Fort Constantine. (L-R) Front row: **Cst. Pinkerton, Cst. Jenkins, Cst. Jenkins, Cst. Telford, and S/Sgt. Hayne;** *Middle row:* **Cst. McKellar, Cst. Sinclair, Cst. Murray, Francis Constantine (boy), Insp. Constantine, Insp. Strickland, Dr. Willis and Cst. Churchill;** *Back row:* **Cst. Brother, Cst. Gowler, Cst. Thornton, Cst. Brown, Cst. Webster, Cpl. Engel, Cpl. Newbrook and Cst. Ward.**

Fort Constantine
11 April 1898

The interior of the square at Fort Constantine, spring 1898. Buildings from left to right are the quarters of: S/Sgts. Engel and Haynes, the Stricklands, the Constantines, Dr. Willis and the store/office.

A more formal portrait of part of the Yukon NWMP detachment, Regina, May 25, 1895. (L-R) Front row: __, **Insp. Strickland, Insp. Constantine, Sgt. Murray Henry Edward Hayne, Cpl. Edward Newbrook;** *Reclining:* **Cpl. Engel;** *Back row:* __, __, **Cst. Telford, Cst. Gowler, Cst. J. Murray.**

"They stood the hard work well" – Building Fort Constantine

…we had to aim at erecting as near a model as was·possible under the circumstances of a decent civilized set of barracks, in which we should be able to conform to the more important of the requirements of discipline and civilization.

— Sgt. M.H.E. Hayne[3]

The men have worked well and hard, long hours and in bad weather. They have kept their health.

— Inspector Constantine, October 1895[4]

The party's new home was a mossy spruce swamp just upriver of Fort Cudahy. As there was no dry ground on which to pitch tents, the Mounted Police thankfully rented cabins from the trading company while they built their own quarters.

This was a major undertaking. Inspector Strickland and a party of eight had to travel about 30 miles further upriver to find construction-quality timber. For three weeks,

The building logs were squared at the sawmill at Fort Cudahy. The slabs were used for roof coverings. Inspector Strickland overlooks sawmill operation, ca. 1896.

Ice jam on the Yukon River, December 1895. Six Mounties on the Yukon River ice, Fort Constantine in the background.

The post buildings were set around a parade square, 100 by 80 feet. Fort Constantine, ca. 1895.

the logging crew endured torrential rains and "flies beyond description" as they cut and rafted over 400 building logs to Fort Cudahy. An additional 250 logs had to be purchased to complete the post.[5] The remainder of the men cleared the site, built drains and levelled the ground using a plough drawn by dogs.

All bitterly lamented the lack of horses as they manhandled the 35-foot logs. The building crew dragged the logs from Fort Cudahy's sawmill to the construction site over a simple trolley with log tracks. A dog team could pull three or four logs at a time. The police made the mistake of all novice builders in the far north—they stripped the ground cover until they reached the rock-hard permafrost. The exposed permafrost eventually melted, causing the structures to sink and tilt in the muddy ground.

In January 1896, Inspector Constantine datelined his annual report from "the most northerly military or semi-military post in the British Empire."[6] He proudly reported that his men had built a guard room, staff-sergeants' quarters, two officers' quarters, assistant surgeon's quarters, hospital, office and store room, carpenter's shop, and wash and bath room. The post took on a smart military appearance with the installation of a 50-foot flagpole and the beginnings of a stockade of vertical poles.

Over the fall and winter, the Mounties redirected their energies to obtaining firewood. During the extremely cold weather of midwinter, the post stoves burned two cords of wood a day. The detachment needed 315 cords to get through the winter.[7] The buildings were not cozy: the green timber walls sweated, the slab and sod roofs leaked in warmer weather, cold came up from the damp ground through the uninsulated floor, and the green firewood gave off little heat.

While most of their efforts were directed toward construction and survival, the Mounties did carry out some traditional police work. There were few crimes, none serious, and little objection to paying customs duties. The very presence of the police put an end to most of the illegal whiskey trade, while those irked by the presence of the force moved downriver to Circle, Alaska. Constantine felt the burden of being the sole civil authority, however. He urgently requested that civil courts be established as well as an office to register legal transactions. Over the next few years, he also asked for a steam launch for summer patrols, a request repeatedly ignored by his superiors in Regina.[8]

The most serious challenge to police authority came in the spring of 1896. A miner with a lease or "lay" on a Glacier Creek claim refused to pay his labourers.[9] The workers demanded their wages from the mine's owners. When the owners refused to pay the debts of their lessee, a miners' meeting determined that the claim should be sold and the labourers paid with the proceeds. The original owners protested to the NWMP. When the so-called new owner came to register his claim, Inspector Constantine refused to recognize the sale or register the transaction.

After the man left, "breathing defiance," Constantine determined it was time to exert police authority. He sent Inspector Strickland with a party of 12 heavily-armed police to the disputed mining claim. They evicted the illegal claimant, occupied the claim and refused to deal with the miners' committee. After two days, the miners gave in and the police action was accepted unquestioned. The police had proved to the miners that they could enforce security of tenure, something the miners' meetings had never been able to do.[10]

"The gold excitement is at fever heat"

There is one thing certain, unless the Govt. are prepared to put a strong force in here next year they had better take out what few are now here. The rush in here will exceed any previous year.

— Inspector Constantine, September 1896[11]

By late summer 1896, Constantine was satisfied with the progress of his detachment. Work on the buildings was almost complete and the post was ready for winter. The Canadian government had finally sent a customs collector north. Unfortunately, by then the Mounties of Fort Constantine barely had a community to police.

On August 17, 1896, George Carmack and his First Nations companions, Skookum Jim and Tagish Charlie, struck the long-awaited bonanza on Rabbit Creek, a tributary of the Klondike River. They had barely registered their claim at Forty Mile when the rush began. The town emptied overnight. As word spread to the outlying diggings, everyone dropped their tools in their haste to stake their own claims.

Constantine was quick to understand the implications of the rush and consequent demands on the police. He immediately wrote Commissioner Herchmer to report the strike, requesting immediate reinforcements and stating the need for additional posts, particularly at the mouth of the Klondike.

As if the prospect of policing thousands of stampeders was not enough to deal with, the presence of gold provided its own problems. That fall, two constables took their discharge. Goldfield labourers earned up to $15 per day and the meager police pay of $1 a day held little appeal. Constantine lamented that he would be unable to induce his force, most afflicted with gold fever, to build a new post at Dawson at their present rate of pay.[12]

It was a grim situation. Food and supplies were running low. The clothing and boots issued to the men had long since worn out and they had to buy their own replacements. The civil duties multiplied. Constantine again appealed for court representatives, stating he did not care to be "judge, jury and executioner."[13] Most crucially, Constantine worried his small force would be powerless in the face of a concerted public uprising. He demanded a Maxim machine gun to even the odds and fretted when his request was not taken seriously.[14] Obviously, Constantine felt that he and his men were in desperate straits—but their greatest challenges still lay ahead.

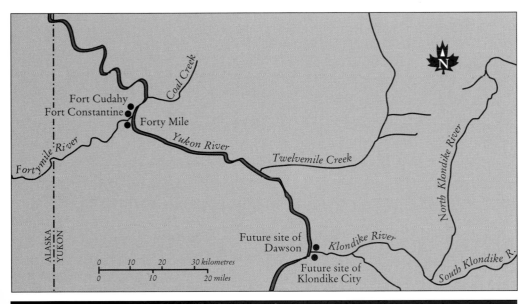

Forty Mile area

First Nations fishing camp at the mouth of the Klondike River in 1895, later the site of Klondike City.

> *Because of his strength of character, sound judgment, and physical strength, he was selected for much of the pioneer work of the force. He was the first to command the Yukon Territory; and in the early days of the gold rush, his tact and firmness established the reputation of that gold camp as the most orderly in the world.*
>
> **— Commissioner A.B. Perry**[15]

When Inspector Charles Constantine was first dispatched to the Yukon in 1894, he was already a 24-year military veteran. He had served with the Red River expedition, as chief of police for the newly-formed province of Manitoba and adjutant with the 91st Winnipeg Light Infantry during the second Riel rebellion. When he applied for a NWMP commission, he was taken on as an inspector.

Constantine was the first Mounted Police officer to travel to the Yukon and he commanded the first Yukon detachment. After a year of northern service, he was promoted to superintendent.

Since supplies and mail, including orders, arrived only once a year, much depended on Constantine's on-the-spot decisions and innate good sense. It is largely due to his unflagging efforts to convince his superiors of the need for more Mounted Police, that the streets of Dawson were safe during the Klondike gold rush. During his time, the Yukon force increased from 20 to 264, with 31 posts throughout the territory and northern British Columbia. When Constantine finally left the Yukon on June 23, 1898 his diary entry simply read, "Left Dawson per Str. *C.H. Hamilton*. Thank God for the release."[16]

Constantine's subsequent career was no less challenging. In 1903, he led an expedition down the Mackenzie River to establish the first police post north of the Arctic Circle. Two years later, he was put in charge of a project to construct a road from Fort St. John through the Rockies to the Yukon. This extremely laborious, and ultimately fruitless, task proved to be too much for Constantine and he contracted the illness that led to his death seven years later.[17]

Sgt. M.H.E. Hayne relaxes outside his quarters at Fort Constantine, ca. 1896.

I and all of us had been eye-witnesses and actors in one of the most astonishing pieces of pioneering that has ever been known. We had been alternately and at once guardians of the law, Her Majesty's representatives, Arctic explorers, pioneers in a new and unknown country, goldminers, and a host of other things besides.[18]

Staff Sergeant Hayne was the first of the Mounted Police writer/photographers to tell the world of his Yukon experiences. In anticipation of his trip north, he ordered a "complete set of photographic apparatus" from Montreal.

Hayne vividly described the difficulties of early northern photo processing in the land of the midnight sun. His first darkroom experiments took place on the *Portus B. Weare* during the

1600-mile trip up the Yukon River. Finding it almost impossible to make his cabin lightproof, he tried the ship's hold where he stood wrapped in a blanket, knee-deep in bilge water while he processed his plates. Despite these efforts, most of his plates were fogged or completely spoiled due to light leakage. Hayne also lost a packet of photographic plates when the heat of the ship's boiler dissolved the gelatine in the film.[19] Fortunately, his later efforts were successful and his photographs are a valuable record of the construction of Fort Constantine, his companions and his surroundings.

Hayne joined the force in December 1882. He served in various locations around the west

before volunteering for the first Yukon detachment. He was the only one of that first group of members to stay on with the force after his Yukon service ended in the summer of 1897. After leaving the north, his active career included service in South Africa, at Wood Mountain and finally, at Cape Fullerton in the northwest corner of Hudson Bay, where he died of uremia at the age of 45.[20]

After his Yukon stint, Hayne narrated his experiences to a London writer, H. Taylor West. His book, *Pioneers of the Klondyke*, was one of the few first-hand accounts available to Klondike stampeders and today remains an important and entertaining historical record for northern researchers.

23

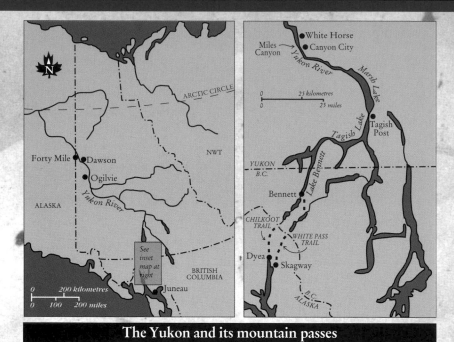

CHAPTER 2

The Yukon and its mountain passes

THE KLONDIKE GOLD RUSH

When weather permitted, an endless line of climbers struggled up the steep slope to the Chilkoot Pass.

"Gold in the Klondike!" The headlines fired the imaginations of depression-weary people the world over. By the fall of 1897, tens of thousands of goldseekers were bound for the Yukon to seek their fortunes. Most took the route through the Coastal Mountains of southeast Alaska over the Chilkoot and White Pass trails.

The small force of North-West Mounted Police faced their greatest challenge yet. They had to safeguard the stampeders on their hazardous journey north, control the criminal element inevitably attracted to easy pickings, and protect Canadian interests in the face of an overwhelming influx of Americans totally unaware, and uncaring, of where Alaska ended and the Canadian Yukon began.

It was a recipe for chaos. The Alaska panhandle town of Skagway was described as "little better than a hell on earth."[1] Murder, robbery and public shoot-outs were common events. The thousands of inexperienced stampeders who did not fall prey to the hazards of Alaska faced 600 miles of gruelling mountain passes, treacherous waterways and ferocious insects.

Even at the end of their quest, the stampeders were not safe. Confidence men, thieves, cardsharps and ladies of dubious virtue also headed north to "mine the miners." The sprawling tent town of Dawson City, built on a swamp, was susceptible to epidemics and fire. Communications were almost nonexistent, supply lines unreliable, and the community was virtually cut off from the outside world.

The fact that the Yukon remained orderly during this tumultuous time was largely due to the presence of the North-West Mounted Police. Superintendent Constantine and his men, already established at Fort Herchmer in Dawson City, kept order, while allowing for the rough and ready atmosphere of a mining camp. His reinforcements arrived swiftly and, after setting up a string of posts, successfully shepherded the great flow of humanity from the mountain passes all the way to Dawson City. The force that had quelled whiskey traders and rebellions on the Canadian prairies was not going to permit a repeat of the American Wild West in its jurisdiction.

25

Terror on the trail – *The summit detachments*

The trail is a terror, there is no doubt of that, and no one can form an idea of it unless he goes over it himself. One of our horses got his foot in a crevice and broke the leg clean off and went on three legs until stopped and shot. Another horse died and the balance are in bad shape; sore backs, cut legs &c., and I am afraid we cannot work them much longer...

Would you let my wife know I am getting on all right. You can imagine how awful it is to lay on your back all day in this little dark shack, thinking, nothing but thinking.

— Ass't. Commissioner McIlree, Skagway, September 1897 *(written while laid up with a bad ankle and diarrhea)*

As for the trail over this pass, I can't find words to express what it is like. The alternate heavy frosts and thaws have made one glare of ice, which the snow covered to depth of a foot or more...The men have no creepers and they would get nearly to the top of a hill only to slide at a break-neck rate to the bottom again.

— Inspector Z.T. Wood, Skagway, December 1897[2]

N. W. M. P.

DAWSON, Nov. 18, 1898.

THE Commissioner of the Yukon Territory orders that no person will be permitted to enter the Territory without satisfying the N. W. M. Police Officers at Tagish and White Horse Rapids that they have with them two months' assorted provisions and at least $500 in cash, or six months' assorted provisions and not less than $200 in cash, over and above the money required to pay expenses from the border to Dawson.

N. B.——This order will not apply to residents of the Yukon Territory returning, if they are identified and prove their competence to pay their way into the country.

By order,

(Signed), **S. B. STEELE,** Supt.,
Commanding N.W.M. Police, Yukon Territory.

This poster is a later version of Commissioner Walsh's famous order.

The Commissioner of the Yukon early in the year (1898) issued an order that no one would be permitted into the Yukon Territory without having a year's provisions; this was strictly enforced, notices had been posted in Skagway, Dyea and other important points.

According to Supt. Sam Steele,

the regulation...was a wise one and has saved the country much expense and has prevented a great deal of suffering in the Yukon this winter...[3]

Stampeders and horses trudge up to the White Pass Summit. E.A. Hegg, photographer.

NWMP checking stampeders' supplies at White Pass Summit. Asahel Curtis, photographer.

The NWMP and Canadian customs house on the Chilkoot Pass, 1898. The Union Jack shows the location of the customs building. E.A. Hegg, photographer.

THE KLONDIKE GOLD RUSH

Raising the flag

In February 1898, two detachments of North-West Mounted Police hauled machine guns up to the coastal mountain passes. They were charged with defending Canadian sovereignty on the main route into the Yukon. This was a key moment during the Klondike gold rush and a major trial of Canadian-American relations. How did such a drastic confrontation come about?

Long before the arrival of Euro-American outsiders in the north, the coastal Tlingit First Nation travelled over three mountain passes into the Yukon to trade, visit and intermarry with the First Nations people of the interior. They controlled access to these important trade and travel routes, later known as the Chilkat (or Dalton), Chilkoot and White Pass trails. When forced to make way for the growing number of traders and prospectors coming into the country, the Chilkat people continued to exercise their sovereignty by charging high fees to pack the outsiders' freight over the steep mountain passes.

These treacherous and stormy trails became the main gateway into the Yukon during the Klondike stampede, the focus of a major border dispute between Canada and Alaska, and the subject of countless stories of hardship and perseverance.

At the time of the Klondike gold rush, no one knew the exact location of the boundary between Alaska and Canada, along what is now known as the Alaska panhandle.[4] The border, vaguely-defined in an 1825 treaty between Russia and Great Britain, remained unclear when the United States purchased Alaska from Russia in 1867. A boundary commission appointed by the United States and Great Britain in 1893 did little to resolve the situation. The potential wealth of the Klondike goldfields brought the border issue to the forefront. Canada was intent on obtaining ocean access. The United States felt its territory should extend well within the Yukon River watershed.[5]

American stampeders, assuming that U.S. territory extended over the passes to Bennett, reacted with indignation to Canadian customs collection at Bennett in November 1897. Alaskan officials laid claim to Lindeman and Bennett by registering a townsite survey for Lindeman with the United States government. Canada's Minister of the Interior, Clifford Sifton, countered by sending two 20-man detachments of Mounted Police, each armed with a Maxim machine gun and Lee Metford carbines, to the summits of the Chilkoot and White passes in February 1898. Each party set up a tent camp, built a small customs shed and, in late February, hoisted the Union Jack and began collecting customs.

At Alaska Governor Brady's request, 200 U.S. army troops were sent north to Skagway and Dyea Inlet to protect American interests. Their commander, Colonel Anderson, asked the NWMP to withdraw from the summits. The Yukon's commissioner, James Walsh, firmly refused. Both sides became alarmed at the potential for violence. In March, Colonel Anderson and NWMP Superintendent Sam Steele, commanding the summit detachments, defused the situation with an agreement to recognize the summits as a temporary boundary. By May, most U.S. soldiers had left and the machine guns had been removed.[6]

Members drill with machine guns at Whitehorse, ca. 1900.

NWMP stand by the Union Jack and the Stars and Stripes on the White Pass Summit, April 9, 1899. E.A. Hegg, photographer.

"Circumstances of the most trying character"

The officers in charge of the summits displayed great ability, using great firmness and tact, were loyally supported by the non-commissioned officers and constables under their command, who under circumstances of the most trying character displayed the greatest fortitude and endurance, amidst the terrific snowstorms which raged round their respective camps.

— **Superintendent Sam Steele**[7]

During the winter of 1897-98, the summit detachments were the most desolate postings in the north. The Chilkoot and White Pass summits, well above treeline, mark the divide between the Pacific Ocean and Yukon River watersheds. Here, moist air from the Pacific Ocean is forced up against the coastal mountains where it cools, then dumps large amounts of snow. The storms worsen into prolonged blizzards when relatively warm Pacific air meets cold Arctic air from the Yukon interior. Heavy snowfall and high winds cause drifting and blowing snow. The winter of 1897-98 seems to have been unusually harsh, even for this normally-stormy area.[8]

On the Chilkoot Pass, Inspector Robert Belcher's tent was soon completely buried under nine feet of snow. The guard had to shovel out the entrance every 15 minutes to prevent it from being completely filled in. Belcher got permission to replace the entombed tent, but continuing storms prevented him from pitching the new one.

Heavy snowfall on the Chilkoot Pass caused a major avalanche on the American side on April 3, 1898. About 60 people, returning to Sheep Camp to escape an increasingly violent storm at the summit, were caught in the slide. Of these, 53 lost their lives. Sam Steele sent a party to look after the effects of deceased Canadian citizens and to notify their relatives.

Over at the White Pass, the Mounties had to get their firewood from Log Cabin, 14 miles away. While setting up camp in a ten-day blizzard, Inspector Strickland worried that he might lose some of his men as they struggled with teams of horses to haul timber over that long distance. The police constantly wore their oilskins to protect themselves from "a kind of wet sleet which froze as it fell" and slept in a "fine drizzle" that came through the inferior canvas of their tents.[9]

As well as marking the bounds of Her Majesty's dominion, the Mounties' main duty was collecting customs. They made every effort to do this with as little delay as possible given the bitter weather conditions, tons of goods and the crush of thousands of stampeders.[10]

The men of the summit detachments suffered from harsh weather and poor living conditions. Common ailments that winter were frostbite, colds, kidney problems, bronchitis and in extreme cases, pneumonia. They more than earned the praise they received from their superior officers.

View of the Chilkoot Pass and Crater Lake.

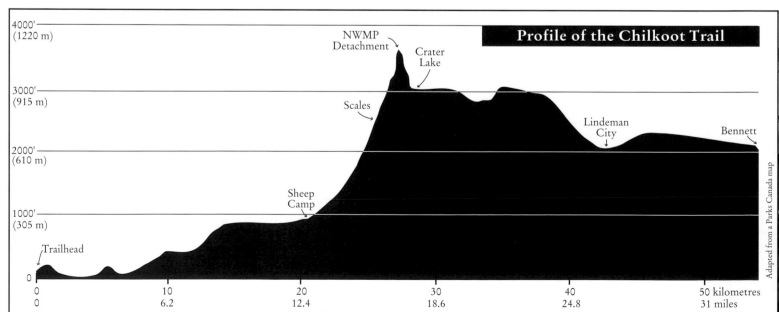

Profile of the Chilkoot Trail

Chilkoot summit detachment

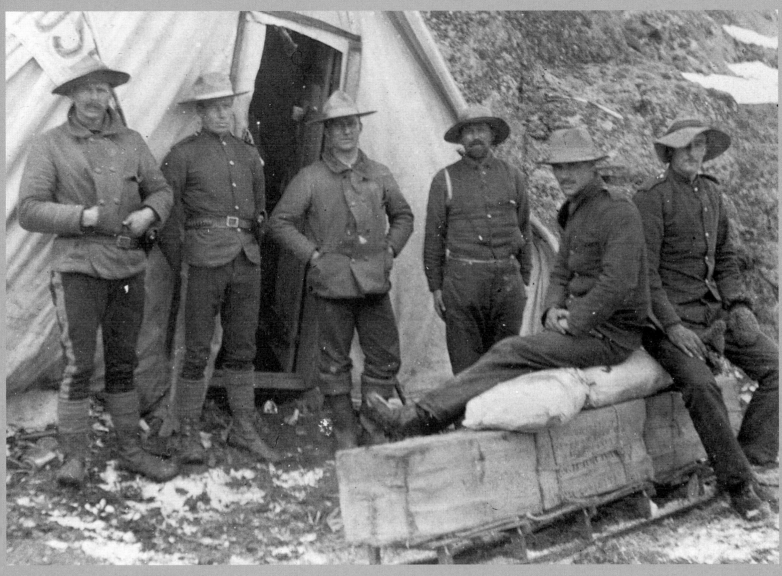

NWMP detachment on the Chilkoot Trail.

Inspector Belcher's hastily-erected customs post was a 12-foot square shack with walls and floor made from rough, green, one-inch lumber, with a canvas tarpaulin for a roof. A rough plank counter divided the beds and supplies from the people who came in to pay duty on their goods. Inspector Belcher and Corporal Still both slept in this building to guard the money collected for customs, which totalled $174,470.32 between February and June, 1898.

Corporal Still spent much of his time shovelling out the snow that blew in through the cracks between the shrunken planks, while trying to protect papers and gear from the morning "rain" that started falling as soon as heat from the stove melted the thick deposit of frost on the inside of the tarp

ceiling. During that stormy winter, there was no chance to completely dry out. Papers were sodden and the men had to sleep under wet and mildewed bedding until spring. Firewood was costly and hard to come by. As the wood only came in small bundles from the American side of the border, the detachment often had to do without during storms when no one could reach the pass.

The detachment's tent camp was set up just north of the pass on the ice of Crater Lake. Although this lower location provided some protection from the violent winds of the pass, the men here had their own problems. During a ten-day blizzard, the lake water rose and flooded the four tents with six inches of water. Since it was impossible to move the tents during the storm, the men hauled in

sleighs to use as platforms to raise their bedding.

During spring thaw, the Chilkoot detachment learned their customs building had been sitting on 20 feet of snow. As the snow melted, the building slowly descended, never tilting more than six inches off plumb, until one corner hung up on a large rock. The men kept propping up the remaining three corners only to find, when all the snow had disappeared, that the cabin was now nine feet above ground!

There were no regrets when, in late June, this miserable shack was dismantled to construct another building nearby and the Mounted Police were able to relinquish the duty of customs collection to civilian officials.[11]

Bennett detachment

At Superintendent Steele's recommendation, the customs posts were moved from the Chilkoot and White Pass summits to Log Cabin and Lindeman in July 1898. By November, with the main rush over, the summit detachments were withdrawn entirely. Daily patrols ensured the flags were still flying, however.

The detachment at Lindeman, consisting of a sergeant and a constable, had to keep about 4,000 people in order, regulate the sanitary condition of the town, see that the sick were attended, and also the burial of the dead, settle hundreds of disputes, give information upon all sorts of subjects, and various other matters besides their regular police duties. A letter signed by all the principal people of the place was sent to you, speaking of the efficient manner in which this detachment had carried out its varied duties in the highest terms.

— Inspector Belcher, 1898[12]

Canadian customs official, Frank Charman, on right and two Mounties, inside the police/ customs post at Lindeman, ca. July 1898.

Exterior of Lindeman detachment and customs post, ca. 1899.

Tent detachment at Lake Bennett, May 1898.

Bennett detachment, 1898. Drawing by E.B. Brown.

I f there was an individual who personified the fortitude and forthrightness of the North-West Mounted Police during the Klondike gold rush, it would be Superintendent Samuel Benfield Steele. Steele was the Officer Commanding of the NWMP in the Yukon during the critical period from July 1898 to September 1899. Considering that the stampede "brought in toughs, gamblers, fast women, and criminals of almost every type, from the petty thief to the murderer," the relatively small force of Mounted Police did an admirable job of imposing order in a potentially chaotic situation.[14] Much of the credit for this is due to the firm hand and decisiveness of Sam Steele.

Steele's military career spanned more than 40 years. After training at the Royal Military School of Toronto, he served with the Canadian militia. When the NWMP was formed in 1873, he signed on as a sergeant major. By the time he was posted to the Yukon, he had achieved the rank of superintendent. After his Yukon service, he went on to South Africa where he commanded Lord Strathcona's Corps. He reached the rank of Major General in World War I and was later knighted.

When he became commanding officer of the Yukon in July 1898, Steele was also appointed a member of the first council of the newly-declared Yukon Territory. He set up and chaired the first board of health, chaired a board of license commissioners, and supervised the winter mail service. He gave a breathtaking description of his rigorous day:

> *...my working hours were at least nineteen. I retired to rest about 2 A.M. or later, rose at six, was out of doors at seven, walked five miles up the Klondyke on the ice and back over the mountain, visited every institution under me each day, sat on boards and committees until midnight, attended to the routine of the Yukon command without an adjutant, saw every prisoner daily, and was in the town station at midnight to see how things were going.*[15]

Steele had a reputation for making up the laws as he went along. Some, such as his decree that only experienced pilots could run boats through Miles Canyon, undoubtedly saved many lives. When the man, dubbed "the Lion of the North," departed the Yukon to rejoin his family after a two-year separation, thousands of Dawsonites lined the wharves to bid him farewell. The town's leading citizens presented him with a purse of gold nuggets in appreciation for his services.[16]

Mount Steele, located in Kluane National Park, is Canada's fifth highest mountain at 16,664 feet above sea level. J.J. McArthur named this peak in 1909, while surveying the international boundary.

Tagish Post, 1898: *"H" Division headquarters*

Raising the flag at Tagish Post. Drawing by E.B. Brown.

In October 1897, Inspector D'Arcy Strickland established Tagish Post as the Canadian customs port for those entering the country via the Taku River, White Pass and Chilkoot trails. At the time, it seemed an ideal location. The narrow Tagish River joining the Tagish and Marsh headwater lakes, was a natural bottleneck on the water route to the Klondike goldfields. The post was pleasantly situated on a slight rise with ready access to water, timber for building and firewood, and hay meadows for horses.

From a strategic point of view, however, it was less desirable, being many miles within Canadian territory. The location of Canadian customs was a key factor in the often-tumultuous negotiations leading to an international boundary agreement in 1903. In a move to assert Canadian sovereignty, customs posts were established at the summits of the Chilkoot and White passes in February, 1898.

Tagish still served a vital function, however. The hordes of stampeders, mountains of supplies and stormy weather made it impossible for Mounties stationed at the summits to do a complete job. Determined

that there be no grounds for charging the police with inefficiency or carelessness, Superintendent Steele ordered an additional "rigid examination" of all goods by customs at Tagish Post.[17]

Steele also ordered Bennett and Tagish detachments to record and number all boats and take the names and addresses of each person in every vessel, about 28,000 people in all. These records later proved invaluable when the NWMP responded to hundreds of inquiries about missing relatives. The entries were not alphabetized, however, making that job especially time-consuming.

Strickland marvelled at the lack of crime at Tagish during the stampede. No thefts were reported and, as magistrate, he was only required to settle a few "petty squabbles," chiefly among partners.[18]

On June 13, 1898, the Yukon became a separate territory. At the same time, it was decided that the 31 far-flung detachments would be more efficiently administered as two separate districts. "H" Division took in the southern Yukon and northern British Columbia from the international boundary up to the Five Finger detachment, while "B"

Division encompassed the northern Yukon including Dawson City and the Klondike goldfields. In July, Tagish Post became the headquarters for "H" Division, with Superintendent Zachary Taylor Wood in command.

When Wood took up his new posting in early September, he faced a formidable task. The four-building detachment was much too small for a division headquarters. With no proper quartermaster's store, no jail, no stables and few habitable buildings, police, prisoners, horses and supplies all had to stay in tents. In a mad race against winter, he oversaw an ambitious construction program. He also directed his men to haul in several tons of hay from nearby meadows and to cut hundreds of cords of firewood. At the same time, lake steamers were working day and night transporting supplies between Bennett and Canyon City before winter freeze-up. The police spent long hours meeting boats and unloading tons of stores which then had to be sorted and sent on to inland detachments.

By December, the post boasted a new quartermaster's store, married quarters for Superintendent Wood and Inspector

View of Tagish Post from across the Tagish River, ca. 1900.

Tagish Post, 1898.

Strickland, single officers' quarters, cow stable, a hay corral, sergeant major's quarters, sergeants' mess, an addition to the men's barracks, horse stable, and store room. Construction of a hospital halted in mid-December when the post ran out of nails, lumber and windows.[19]

The police ran the Tagish post office, recorded mining claims, monitored north and southbound traffic, and conducted the normal duties associated with maintaining law and order. In November 1898, they began mail delivery. Over the winter, they also provided room, board and transport to travelling government officials and their friends. Wood made it clear he did not relish this obligation:

…we might possibly perform the work satisfactorily, were it not that so many persons passing out and in have orders for transport, food and lodging. Both our outcoming and ingoing Mails have been delayed to provide transport for these persons. Twelve people have passed out during the past month with orders for food and lodging and some for transport; three of these have come to me with complaints of the behaviour of different N.C. Officers and Men after living on them for months.[20]

By the summer of 1899, Tagish Post was a self-contained little community of 43 Mounties and nine horses. The Yukon's new Commanding Officer, Superintendent A.B. Perry, declared that it was a "healthy and charming spot" and that Superintendent Wood had made it "one of the most attractive posts in the force."[21]

By this time, however, the post's usefulness was nearly at an end. Construction of the White Pass and Yukon Railway from Skagway to Whitehorse meant most traffic in and out of the Yukon would bypass Tagish. Superintendent Perry recommended the transfer of division headquarters to the rail terminus at the new community of Whitehorse. By 1900, the bustling post at Tagish had been partially dismantled and only a small force was stationed there over the next few years.

Tannis, Roland and D'Arcy Strickland at Tagish Post.

Inspector Strickland was a key player in the events that shaped the early history of the NWMP in the Yukon. In 1895, he and his wife, Tannis, accompanied the Yukon's first detachment of Mounted Police to the Fortymile area. In the fall of 1897, Strickland supervised the construction of Tagish Post, later the division headquarters for the southern Yukon. He commanded the customs post on the summit of the White Pass in February 1898, but was forced to leave at the end of March when he became dangerously ill with bronchitis. During the great stampede to the goldfields during the spring and summer of 1898, Strickland was back in charge at Tagish Post. He ensured that the men of the detachment checked vessels and registered the names, addresses and next of kin of nearly 28,000 goldseekers. As the postmaster for Tagish, he later had to deal with hundreds of pounds of mail for those same people.

D'Arcy Edward Strickland, a graduate of the Royal Military College at Kingston, was appointed an Inspector in the North-West Mounted Police in 1891. After leaving the Yukon in 1900, he served at Prince Albert, then went on to the Boer War in South Africa as Adjutant of the 5th Canadian Mounted Rifles. He then commanded "G" Division, at Fort Saskatchewan, from 1904 to 1908. His sudden death at the age of 40, was attributed to "cardial dropsy."[22]

Carrying the mail

...the hard work...was on the trail, travelling all hours of the day and night, and in all kinds of weather, most of it extremely cold. I do not think that anyone who has not had some experience in the Yukon territory could appreciate the hardships and dangers of travelling here during the night with the thousand and one chances of getting into the river...

— **Supt. P.C.H. Primrose, 1899**[23]

In November 1898, the police took on the responsibility of carrying the winter mail. Members and special constables made dogsled patrols to deliver the mail between Dawson and Skagway, a distance of about 600 miles. Twice a month, relays of north and southbound patrols travelled from detachment to detachment by dog team on rough trails or over the Yukon River ice. Over the winter of 1898-99, the Yukon force travelled 64,012 miles, carrying over six and a half tons of mail by dog team.[24]

Nearly every trip was a saga of hardship. During a mid-November mail trip from Bennett to Tagish, Sergeant Pringle and Special Constable Albrecht took four days to navigate 50 miles on the lakes. Twice, heavy waves swamped their canoe, then at the foot of Tagish Lake they had to chop through ice for two miles to reach the shore. The postmaster, Inspector Strickland, and two men had to spend over a week drying and sorting 642 pounds of soaked and frozen mail.

On November 30th, Corporal Richardson and dog driver Bell were travelling south on the Yukon River ice near Hootalinqua when the river ice suddenly began to move, broke up into pieces, then swept them downstream. The men saved themselves by clinging to a tree limb but were unable to rescue their dogs or the outgoing mail.

Corporal Spreadbury, Special Constable Loucks and ex-Special Constable Christiansen left Tagish for Bennett on December 4th, to deliver mail and purchase Christmas supplies for the division mess. After an arduous four-day trip, Spreadbury and Christiansen collapsed on the lake ice within sight of the lights of Bennett. Loucks pushed on to get help for his exhausted comrades. Fortunately, they soon revived under the medical care of police surgeon, Dr. Louis Paré.[25]

In June 1899, the mail service was contracted out to the Canadian Development Company. The police were never able to completely shake this duty, however, and even briefly resumed the Whitehorse to Dawson mail run in 1905. Up until the late 1940s, members in remote detachments routinely carried mail to the trappers, First Nations people, missionaries and prospectors they visited during patrols.

Collecting customs at Tagish Post, 1898.

Louis Alphonse Paré was one of the small group of doctors assigned to tend the health of members of the force in remote areas. As well as handling a great variety of medical cases, ranging from scurvy and typhoid fever to the amputation of frostbitten limbs, the detachment surgeon was also responsible for post-mortem examinations, care of sick prisoners and "lunatics," and monitoring the detachment's diet and sanitary arrangements. Many of these men also spent much time treating other government employees, civilians and First Nations people.

Dr. Paré was from Lachine, Québec. He was appointed assistant surgeon with the North-West Mounted Police in 1887. In November 1898, he received word at his posting in Maple Creek, Saskatchewan, that his services were urgently required at Tagish Post in the Yukon. He left immediately, arriving at Tagish Post on December 20th. The post had been without a regular doctor for over a year. Several men were laid up with or just recovering from typhoid fever. The seriously ill were sent 50 miles to Bennett or, in the absence of a doctor, were granted sick leave to go to Skagway or take a ship down the coast.

During his first year at Tagish, Paré treated 274 cases in the new hospital. He attempted to improve the members' diet, observing that "navvies on the railroad" ate better than the police. He strongly urged that the ubiquitous "evaporated" potatoes, tinned meats and bacon be supplemented with more fresh produce and fresh meat.[26]

Paré stayed on in the Yukon until his retirement in 1911, being promoted to full surgeon in 1904. On several occasions, Commissioner Perry cited his good service and devotion to duty. [27]

Assistant Commissioner Z.T. Wood, C.M.G., died at Asheville, North Carolina, on January 15 last, where he had gone in search of health. His death was a distinct loss to the force and was lamented by all ranks. He had served for upward of thirty years, and during that long period was ever distinguished for his devotion to duty, his loyalty to the force and his upright character.

— Commissioner A.B. Perry, 1915[28]

Bravery and stamina were not the only qualities required of a Mountie in the Yukon. The ability to deal with mountains of administrative matters, to make do with few resources, and above all, to adapt to a changing environment were essential characteristics in a leader. Z.T. Wood was such a person and more than any other, he carried the Yukon force into the 20th century.

Zachary Taylor Wood, grandson of U.S. President, General Zachary Taylor, was born at Annapolis Naval Academy, Maryland. His life reflected his military heritage. After graduation from the Royal Military College at Kingston, he served with the 90th Regiment of Infantry during the Riel Rebellion. In 1885, he was appointed an inspector with the North-West Mounted Police and held various commands throughout the west.

In September 1897, Wood left Calgary, leading ten members, 84 dogs, nine dog handlers and stores—all en route to the Yukon via Skagway. Wood had expected to return after the safe delivery of his party, but the Yukon's commissioner, Major Walsh, decided he was urgently needed in the north. The Yukon was to be Wood's home for the next 15 years. For most of the frantic winter of 1897-98, he ran an office out of Skagway. There he acted as the force paymaster, arranged to forward men and supplies into the Yukon, and provided information to the steady stream of travellers. Of course, the force had no legal authority in Skagway during its lawless heyday, and members wore plainclothes while stationed in the Alaskan town. On one occasion, Wood's Skagway office was caught in the midst of a gunfight. The staff hit the floor as bullets whizzed through the walls.

According to another oft-recounted tale, Wood and a small force of men successfully eluded Soapy Smith and his outlaw forces while transporting $150,000 in Canadian customs dues and license fees through Skagway en route to Victoria.

In the summer of 1898, Wood was appointed Superintendent of "H" Division, in charge of all detachments in the southern Yukon. Wood became commanding officer for the entire Yukon in 1900, a post he held for 12 years. From 1902, he held the rank of assistant commissioner.

During this time, the Yukon's population dropped radically, as did the numbers of Mounted Police. The area to be policed and patrolled did not shrink, however, and neither did the range of duties. While Wood may have lacked the flamboyance and dash of Sam Steele, his ability and adaptability did much to establish the solid reputation of the force in the Yukon during the early years.

His son, Stuart Taylor Wood, grew up in the Yukon and later served as the RCMP Commissioner from 1938 to 1951.[29]

Miles Canyon/White Horse Rapids detachment: 1898

Canyon City, ca. 1898. The NWMP cabins are just to the right of the long roadhouse building at left.

After the ordeal of the passes, Klondike goldseekers temporarily settled along the shores of nearby Lindeman and Bennett lakes, creating vast tent cities. While waiting for the lake ice to break up, they built boats for the next leg of their journey through the great headwater lakes and down the Yukon River to Dawson City. When the ice finally went out in May 1898, a vast armada took to the water. The thousands of boats, of all descriptions and levels of seaworthiness, included substantial steamers, bulky scows, overloaded canoes and crude rafts.

These vessels soon reached Miles Canyon and White Horse Rapids, the most hazardous section of the route. Here, the Yukon River dashed through the steep volcanic walls of Miles Canyon before the foaming waters spread out over the rocky ledges of White Horse Rapids, a six-mile roller coaster. While many chose to take the portage route on the

east bank of the river, the impatient braved the rapids. Often, they paid for their inexperience with lost gear, smashed boats and in extreme cases, their lives.

In the fall of 1897, Inspector Strickland had sent two Mounties with six months' rations to build a "shack" and assist winter travellers at White Horse Rapids. The following May, Superintendent Steele detailed two police to the head of the canyon at the site that became known as Canyon City. Their orders were to warn the stampeders of the impending danger and ensure that "there was no overcrowding or unnecessary haste" in entering the canyon.[30] When Steele visited the site a month later, he learned that the Mounties had spent a large part of their time rescuing those who had foundered in the rapids. About 200 boats had been wrecked, 52 outfits of supplies had been lost and five men drowned. Steele lost no time in

implementing stronger measures. He posted an edict that only experienced pilots, registered with the Mounted Police, were permitted to navigate vessels through the canyon and rapids. Women and children had to walk around the rapids via the portage route. The charges for piloting were $150 for steamers, $25 for a barge or scow, and $20 for a small boat. Those unable to afford the charge were piloted for free by Constable Edward Dixon and others.[31]

By this time, Norman Macaulay had established the "Canyon and White Horse Rapids Tramway." For a fee, horse-drawn carts hauled goods and small boats over a simple log track from the cluster of log buildings and tents at Canyon City to White Horse, the small settlement that grew up at the downstream terminus of the tramway. The tramline operation boomed to the extent that Macaulay paid $60,000 to buy out the rival

Shooting Miles Canyon in an empty scow at high water.

Hepburn tramway on the west side of the river and consolidate his monopoly on goods being shipped around the rapids.

By August, the detachment was increased to one non-commissioned officer and three constables. A new barracks building housed the men's quarters, mess room, kitchen and an office. A smaller building served as a storehouse. At White Horse, a constable resided in a small 10-foot by 12-foot shack. By the end of the summer of 1898, only three

Mounted Police remained at the Miles Canyon/White Horse Rapids detachment. They turned their rations over to Norman Macaulay and took their meals at his Canyon City roadhouse.

This was one of the busiest detachments during the gold rush. Police checked all vessels to ensure they were not overloaded or carrying illegal liquor shipments. Constable Edward Dixon worked almost full time as a river pilot, steering boats downriver to White

Horse then returning the five miles to Canyon City by horseback along the tramway. The Mounties routinely handled numerous inquiries about conditions on the trail ahead and generally assisted travellers on their way.

By the end of the 1898 navigation season, more than 7,000 vessels had passed through Miles Canyon and the White Horse Rapids. After Steele's edict, there were few accidents and no further lives were lost.[32]

Murder at White Horse Rapids

On the afternoon of August 27, 1898, the NWMP at White Horse investigated their first murder. The perpetrator and victim were both employees of the Bennett Lake and Klondyke Navigation Company. James Cowie, steward of the steamer *Ora*, learned that T.C. Burnett, the former cook, had accused Cowie and the purser of taking monies illegally. In his official report, Sergeant H.G. Joyce explained what happened next:

> …today Cowie found Burnett in the Store Tent of the B. L. & K. N. Co. and the two engaged in a fight. Burnett not being the better man had his face bruised. Shortly afterwards, Burnett on boarding the steamer carrying two small bags it is said was again about to be aggressed by Cowie when Burnett drew a Revolver and shot Cowie in the region of the abdomen.
>
> Burnett was disarmed by W.D. Oregel and Wallace, store Keeper for the B. L. & K. N. Co.
>
> Burnett was arrested by Const. Lindbladt, Const. Dixon appearing on the scene immediately, and held prisoner until I arrived from the Detachment…The first intimation I received of the affair was from the Purser of the *Ora*, <u>H. Freese</u> who on hearing the shot came to the Detachment on the run for a doctor.[33]

Cowie died within 24 hours. Burnett was transported under guard to Tagish to await preliminary examination. Tagish Post was ill-equipped for such a case. Lacking a jail, the prisoner was detained in a tent—inadequate quarters in cold autumn weather—and two men had to be taken from other duties to stand guard. While awaiting a judge, several witnesses were detained in the Yukon despite their anxiety to travel outside before winter. Finally, in October, Burnett was transferred to more secure quarters in Dawson to await trial for manslaughter the following year. The case ended up being discharged in 1899, possibly due to the lack of witnesses.

The original townsite of White Horse at the downriver terminus of Macaulay's tramway, 1899. A few years after the settlement moved across the river, its residents changed the name to Whitehorse.[34] H.C. Barley, photographer

THE LANDING AT WHITE HORSE.

H.C. BARLEY.

Flotilla of stampeders on Lake Laberge, 1898. Larss and Duclos, photographers.

716. #39 LAKE LEBARGE.

YRIGHT 1898.

LARSS & DUCLOS
PHO.
DAWSON
Y.T.

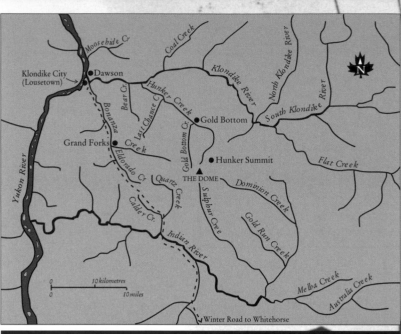

CHAPTER 3

Dawson City and the Klondike goldfields

During Victoria Day celebrations, NWMP fire a cannon at Fort Herchmer while Dawson residents look on, May 24,1900.

Dawson City

The population has jumped during the past few summer months from a few hundreds to at least 5,000. Dawson a year ago, consisted of half a dozen small log cabins; to-day it has a number of substantial buildings, hundreds of cabins, and a population of from 1,500 to 2,000. Both the trading companies have built fine stores and extensive warehouses. The majority of the newcomers are from the United States, many of them could well be spared in any community. The rush has brought in toughs, gamblers, fast women, and criminals of every type, from the petty thief to the murderer.

— Supt. C. Constantine, January 1898[1]

Over the winter of 1896-97, rumours of the rich strike on the Klondike spread throughout the north. Miners and would-be miners raced to the area to stake every bit of available ground. The very names given to the creeks evoked fabulous wealth: Bonanza, Eldorado, Gold Run, Eureka and Gold Bottom. When the news reached the outside world in the summer of 1897, many goldseekers left immediately, reaching the Klondike by fall. The vast majority of the stampeders headed north over the following winter, however, reaching Dawson City during the spring and summer of 1898. They found almost all the gold-bearing ground already taken and the Mounted Police waiting, if not entirely ready, for the great flood of humanity.

The Canadian government had acted on Constantine's plea for more Mounted Police and government officials, realizing the great potential for revenue from "the marvellous discoveries of gold" and the need for law enforcement during the ensuing rush. Clifford Sifton, the federal Minister of the Interior, obtained cabinet approval to increase the police force to 100, improve the lines of communication between Dawson City and the Pacific Coast, and authorize the required funds.[2] He also sent five officials, including the Yukon's first gold commissioner, Thomas Fawcett, to take over some of the civil duties overwhelming Constantine.

Two parties of Mounties travelled over the Chilkoot to the Klondike in 1897: Inspector W.H. Scarth was in charge of 19 replacements for the original detachment, while Inspector Frank Harper, arriving October 1897, brought 20 additional reinforcements. The newly-promoted Superintendent Constantine did not exactly welcome Harper's party with open

*Dawson bound! The **Islander** leaving Vancouver with Inspector Harper and his party of Mounted Police, August 1897. Tappan Adney, photographer.*

REINFORCEMENTS MEET THE GREAT STAMPEDE

arms. They arrived empty-handed to a detachment preparing for another winter of food shortages. Constantine claimed that even the four dogs they brought in were "small, ill-conditioned and of very little use."

Nonetheless, Constantine managed. He convinced 300 destitute stampeders to move on to the better-supplied downriver communities of Fort Yukon and Circle. Many of those arrested for theft and other crimes also had to be shipped out as the police could not spare any rations to feed prisoners. An additional 600 stampeders left voluntarily just before freeze-up when the food shortages became apparent. By the spring of 1898, hungry miners with pockets full of gold gladly paid up to $18 for a dozen eggs and $25 for a can of oysters.[3]

Shortly after the spring break-up of the river ice, the hordes began arriving. A vast tent city sprang up and spread over the surrounding hillsides like a snowfall.

The long, hard journey took its toll on tempers. Many partnerships and marriages broke up on the shores of the Yukon River and the Mounties refereed many disputes over the division of food and supplies.

The town of Dawson was built on a swamp and its gold-fevered residents paid little attention to sanitary arrangements. According to Acting Assistant Surgeon Richardson, the situation was ripe for an epidemic. The following summer, his words proved prophetic with "the deposit of nearly 20,000 souls upon the swamp that mainly constitutes the Dawson town site."[4]

By August, the police hospital was one of three hospitals full of typhoid victims. As head of the Board of Health, Superintendent Sam Steele gave orders regarding garbage disposal, drinking water and other sanitary arrangements, keeping the situation from getting even worse.

In October 1898, the overworked 51-member force in Dawson was augmented by 50 soldiers of the Yukon Field Force. Together they patrolled the town, fought fires, protected gold shipments, guarded prisoners and ensured residents could walk the streets in perfect safety. For several months, they had charge of the largest city "west of Winnipeg and north of San Francisco." They met a tremendous challenge and passed it with flying colours.[5]

Front Street, Dawson City, ca. 1898. E.A. Hegg, photographer.

51

Fort Herchmer

Boating in the parade square! Fort Herchmer during the spring flood, 1898.

Last spring the Yukon River at Dawson was very high, flooding the barracks. The orderly-room, hospital, sergeants' quarters and store-room had about two feet of water in them. We had to take all the provisions and put them on the roofs of the different buildings. My own quarters I could only leave and return to by canoe…A considerable portion of the town was flooded. It was about ten days rising to its highest point, and dropped in about twenty-four hours…

— Insp. Frank Harper, 1898 [6]

Shortly after the initial gold discovery on Bonanza Creek, Alaska Commercial Company trader Joe Ladue staked a townsite in the moose swamp where the Klondike River flows into the Yukon. This was subsequently surveyed by William Ogilvie and named Dawson City after George Dawson of the Geological Survey of Canada and leader of the 1887 Yukon expedition. Forty acres of the new townsite were set aside as a government

reserve. Here, in the spring of 1897, the Mounted Police began construction of the new police post, Fort Herchmer, named after the commissioner of the force.

The Mounties assigned to build the post repeated their efforts of Fort Constantine, although if anything their labours were more intensive. Lacking a sawmill, all logs had to be handhewn on three sides. Three small buildings were moved from Fort Constantine upriver to the new site, while some windows had to be salvaged from other structures. By fall, there were nine buildings on the site. As these were still not adequate to house all the men, nor were there sufficient rations in Dawson for the whole force, Constantine assigned Inspector Scarth and 12 members to spend the winter at Fort Constantine.

The post in Dawson had to be enlarged by 15 additional structures the following year to accommodate more police and the 50

soldiers of the Yukon Field Force. As well as barracks, officers' quarters, and offices, the post housed its own hospital, a large quartermaster's store and a sizeable guard room or jail. In 1898, the 24-cell jail had to be expanded with an extension holding another 34 cells. In July 1898, Fort Herchmer also became the headquarters of "B" Division, the administrative centre for the northern Yukon detachments. From this post, police and orders were dispatched to the goldfields and along the Yukon River. By 1899, Fort Herchmer housed a contingent of 64 Mounted Police.[7]

Officers of "B" Division, Dawson, 1900.
(L-R) Insp. Wm. H. Scarth, Insp. Z.T. Wood, Insp. W.H. Routledge, Insp. Cortlandt Starnes, A/Surgeon Dr. W.E. Thompson.

Constables at Fort Herchmer assume a less formal pose.

Fort Herchmer, Dawson City, ca. 1899.

REINFORCEMENTS MEET THE GREAT STAMPEDE

Dawson town station

The police duties in the town of Dawson are provided for by one non-commissioned officer and eight men, and a special constable as cook for the detachment. Four men are on duty during the day, and are relieved at seven in the evening by another four...Considering the extent of ground over which this town is spread, and the number of dance halls, &c., it keeps four men well employed to try to cover the ground, and I am pleased to say that they do their work in a most efficient manner, and show no partiality in the performance of their duties.

— Supt. P.C.H. Primrose, 1899[8]

In 1898, Sam Steele rented a cabin in downtown Dawson for use as a town police station. When the building burned down during one of the town's frequent fires, he replaced it with a smart new cabin. The following year, the detachment was enlarged with a kitchen addition.

The small town force patrolled the streets around the clock and made regular visits to potential trouble spots—the many gambling and dance halls, theatres, saloons, restaurants and hotels. Detachment members earned extra money from the city for this work.

Dawson residents gave up the town charter in 1904, as their population plummeted. When territorial authorities took over municipal government, the town station police lost their extra allowance from the city. Assistant Commissioner Wood proudly reported,

however, that his Mounties remained every bit as conscientious in carrying out their duties.[9]

NWMP band leading a parade in Dawson during the Victoria Day celebrations, May 24, 1899.

The Dawson town station detachment, ca. 1899.

54

Crime and punishment

As Dawson's population grew, so did the number of shady characters and crimes. Until the rush, miners could safely leave their cabins or caches for months at a time and return to find their tools and goods intact. As the population skyrocketed, however, robberies became common. The police imposed stiff sentences on convicted thieves. The prospect of a long jail term with hard labour on the police woodpile did much to curb theft. Plainclothes detectives gathered information on the backgrounds of suspicious characters. In this way they identified a number of former murderers, armed robbers and other desperados who were then arrested, fined for vagrancy and often given a "blue ticket" ordering them out of the country. In a few cases, people were swept up in this clean-up for little reason other than the police did not like their looks.[10]

While the police tolerated some of the rowdier entertainments of a mining camp, they did set limits. Police monitored performances in the music and concert halls to prevent "improprieties of any character" and strictly enforced Sunday closures. Women were not allowed to gamble or drink liquor in dance halls. Although the police fined many women convicted of being an "inmate of a house of ill fame," they made no serious effort to stamp out prostitution. Instead, the practice was pushed out of sight when houses of prostitution were banned from within the city in 1901. There was some consternation when many moved to West Dawson—directly across the river from the town—within plain view and hearing of "respectable" citizens. Eventually, however, the red light district was confined to Klondike City, just upriver from Dawson, a region soon dubbed "Lousetown."[11]

By the early 1900s, Dawson was a much more sedate town. Its families, schools, and substantial government buildings reflected permanence and stability. The town was also embarking on its long, slow decline. As the miners and wilder element moved away to other goldfields, rowdy behaviour became less tolerable to the majority of its residents. Many of the pimps or "macques" were chased out of town. Gambling and prostitution were banned. Although neither activity ever ceased entirely, the Mounted Police had moved on to a new phase of law enforcement.

Prostitutes in Lousetown.

Glimpse of the last public game at Dawson at the Dominion Saloon, 12 p.m. March 16, 1901. Lars and Duclos, photographers.

The fate of the first Yukon detachment

…we were now veterans returning home with the spoils of war, instead of pioneers toiling slowly towards an unknown land with staff and scrip and fixed rations for a limited time only.

— S/Sgt. M.H.E. Hayne[12]

By the spring of 1897, after two years of short rations and hard work, members of the Yukon's first NWMP detachment were more than ready for a break. When Inspector Scarth led in their relief force in early June 1897, all the constables and NCOs, except Staff Sergeant Hayne, took their discharge from the force. Most chose to stay in the Yukon to go mining. Inspector and Mrs. Strickland headed out with their new baby to personally report to NWMP Commissioner Herchmer in Regina and take a much-needed

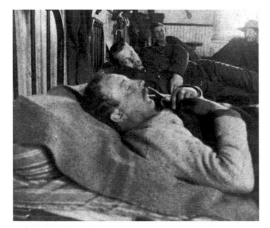

rest. The remaining four members sold their claims or left them with partners, then boarded the *Portus B. Weare* on the first stage of the long trip outside.

Their shipmates included many newly-rich Klondike miners. For the first time, the small supply steamer bore a much heavier cargo on its outbound voyage—a fortune in gold dust and nuggets. The purser's cabin required extra bracing under the deck to support the ton and a half in gold nuggets held in storage. Elsewhere on the vessel:

> *Blankets full of gold lay about on deck in absolute security and unconcern. Their own weight was a sufficient safeguard against any attempt at unlawful removal. It took two men to lift one of these improvised sacks.[13]*

At St. Michael, Alaska, the Klondikers transferred to the steamer *Portland* for the month-long voyage down the coast. Staff Sergeant Hayne was aboard the *Portland* when it steamed into the harbour at Seattle on July 17, 1897, bearing the cargo of wealthy Klondike miners and three million dollars in gold. Hayne gave this account of their reception at the docks:

> *Our fame had preceded us, though ours was the first steamer to return from the Yukon. The crowd of people was a sight to see. I believe the whole town turned out to*

greet us. The reporters were absolutely merciless, and a source of very great annoyance. Nothing would shake them off. Threats, expostulations and entreaties were alike in vain.

> *"For pity's sake, man," I cried, "let me get ashore at any rate." But they clung to us like limpets.*

> *"Look here," I cried at last in desperation, heading for the nearest hotel, "I have been for two years in a country where the only drink is poison. Let me at least have a thimbleful of good Scotch whisky before I suffer the torment of an interview."*

> *Six men accompanied me to the bar, and each one simultaneously planked down twenty-five cents on the counter, and six voices exclaimed in chorus: "Say, Miss, give this man a drink!"[14]*

Relaxing in barracks at Fort Herchmer.

*The departing police detachment retraced their voyage of two years before aboard the trading vessel **Portus B. Weare**. This time, the 1800-mile trip went much faster not only because the boat was travelling downriver, but also because the men knew their long tour of duty had ended.*

Shipment of gold dust worth $750,000 stacked in front of the Canadian Bank of Commerce at Dawson, September 20, 1899. Goetzman, photographer.

Officer at his desk in Dawson.

Yukon Field Force

On May 6, 1898, Corporal John A. Tinck stood at rigid attention before the Earl of Aberdeen, Governor General of Canada. His Excellency was addressing Tinck and 200 troops from the Royal Canadian Dragoons, the Royal Canadian Artillery and the Royal

Regiment of Canadian Infantry just before their departure from Ottawa to the Yukon. The encouraging words and good wishes of the country's head of state did little to inform the men of exactly where they were going or what they would do once they got there. Perhaps it was just as well.[15]

By late winter, the hordes of goldseekers pouring into the Yukon had not abated. The federal government felt that the North-West Mounted Police might be overtaxed. The government authorized the formation of a military body, the Yukon Field Force, to support the Mounted Police in the Yukon. Its men were drawn from military bases in Fredericton, New Brunswick, St. Jean, Québec, and Kingston and London, Ontario. Their commander was Lieutenant Colonel T.D.B. Evans. He had been instructed to lead his men north via an untried "all-Canadian" route

into the territory. They would travel from Vancouver up the west coast to Wrangell, Alaska, inland along the Stikine River to the head of navigation at Glenora, then march overland to Teslin Lake. Their destination was Fort Selkirk, a small fur trading community on the Yukon River about halfway between Whitehorse and Dawson City. It had been identified as a possible capital for the new territory. Six women accompanied the group—four members of the Victorian Order of Nurses, Inspector Starnes' wife Marie, and Faith Fenton, a reporter for the Toronto *Globe*. Fenton's dispatches later told the world about

The **Stikine Chief,** *the steamer that carried the soldiers up the Stikine River.*

Lt. Col. T.D.B. Evans, commanding officer of the Yukon Field Force.

conditions in the Klondike as well as the fortunes of the Field Force.[16]

John Tinck began his trip north with a promotion to the rank of acting sergeant and, as he states in his diary, "good health and spirits."[17] The 34-year-old Tinck, a soldier since age 18, was also a writer and artist. He documented his northern adventure in a journal, made some watercolour paintings of scenes along the way, and composed a heartfelt poem on the subject of field rations. Here is the odyssey of the Yukon Field Force as seen through Tinck's eyes. The first diary entries cover the 24-day march from Telegraph Creek on the Stikine River, overland to Teslin Lake.[18]

June 7th *Heavy marching Order at 10 am with Straps – large Kit Bags containing Blankets, Oil Sheet and all belongings weighing about 85 lbs. Lce-Cpl. Grey No. 4 Coy., Fredericton discharged for refusing to Carry the Heavy pack. No. 2 and 3 Coy's marched abought 4 Miles two out and two back.*

Said Lce. Cpl also reduced.

June 14th *Left Telegraph Creek 7:45 am. 33 N.C.O.'s and men, Major Talbot, Sgt. Major Young and two Nurses with Mrs. Stirnes reaching the Summit at 4:25 after A very heavy march under A very hot Sun 12 miles. after pitching the necessary Tents, five in number, we had supper which consisted of Vegetable Butter Soupe Tea Prunes and Hard-Tack. every man in good health. Some A little sore, all very tired.*

June 15th *Revielle at 4 o'clock in the Shape of A Stampede of pack mules through our lines tripping and falling over the guies [tent guy lines]. after packing our blankets and kits we struck tents and had Breakfast which consisted of Wet Hash (which consisted of Meat Potatoes & Prunes) hard tack Butter and Tea Sugar and Condensed Milk…*

June 21st…Started on the Trail at 7 [a.m.] traveling until 5 pm through Swamp nearly all Day. quiete A common occurrence to have two and three mules down in the mud at once. Making between 18 and 20 miles. Mosquitoes verry Bad all Day and evening.

June 22nd *…N.C. Officers & men to carry Cpl. Thompson of the Québec Battery over the Trail.*

Helpless with Rheumitism…The Stretcher Party Reaching camp at 4:30 am 23 inst. every man tired out. receiving an immediate Order to look alive and get Something to eat, must pull right out again leaving Camp again at 7.45 still in heavy marching Order. Pitching Camp again at 12.30 pm where we remain untill 25th much to the Satisfaction of all in camp, every man being so very Tired.

June 25th *Robbed wild Bees nest in dry Moss. Got A few Cups of honey, divided it up with Pte. Warr.*

July 1st *Left Camp at 10.55 am arriving at Teslin Lake at 8.55 pm after making abought 12 miles. All in good health and Spirits but very tired.*

July 10th *Church Service 11 am by Col Stevens. Reading and Hymns. Shall we gather at the River/Jesus lover of my Soul.*

July 13th *Heavy Wind Storm passed over camp abought 7 P. M., all hands called out with axes cutting down and preventing trees from falling upon the tents.*

Yukon Field Force soldiers in camp on the Stikine trail.

One heavy clap of Thunder and one Flash of Lightening.

Tinck was a member of the advance party that travelled to Selkirk aboard the *Anglian* on the maiden voyage of the first steamer on Teslin Lake. Two of the nurses, learning of the typhoid epidemic in Dawson, left immediately to work at police barracks and the Good Samaritan Hospital. The remainder of the men built rafts and arrived a month and a half later.

July 21st Left Teslin City 2.20 pm. 59 N.C. & Men on Board the Steamer Anglian for Fort Selkirk.

July 23rd Stopped at Hootlanqua [Hootalinqua] City. quite A large Camp 2 Mounted Poliece Stationed there. At 8.20 pm Stopped to take on wood & cut it. went ashore gathered A few Flowers and feed of Black Currents. very tart but not too Bad. –

July 24– Went on rock at or just below five finger Rapids at 9.45. forced to take cargo ashore. not until four pm did we have the good ship afloat. large hole in her Bottom. ate A quantity of red Berries.

July 25th Arrived at Fort Selkirk at 5 pm. All in good health and Spirits Advanced Party.

At Fort Selkirk, the men began erecting several buildings around a large parade square at the east end of the townsite. A sawmill was set up and civilian contractors joined the soldiers in constructing a complex of 11 log buildings.

The arrival of 200 men had a great impact on this small community inhabited by a handful of whites and a large seasonal population of First Nations people. Selkirk First Nation people still tell stories about the soldiers. They point out two holes in the basalt wall across the river, apparently targets for the Force's seven pounder field guns. People thought the soldiers were fighting each other during training exercises. Others noted the rowdy behaviour of men who frequented the settlement's saloons. For the soldiers, Fort Selkirk became the place where they first lost one of their comrades.[19]

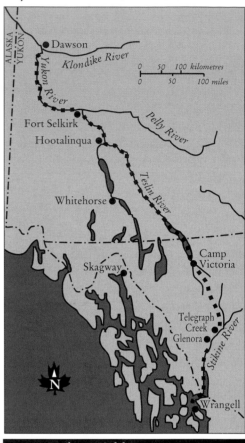

Yukon Field Force route

Yukon Field Force soldiers haul logs up the riverbank at Fort Selkirk.

Building the YFF compound at Fort Selkirk.

Sept. 8th *Pte Hurley Seven Days Cells. first to occupy New Cells.*

Sept. 11th *Main Body arrived at 1.35 pm with foure Scows and foure Small Boats.*

Sept. 27th *Gunner Corcoran found dead in his Tent at Reveillie. Artillery from Quebeck.*

Sept. 29th *First military funeral in the Yukon at 11.30 am that of Gunner Corcoran Quebeck.*

In September 1898, Supt. Sam Steele requested 50 soldiers of the Yukon Field Force to reinforce the 51 overworked Mounties at Dawson. Even this increased force proved inadequate and another 16 soldiers were transferred from Selkirk the following January.[20] While in Dawson, the men's duties included guarding prisoners, providing night guards for the town's two banks, fighting fires and escorting gold shipments from the outlying creeks.

During that winter, Tinck served as prisoner escort, bank guard and member of a dog team patrol to Circle City from December 17, 1898 to January 17, 1899. The steamer

Seattle had gone aground at Circle City on her last trip upriver. The patrol's mission was to furnish guards to protect the vessel's cargo which included 250 tons of supplies for the Yukon Field Force and 50 tons for the NWMP. Tinck's Christmas dinner, taken on the trail, consisted of two pieces of hardtack and a slice of boiled ham.[21]

Tinck also recorded several major events, including two large downtown fires, a number of deaths, the territory's first executions and the first balloon and parachute flights in the Yukon. Two more members died at Fort Selkirk from "galloping consumption" and "disease of the stomach." Three of the Dawson soldiers came down with typhoid fever, one catching the disease while in the hospital for another complaint. The anniversary of Tinck's departure from Toronto coincided with the excitement of the spring break-up of the Yukon River ice.

Oct. 1st *Left Fort Selkirk. 50 N.C. Officers and men onboard the Steamer Gold Star arriving in Dawson City 3.30 pm the 2nd Oct.*

1899

April 2nd *Easter Sunday. for Dinner the Sgts. had Roast Cariabo [caribou] dried Potatoes (in flakes) Canned Corn Bread Butter Tea Sugar Beer with Fruit Pudding…*

April 26th *Fire broke out at 7.30 pm on front Street with considerable wind blowing destroying one hundred and eleven Buildings. Damages over one Million Dollars. I mounted Guard at 12 P. M. with Six men Guarding the Vault of the Bank of B.N.A. [British North America], the Building being destroyed by the Fire the Vault falling to pieces with the intense heat exposing enormous wealth in Gold Dust and Nuggets…*

May 3rd *Dawson, Y.T. 9.10 am just one year ago I steamed out of the Union Depot Toronto. the weather here is fine with A cold wind blowing. Health and prospects good but no Money as yet. good outlook.*

June 17th *Gr. [Gunner] Enfield absent untill brought in by escort after contracting debts to the amount of six hundred dollars by issuing bogus cheques on the Bank of Commerce where he had no account.*

June 20th *Gr. Enfield deserts his Post while on Sentry outside of Bank of Comm. appearently deserted.*

Canadian Bank of Commerce fire at Dawson, January 10, 1900. NWMP on guard to prevent looting. Larss and Duclos, photographers.

RUINS OF THE BRANCH OF THE CANADIAN BANK OF COMMERCE, FIRE OF JAN. 10TH. 1900.

June 25th 99 Fresh Eggs for Dinner, three each, great treat $1.50 per Dozen.

August 4th One white man and two Indians Hung for Murder, drop falling at 8.30 am the first to hang in Dawson or to be executed in any way in this Territatory.

Aug 28th Capt. Bennet arrived with the order for, and names of Officers, N.C.O.s and men of A Coy who are to leave for the outside not later than 1st or 2nd of Sept. via Steamer Victorian.

By the fall of 1899, the Canadian government no longer felt it necessary to commit one quarter of its militia forces to the Yukon. Field Force headquarters were transferred to Dawson and half the force shipped out. The remainder left in June 1900.

When Tinck left Dawson on September 1, 1899, his journey outside was a pleasant contrast to the arduous trek north. The troops travelled up the Yukon River by steamer and then rode over the newly-completed railway between Bennett and Skagway to take a coastal vessel to Vancouver. The last leg was the Canadian Pacific Railway trip from Vancouver to Toronto marking the end of the journal as well as the completion of Tinck's Yukon adventure.

Yukon Field Force Band, Dawson, 1900.

Members of the Yukon Field Force sitting down to Christmas dinner in their festively-decorated mess hall, December 1899. The cannon in the foreground was brought inside to keep warm.

CHRISTMAS DINNER
DAWSON Y.T.

Soldiers Rations (an excerpt)
by John A. Tinck

Then the soldiers from the east
Were drafted or at least were to Klondike far to
go
They had to take their stuff
So they could take enough
In the most evaporated form you know.
So whether it was meat
Or molasses for a treat
Or whether it was bacon, eggs or brown
So that it would safely pack on a mule's
uncertain back
T'was the most compressed and evaporated
form
With evaporated flapjacks
Evaporated tin tacks
Evaporated peaches and evaporated prunes
Evaporated rice, beans, whisky; beer and ice
cream
Evaporated flutes that play evaporated tunes.

Yukon Field Force celebrate Christmas in Dawson, 1899.

Members of the Yukon Field Force in Dawson, ca. 1898.

CHAPTER 4

*A great deal of our work is in
connection with customs. Some of our men
are employed on customs duties entirely,
giving none of their time to police work.
This is a great inconvenience to us, as we
are compelled of course to pick our most
intelligent men for such duties, men, that
short-handed as we are, we can ill spare.*

— Ass't. Comm. Z.T. Wood, 1902[1]

Customs inspection at Forty Mile, 1933.

*Chauffeur duty. A Mountie drives Martha Black, wife of the
Yukon Commissioner, around Dawson to deliver flowers,
ca. 1915.*

The frenetic pace of the Klondike gold rush was
soon over. By 1900, most of the gold seekers
had gone. Dawson City was now a respectable town
with churches, schools, and families. A few large
companies controlled most of the goldfields using
mechanized methods of mining. The Yukon's
population dropped from a high of 30,000 in 1898 to
about 10,000 in 1904.[2] Federal spending in the Yukon
collapsed, including the Mounted Police budget. Large
detachment buildings were abandoned or sold as they
became too expensive for the smaller force to
maintain. Many posts were closed entirely. Others—
along the winter road to Whitehorse or at the scene of
a new gold strike—were open only for a few months of
the year.

The duties of departing civil servants fell to the
ever-dwindling police force, who resented the
unwanted burden. In 1903, Ass't. Commissioner Z.T.
Wood complained about the poor treatment of police
by civil servants, and the lack of respect shown his
"semi-military" organization:

> *A common cause for complaint among our men is
> that when detailed to assist another department they
> are invariably compelled to do the most unpleasant
> and menial portion of the work, and are often
> ordered about by some of the employees of the
> department they are assisting in a hectoring and
> domineering manner.[3]*

When World War I broke out, many Mounties,
gripped by patriotic fever, wished to serve their country
overseas. Canada's prime minister, Robert Borden,
declared that the Mounted Police were needed on the
home front. Many disregarded this order and deserted
the force to go to war. After heavy casualties, the
Canadian government relented and in 1918, two
squadrons of RNWMP troops went overseas.

The economic downturn following the Klondike
gold rush affected all parts of the Yukon. The reduced
Mounted Police force also changed and adapted.

Guarding the goldfields – Grand Forks detachment

Panorama of Grand Forks, 1898. E.A. Hegg, photographer.

The first Grand Forks detachment.
(L-R) Sgt. Marshall, –, –, –, –, Cst. J.R. Patterson, Kid Owen.

While Dawson was the supply and transport centre for the Klondike goldfields, the actual mines were miles away up the creeks. Before roads were built to the main mining areas, a trip to Dawson meant a few days hard travel by foot or dogsled. Consequently, small communities grew up around the more populated mining centres. The establishment of a roadhouse or store was often a magnet for further settlement, including a North-West Mounted Police post.

The most prosperous mining operations were located on Bonanza and Eldorado creeks. During the winter of 1897-98, Inspector Harper visited the gold creeks:

> *On Eldorado and Bonanza where the greater part of the work was done, I found the miners all well supplied with provisions, especially the mine owners, who are very hospitable and entertained one in a princely manner, making one think that no such thing as starvation could exist in the Yukon Territory…Every one seemed to have work and at a good rate of wages.[4]*

Entrepreneur Belinda Mulrooney built a roadhouse at the confluence of Eldorado and Bonanza creeks. This site became the town of Bonanza or, more commonly, Grand Forks.

Grand Forks NWMP detachment, June 1, 1904.

Group of NWMP pose before the second detachment building, Grand Forks, ca. 1901.

It was a thriving community in 1899. Cabins covered the hillsides while the Gold Hill Hotel, Grand Forks Hotel, Bonnifield Saloon, two blacksmith shops, Eldorado Hotel and Restaurant, the NWMP detachment and a mining inspector's office lined the main road through the town. At its peak, the valley's population numbered about 10,000.[5]

In 1898, the North-West Mounted Police purchased a log building across the dirt street from the "row" occupied by the prostitutes. Two years later, the detachment building had been undermined and condemned as unsafe. The Mounties then moved into a former hotel which in turn began sinking as underground

mining operations progressed underneath the structure. By the following spring, it too was on the verge of collapse.

The Mounted Police decided they needed their own detachment building. In April 1901, they found a site and arranged to build a new detachment and stable on a hillside overlooking the town. The handsome two-storey frame building cost just under $6,000. It housed two bedrooms, an office, kitchen, dining room and cells on the ground floor and a large barrack room and storeroom upstairs. Outside of Whitehorse and Dawson, it was the only detachment lit by electricity rather than coal oil lamps. It was staffed by an inspector, a sergeant and four constables, with a dog team and two canoes for transport.[6]

The Mounted Police at Grand Forks carried out regular police duties such as investigating accidents and deaths, checking for liquor and gaming infractions, and patrolling outlying areas.

As well as keeping law and order, members in the goldfields detachments collected gold royalties—the percentage of the miner's take due to the Canadian government. An armed guard, consisting of a corporal and three members, transported the gold. Many miners sent their own bullion to Dawson with the police guard. In 1899, Inspector Belcher collected over $440,000 in

royalties from the miners of Bonanza and Eldorado creeks and their tributaries. In September 1901, the Grand Forks area provided more than 70 percent of the royalties collected by seven goldfields detachments.[7]

The royalty fee was later reduced from ten to five percent, then replaced by a gold export tax of two and one-half percent. The police no longer had to monitor each mine's output to see that full royalty was paid. Instead they had to ensure people departing the territory were not smuggling out undeclared gold.[8]

By 1906, Grand Forks was in decline. Only three members staffed the detachment. Large mining companies moved in and the heyday of the independent miner ended. The Guggenheim brothers gained control of most claims on Bonanza, Eldorado and Hunker creeks and the claims lay idle until their new owners were ready to start operations. In the meantime, the great exodus of people from the Dawson district meant many of the well-known creeks were "practically abandoned."[9]

On the afternoon of July 11, 1911, Constables Mapley and Fyfe were working in the Grand Forks detachment stables when they noticed smoke billowing from the Yukon Gold Company bunkhouse. They raced to the building and discovered an upstairs storeroom full of burning mattresses and blankets. After rousing the sleeping night shift crew, they tried to fight the fire. But flames quickly spread to the neighbouring buildings, including the Mounted Police barracks at the rear of the bunkhouse. Fyfe and Mapley worked with Grand Forks citizens and Yukon Gold employees to contain the blaze and salvage records and supplies from the burning detachment. When it was all over, 16 buildings had been destroyed and three cabins razed to prevent further spreading of the fire.[10]

The fire hastened the inevitable closing of the Grand Forks detachment. By this time, only 41 remained in the Yukon. It had become harder to police the widely-scattered population with ever fewer resources. A cabin was rented for a summer detachment for a few years, after which the area was covered by sporadic patrols from Dawson.

Sluice sleuth

One of the more common and difficult-to-detect crimes in the Klondike was the theft of gold from miners' sluice boxes and mining claims. It was hard to prove that gold came from a particular claim and, unless the theft had been witnessed, evidence was hard to find. Members in plainclothes and detectives monitored shady characters and suspicious activities but many such thefts remained unsolved.

One successful investigation in 1911 concluded with the arrest of Jack Williams and James Stott, sub-foreman and labourer of the Yukon Gold Company. When the company manager suspected that his employees were stealing gold, he made wax impressions of several gold nuggets which were then used as bait on the claims. Constable Victor Christensen was detailed for plainclothes duty and hid himself where he could watch the suspects unobserved. When Williams and Stott helped themselves from the salted claims, they were immediately arrested and charged. Both were found guilty and sentenced to two years hard labour. Judge Macaulay complimented Constable Christensen for "his intelligent, impartial and straightforward evidence in the case."[11]

Grand Forks NWMP detachment, 1904.

Interior of RCMP detachment at Grand Forks.

The Dewey Hotel

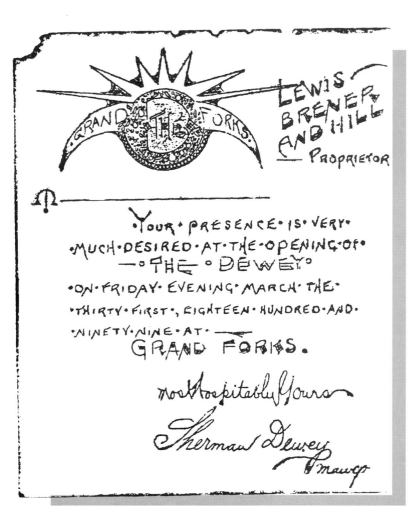

GRAND FORKS

LEWIS
BRENER
AND HILL
— PROPRIETOR

·YOUR· PRESENCE· IS· VERY·
·MUCH· DESIRED· AT· THE· OPENING· OF·
— ° THE ° DEWEY°
·ON· FRIDAY· EVENING· MARCH· THE·
·THIRTY· FIRST·, EIGHTEEN· HUNDRED· AND·
·NINETY· NINE· AT· —
GRAND FORKS.

Most Hospitably Yours

Sherman Dewey
Manager

NORTH WEST MOUNTED POLICE

GRAND FORKS, 3rd, August, 1901

To/

Const. Patterson, N.W.M.Police.

Deputy Chief Constable, of Grand Forks,

Yukon Territory;

Whereas, complaint has been made to me in writing, in accordance with Section 575, of the Criminal Code, that a room is kept in the Dewey Hotel at Grand Forks, in the Yukon Territory of Canada; and used as a common gaming house, as defined in Section 196 of the Criminal Code:----

Now, therefore, this is to authorize you, in accordance wity the provisions of said Section 575, of the Criminal Code; to enter such room, kept as aforesaid, with such Constables as you deem requisite, and if necessary to use force for the purpose of effecting such entry(whether by breaking open doors, or otherwise)---and to take into custody all persons who are found therein, and to sieze all tables and instruments of gaming, and all moneys and securities for money; and bring them before me that proceedings may be taken as the law directs; and for so doinig this shall be your sufficient Warrant.

Given under my hand this 3rd day of August, 1901, at Grand Forks, in the Yukon Territory, Canada.

a Justice of the Peace, in and for
the Yukon Territory

Grand Forks

Invitation to the grand opening of the Dewey Hotel.

"Warrant to Search" the Dewey Hotel in Grand Forks, dated August 3, 1901, signed by Inspector W. Routledge.

Grand Forks, July 1, 1903. Crowd lines the street in front of the Dewey Hotel.

AFTER THE RUSH

Whitehorse: "H" Division headquarters

NWMP tents at Whitehorse, October 1900.
H.C. Barley, photographer.

Town of Whitehorse. View of barracks square
from the escarpment. E.J. Hamacher,
photographer.

> *The change of location of the Post from
> Tagish to this point at the most
> unfavourable season of the year, has been a
> great test of the endurance and fortitude of
> our men, the difficulties having been
> overcome with cheerfulness. Though our
> sick list was somewhat swollen by the
> unusual exposure, it is not to be wondered
> at, as the men were taken from warm
> comfortable quarters to lie under canvas,
> most of them being quite new to the country
> and unacclimatized.*

— Assistant Surgeon Paré, 1900[12]

After only two years of operation, Tagish Post, the original headquarters of "H" Division, was practically abandoned. With the completion of the railway from Skagway to Whitehorse, all incoming traffic travelled overland, bypassing the headwater lakes system and the police post on the Tagish River. By 1899, the NWMP realized the new townsite being laid out at the railway terminus was a much better location.

The transfer of "H" Division headquarters was not painless. By the time a site was selected in downtown Whitehorse in 1900, it was early fall—not the best time to move into tents. The police dismantled many of the Tagish buildings and attempted to raft the logs to Whitehorse. The rafts proved too large for Miles Canyon, so they had to be taken apart and rebuilt at Canyon City. Even then, three rafts shattered in the turbulent rapids of

the canyon. The logs drifted past Whitehorse. The NWMP then called on the engineer and carpenters of the Department of Public Works for help. Using lumber purchased from local mills, Mounties and DPW employees managed to erect eight buildings by November.[13]

NWMP going through the routine of the mounting and relief of the night guard and picket in front of the Whitehorse guardroom, ca. 1902.

The Whitehorse canteen, May 1903.

> The [Whitehorse] *canteen is a great boon to the division, especially to the men on detachment. Situated as they are, along the river between the White Horse and Dawson divisions, they would otherwise be unable to purchase the little luxuries that make life pleasant.*
>
> *A good stock of canned fruits, milk and vegetables are kept on hand, also several kinds of canned meats and fish. These articles are much appreciated as they make a change from the regular issue of rations.*
>
> **— Supt. A.E. Snyder, 1902** [14]

71

It was an exciting time in the fledgling community. The railway had been completed in July 1900. The population grew rapidly and the price of real estate soared. The town thrived due to its strategic position as both the terminus of the railway and head of Yukon River navigation. Within a year, this route to Dawson replaced the long haul via St. Michael, Alaska and the lower Yukon River as the main route into the territory. Optimism soared even higher with the discoveries of large copper ore bodies nearby, drawing investors and workers.[15]

From 1900 to 1910, Whitehorse was the headquarters for "H" Division. This covered the vast area of southern Yukon up to Five Finger Rapids, west to Kluane and even parts of northern British Columbia. In 1901,103 members served in "H" Division at 18 detachments. Superintendent Primrose commanded 43 Mounties at division headquarters while another four occupied the Whitehorse town station or community detachment.

By 1910, only 50 Mounted Police remained in the entire Yukon. Whitehorse was merged into "B" Division at Dawson and, for a few years, was a sub-district with only two one-man detachments, Carcross and the Whitehorse town station. Only 15 members remained to patrol and police the rest of the huge sub-district.[16]

NWMP haul a two-storey building into the Whitehorse compound with a windlass, ca. 1902.

Whitehorse NWMP office, June, ca. 1903. J.E. Lee, photographer.

By the end of World War I, the Yukon economy was in decline. With the exception of the Whitehorse copper industry, the Yukon reaped none of the benefits of wartime mobilization. Gold mining came to a virtual standstill with an inflationary economy, the loss of experienced workers, and a fixed price for gold. Most young men who signed up for the armed forces never returned to the territory.[17]

Over the next two decades, a much smaller police force served a diminished and aging population, including many old-timers who had stayed on after the gold rush. The Mounties were still expected to handle a multitude of civil service duties as well as law enforcement. But Whitehorse had become a quiet little town, livening up only during the summer shipping season. It remained that way until the next world war woke it abruptly from its sleep.

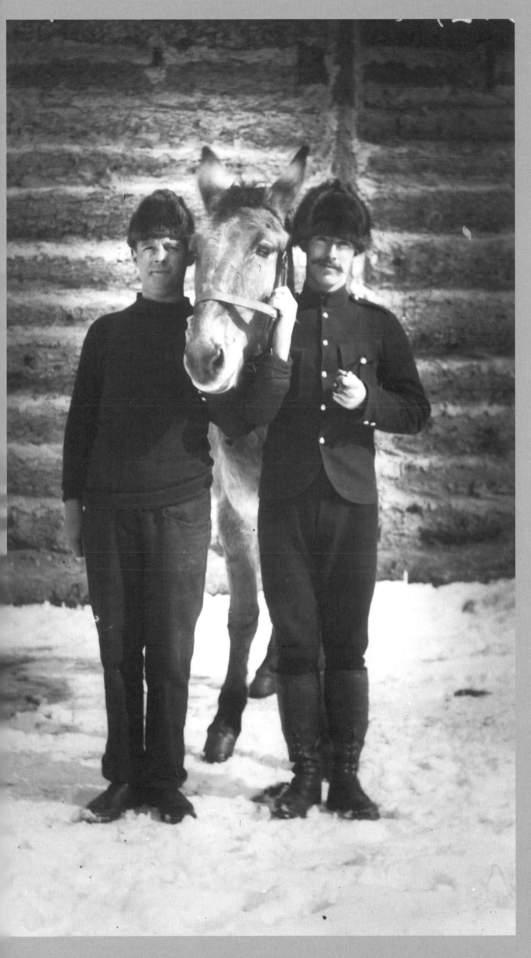

Two members pose with the Mounties' best friend, ca. 1902.

Writing reports in the "H" Division office, ca. 1902.

73

Lower Labarge: *A seasonal detachment*

After a long icebound winter, Dawson residents eagerly awaited two events every spring—the break-up of the Yukon River ice and the arrival of the first boats from Whitehorse bearing fresh fruit, vegetables and eggs. After a winter of dried and tinned foods, Dawsonites paid top dollar to the first entrepreneur to arrive with fresh apples. Consequently, the various boats raced to be the first to reach Dawson as soon as the Yukon River was navigable. The big hold-up was Lake Laberge,[18] 50 miles below Whitehorse, which remained icebound for weeks after the rest of the river had opened.

Many companies wintered their steamships at Lower Labarge, at the foot of the 30-mile-long lake. The steamship companies could get a head start on spring navigation by freighting cargos over the lake ice to open water at the Thirtymile River. Other travellers sledded their boats and canoes over the lake to open water, a task which grew more dangerous as the ice gradually rotted. For a short period every spring, Lower Labarge was a busy and exciting place. Ships' crews readied their vessels for the water, the roadhouse did a booming business, and the telegraph office clattered with outgoing and incoming messages.

In April 1915, Inspector Arthur Acland assigned Constable William Kellock McKay to the Lower Labarge detachment. The Yukon River had opened at Whitehorse on April 3. Four days later McKay was on his way—travelling part way by horse and wagon, then on foot over the ice, helping his dog pull a sleigh loaded with 150 pounds of gear.

This was McKay's first posting outside of Whitehorse and he revelled in the freedom from headquarters routine. During his two months at Lower Labarge, he made numerous foot patrols up and down the river. He searched for a missing man, registered all small craft floating by, buried the body of a drowning accident victim, hunted ducks, monitored a forest fire, and visited the camps of travelling First Nations people. McKay helped an alcoholic telegraph operator dry out, socialized with the ships' crews and caught numerous rides on boats of all sorts. His diary gives a flavour of life at a one-man Yukon River detachment.

Readers should note that the stretch of the Yukon River between Whitehorse and Lake Laberge was commonly referred to as the Fiftymile, while the rapid, winding section from Lake Laberge to Hootalinqua—the small settlement at the confluence with the Teslin River—was called the Thirtymile. The Mounted

Police assigned numbers to all small vessels either at Whitehorse or Lower Labarge.[19]

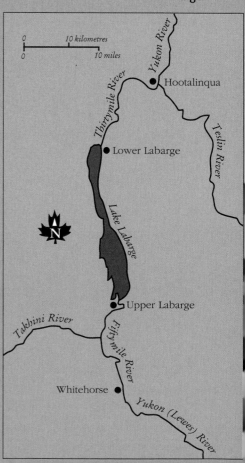

Lower Labarge post and area

Lower Labarge detachment, ca. 1898. Paintings by E.B. Brown.

Tues., April 13 *Patrol down 30 mile. Leave Lower Labarge at 7.45 on raft. Arrive Scott's cabin 2.30 pm. Hard job stearing raft through the rapids. Get out once to push raft off snag. Water v. cold. Can't get in Scott's cabin - sleep outside - no blanket - build large fire and make fir bough wind break and reflector. Have to sleep in wet clothes - burn one pair socks in drying.*

Fri., April 14 *Leave cabin 6.30. Arrive across river 7.30! Start for Lower Labarge on foot. Follow telegraph wires 4 m. shore ice 7 m. trail 4 m. Arrive back 2 pm. Wanted to get to Marion Davis' Cabin but find have only been to Scotts Cabin. 30 mile trip and miss the cabin by one mile -! This means another trip.*

Sat., April 15 *Start cutting operator off his hooch. Pretty bad to-night. gets a go of the shakes, doctor 60 miles off! 50 mile open as far as Lake Labarge. 30 mile open as far as big Salmon.*

Fri., April 23 *Fearful wind all day and nothing doing except writing reports. Originals alright but duplicates and triplicates are the limit.*

Sat., April 24 *First boat 1-15 leaves Lower Labarge for Dawson. Lindston brothers and James McGavin an old timer prospector and trader.*

Has travelled all over Yukon, Alaska - Mackenzie R. and N.B.C. [northern British Columbia]

Mon., May 24 *Roadhouse closes…Start Boarding with [telegraph] operator.*

Only 3 now in Place…The good old batching life starts again. Am living in a little 15'x12' log shack where I am now writing. Must say I do love the life.

Wed., June 2 *Leave Labarge 1 am and mush 17 miles down river to Tanana wreck arriving there at 6 am. Take statements from men in launch who had found Body. Get coffin made by a carpenter there. Leave wreck at 3 pm in row boat with coffin and 2 days grub. Go down river 5 miles as far as "Eagles Nest at Cape Horn". There in an eddy on Right bank find Body in water tied to a stake with a canvas on top of stake. Pull body out of water. Floating low in water face downwards hands by side…*

Fri., June 4 *Dig grave on Telegraph right of way mile above wreck, 16 miles above Labarge.*

Nesutlin [Nasutlin] and Whitehorse arrive during afternoon. Go down again to coffin on Nisutlin getting there about 11 pm. They drop me in small boat. I camp there for night - build fire and have meal then sleep on the shingle. ground very damp and surroundings not of the pleasantest!

Sat., June 5 *Nisutlin returns at 8 am. put coffin on Board and return to wreck. Put coffin off at grave. Get two men working on Tanana to identify body. Take body out of coffin and remove canvas. Face covered with blood and body smells very bad. Men identify body as that of Marion Davis. Put body in grave and fill grave in.*
Paint headstone on bottom of milk box.
Marion Davis
Drowned
Buried June 5th 1915 -

Monday, June 7 *Dawson and Alaska pass in early morning. leave wreck at 9 am and walk back to Labarge arriving 2 pm. make own trail most of the way.*

Tuesday, June 8 *Pack up Kit preparatory to closing detachment and returning to Whitehorse.*

Visit "Hoochi Bill" and squaw camped at Lower Labarge.

Wed., June 9 *Hoochi Bill and squaw and two other Indian families go down River to Big Salmon on Rafts.*

Leave Labarge on Steamer Casca for Whitehorse at 5 pm. Supt. Moodie and Insp. Bell on Board

Thurs., June 10 *Arrive Whitehorse 4 am. Report at guardroom at 6 am. Play tennis in evening.*

During his 17 years in the Yukon, Arthur Edward Acland rose through the ranks from a constable at Dalton Trail Post to commanding officer of the Whitehorse sub-district office. His postings took him all over the territory: Tagish, Whitehorse, Hootalinqua, Livingstone Creek, Kluane, Conrad, Dawson, and Yukon Crossing. Over the summer of 1910, he commanded a summer patrol from Dawson to Fort McPherson and back.

Born in England, Acland emigrated to Canada with his family in 1886. He enlisted with the NWMP in February 1898, after two years with the Royal Canadian Dragoons. He married in 1912, also the year of his promotion to inspector in charge of the Whitehorse Sub-district. The couple had one daughter, Margaret.

In August 1914, Acland was hospitalized for three months with typhoid fever. His was the most serious case of an epidemic caused by drinking river water pumped from an intake in front of town.

After his transfer to Depot Division in Regina in 1915, his distinguished career continued for another 18 years until his retirement in 1933 with the rank of assistant commissioner.[20]

Constable Acland notching a log near Dalton Post, June 1899. H.C. Barley, photographer.

Constable William Kellock McKay

*Birthday and anniversary of joining the force.
York, Craig, Williamson and self go down
town and "celebrate".
Result $10 for breakages.*

**— Wm. McKay's diary entry for
August 17, 1915**

*After this war people may consider a
person joined the M. Police as a means of
getting out of going to the war...You may
say what does it matter what people say –
but I should hate them to say or think a
thing like that of me...I know it will be a
hard pull to you both – you dear old people
and I dread to hear what you will say. But I
have stood out of it long enough – 2 years –
far better men than me have gone to it and
it is now up to me –
...after the whole business is over you
will think better of me as under the old
conditions I felt I was only half serving my
King and country –*

**— Wm. McKay writing his parents in March
1916 after his desertion from the RNWMP[21]**

Constable William K. McKay, 1914.

In many ways, William Kellock McKay was
a typical high-spirited and idealistic young
man of his time. An English emigrant, he joined
the RNWMP in August 1914, probably as soon
as he was legally able to do so. After training,
his first posting was Whitehorse. He recorded
his experiences over the following year and a
half with his diary entries and photographs. He
left a vivid record of the events of the time: the
death watch over a convicted murderer,
arduous patrols, and the range of day-to-day
duties in the Whitehorse Sub-district. He also
recorded the constables' amusements: swimming at a nearby lake, tennis, poker games, an
electioneering meeting, dances, picnics and
initiation into the Moose Lodge.

The Great War cast a shadow over this
otherwise light-hearted account. McKay made
note of the friends and comrades who died at
the front and members who tried to desert to
enlist for overseas service. As he later wrote his
parents, he had planned to desert long before
he finally boarded the train to Skagway on
February 14, 1916. When the Canadian
Immigration officer tried to apprehend McKay
at the Alaskan border by ordering the train to
back up into Canadian territory, he jumped off
the train on the American side and waited until
the train was underway before reboarding.

He travelled down the coast to Seattle,
across the United States to New York, then by
steerage passage to Liverpool, and he finally
reached London on March 16th. He had
travelled the whole way from the Yukon with
"only the clothes I stood up in with a fur coat,
fur cap and moccasins." The following day,
McKay enlisted with the 1st King Edward's
Horse where he served with distinction for the
remainder of the war. In 1920, the Canadian
government granted McKay a free pardon for
his desertion from the police force on account
of his services rendered in the war.

Yukon Mounties and the Great War

At the start of the war, members were forbidden to join the armed forces because the Canadian government felt the police were needed at home. As the war dragged on, however, more soldiers were required and the decision was reversed. On April 6, 1918, permission was granted for all ranks to volunteer for overseas service. The resulting exodus meant the closure of 87 detachments across the country.[22]

RNWMP members of "B" Division at Skagway, on their way overseas to join the Canadian Light Infantry. Names of members are handwritten around the border.

War brought new duties at home as well as overseas. Constable York guards two prisoners of war working on the railway south of Whitehorse: Austrian Tom Bokovitch and a German prisoner, ca. 1914-15. Alex Gagoff, a Russian, shot Bokovitch and three other crew members on September 30, 1915.

THE WEEKLY STAR.

Whitehorse, Y. T., Friday. Oct. 1, 1915   No. 24

ALEX GAGOFF

When Alex Gagoff goes to the scaffold this morning, and he will have made the trip ere any but the earliest risers among the readers of this paper see this, he will expiate his crime of quadruple murder, the most flagrant violation of God's command, "Thou shalt not kill," ever committed in the north and rarely equalled in the annals of crime.

Gagoff nurtured a fancied grievance until it bred a murderous spirit in his heart and in that mood he came upon four unarmed and harmless men and shot all of them to death, later gloating over his horrible act, convicting himself out of his own mouth. So far as known he has never expressed regret for his wholesale slaughter; rather, he has persistently justified himself in the somewhat egotistic assertion, "Me show them Alex is a good man." While his poor victims will never know it, Alex will be a "good man" henceforth.

Never was an accused man given a fairer or more impartial trial than that accorded Gagoff. The law was more lenient to him than he was to himself. He apparently reasoned that he had forfeited his right to live, but justified himself in that he had avenged fancied wrongs. In his opinion, the result justified the means employed to bring it about.

Far away from the land of his birth, the Russian steppes, where he was reared, and where he served in that world-famous military organization, the Cossacks, Alex Gagoff, by the time this greets the readers' eyes, will have answered to man for his crime against man. His arraignment by and his answer to God is another matter.   *E.J. White – Editor*

ALEX GAGOFF

Gagoff Hanged This Morning

To the extent that the taking of one life would atone for four others, the murder of the railroad section crew three miles south of town on the 30th of last September was expiated this morning when, promptly at 7 o'clock, Murderer Alex Gagoff was launched into eternity, being hanged by the neck until dead as the sentence of the court decreed he should be.

With firm, unfaltering steps, marching between two stalwart members of the R. N. W. M. P., Gagoff mounted the steps of the scaffold and took his place on the trap door. Official Hangman Ellis, who came all the way from Ottawa to perform the work of less than a dozen seconds, adjusted the black cap. Sheriff George Brimston then asked the man who stood on the threshold of death if he had anything to say. The question was repeated in the Russian language by Interpreter Zarnowsky. Gagoff answered in Russian, "No." In a clear voice Sheriff Brimston said, "May God have mercy on your soul!" Immediately Hangman Ellis sprung the trap and Alex Gagoff was launched to his death. The drop was 7 feet, 10 inches. His neck was broken and death was instantaneous. Dr. Clarke kept his hand on the pulse, which ceased to beat in 14 minutes. The body was then cut down and placed in a box.

Captain Bell, acting coroner, empanneled the following jury: Wm. Drury, C.H. Johnston, S. Coulter, F.E. Harbottle, F. Langholz and Al Stewart, who viewed the body, returning a verdict that the deceased came to his death by hanging in accordance with the decree of the court. The body was buried immediately beneath the scaffold.

Gagoff slept well through all of last night. He awoke at 5 this morning and later ate a breakfast consisting of two eggs, toast and a cup of coffee.

Those who had not seen Gagoff since his trial and conviction last fall were surprised at his appearance this morning, he having fallen off fully fifty pounds during his confinement.

In addition to those whose duty required their presence, the execution was witnessed by only a half dozen spectators. The temperature was 36 below zero.

Constable Thomas A. Dickson

Five generations of Yukoners can trace their ancestry to a remarkable Mountie and his First Nations wife. In 1888, Tom Dickson and his brothers, Adam and George, left their lumbering jobs in Keene, Ontario to join the North-West Mounted Police. Their younger brother, Andrew, would follow in their footsteps twelve years later. During his service at various posts throughout the west, Tom gained a reputation as an excellent marksman and horseman. In 1898, he headed for the Yukon, where he helped build Tagish Post and Carcross detachment. On January 7, 1900, Dickson arrested one of the Yukon's most infamous murderers, George O'Brien. According to family legend, Constable Dickson declared, "Hands up or your lights out!"[23]

He left the force in 1900 to marry Louise, a Tagish First Nation woman. Louise's uncle, Skookum Jim Mason, was one of the discoverers of Klondike gold. Skookum Jim employed Dickson as a bodyguard and to protect his gold. Dickson also ran a fish camp on Tagish Lake with his three brothers, all of whom had left the NWMP by this time. In 1902, Andrew and another man were canoeing on Tagish Lake when a sudden gale blew up and swamped their boat, drowning them both.

Not long after this, Tom and Louise Dickson settled in the Kluane area near Burwash Landing, where they raised 13 children. Tom became renowned as one of the Yukon's first big game guides. The family kept busy caring for their horses, big game outfitting business, mink farm, garden and trapline.

Constable Tom Dickson soon after his enlistment in 1888.

Louise Dickson with her children Grace (Chambers), Sue (Van Bibber), Kluane (Hash) and Buck at Burwash Landing.

Detachment album

Hootalinqua, ca. 1901.

Big Salmon NWMP Post, 1898. Detachments were set up along the Yukon River at approximately 35 mile intervals. The Yukon's first Commissioner, James Walsh, spent most of the winter of 1897-98 at this post, after being stranded by the Yukon River freeze-up en route to Dawson.

Claude Tidd standing by the newly-completed addition at the rear of the Ross River RCMP post, May 1923.

The Five Finger detachment, on the Yukon River downstream of the Five Finger Rapids, marked the boundary between the "B" and "H" police divisions. This post was also the inland terminus of the Dalton Trail.

CHAPTER 5

During the 1911 smallpox epidemic at Rampart House, Mounties patrolled to outlying camps, warning people to stay away from the quarantined settlement.

First Nations/NWMP relations

The arrival of the North-West Mounted Police marked a new stage in the interaction between two very different cultures. The Yukon's First Nations had been dealing with non-native traders, missionaries and prospectors for more than 40 years. The police, however, symbolized Canadian authority and, given their wide range of duties, were often the sole government officials most people encountered. Only four years after the arrival of the first two Mounties, the Canadian judicial system tried and executed two First Nations men for actions taken to support their own traditional justice system.

Relations between the Mounted Police and the indigenous people varied. Many senior officers looked upon Yukon First Nations people as an unwanted responsibility and treated them as demanding children. On a personal level, however, many individual Mounties established good relationships with their Aboriginal neighbours and were well-liked by the native community. A number of ex-members married First Nations women and adopted their lifestyle. Men such as Harold Frost of Old Crow and Thomas Dickson in the Kluane area and their families were well-respected by both First Nations and non-native people despite the prejudice of the time against mixed marriages.

Few early North-West Mounted Police tried to learn the customs and culture of the people living in the Yukon. Reflecting the colonial attitude of the time, they saw themselves as bringing justice and order to a lawless country. The police did not consider that the First Nations people already governed themselves and that now they were faced with foreign laws imposed by outsiders. Many NWMP officers disparaged the native people, often basing their opinions on the few who had been exposed to alcohol and disease. The Mounted Police did not realize that most First Nations people were leading self-sufficient lives far from the new white settlements. Inspector Constantine's description of the few First Nations people he met at Forty Mile sets a tone found in many early reports. He describes them as "…a lazy, shiftless lot and are contented to hang around the mining camps. They suffer much from chest trouble and die young."[1]

The first encounter between the NWMP and northern First Nations people took place at Dyea, Alaska where Inspector Constantine met the Chilkat packers at the foot of the Chilkoot Trail. His description of this transaction reflects the ambivalence of the force when dealing with First Nations people. Constantine relied on the physical abilities of these people and their knowledge of the trail to get his supplies into the Yukon, but resented the fact that they were astute negotiators prepared to bargain hard. He grumbled that the Chilkat people:

…seemed to take in but one idea, and that is how much they can get out of you,

and being at their mercy as to packing I had, as a rule, to submit to their extortion.[2]

Constantine did pay the 15¢ per pound charge, but left behind 300 pounds of his 1000 pound outfit at Dyea. He didn't realize he was getting a bargain. When the first gold rush stampeders began clambering over the trail three years later, the price would rise to 38¢ per pound and higher.[3]

Part of Constantine's orders were to look into the condition of the First Nations people in the Fortymile area, but on no account was he to give them any indication that the "Government would do anything for them as Indians." In other words, the Canadian government was not prepared to recognize their inherent rights to the land or grant any compensation for the disruption caused by the flood of newcomers. Unlike the prairies, the federal government never did extend the treaty system to Yukon First Nations people. While some small reserves were set aside, most were never occupied. The government did not even appoint an Indian superintendent to handle First Nations affairs until 1914. Until then, the government put the police in charge of giving relief to any natives in need, an unwanted responsibility.[4]

The Canadian government policy, implemented by the NWMP, was quite different from the good working relationship developed with First Nations special constables.[5] When the police first came to the Yukon, they brought their own special constables with them from the prairies, mostly dog drivers and tradesmen. In 1898, they began to hire local First Nations people as guides and interpreters. The First Nations became an important part of the police support system. The knowledge and support of guides and special constables meant the difference between life and death on the trail. The police also relied on First Nations people for winter clothing, snowshoes and other implements necessary to life on the land. Although these individuals did much to bridge the cultural gap between the Mounted Police and local First Nations, there has been little formal recognition of their contribution.

Enjoying a social evening. A Mountie dances with a little girl while Inspector Fitzgerald (right), another member, and their First Nations companions look on.

The Nantuck case

Many Mounted Police histories cite the Nantuck case as an early example of bringing effective law enforcement to the north. This incident also illustrates the conflict between two different systems of justice.

The Mounties charged four First Nations men with murder. Three were found guilty and the fourth, a fourteen-year-old boy, was convicted of the lesser charge of manslaughter. In February 1899, two of the men, weakened by their long confinement, became ill and died of "pulmonary troubles" in the Dawson jail. The remaining two were hung in August 1899 along with another convicted murderer, the territory's first executions. At the time, local newspapers cited this as an example of the swift punishment meted out by the NWMP.

In May 1898, two prospectors, Christian Fox and William Meehan, camped on the McClintock River near Marsh Lake for several days. Four native men met and visited them. On the morning they were to leave, the First Nations men shot at the two prospectors in their boat. Meehan died and Fox managed to

escape. The police apprehended the suspects within a few weeks. After being held at Tagish Post for a month, the prisoners were sent to Dawson for trial. The four brothers, known as Joe, Jim, Dawson and Frank Nantuck, said little in their own defence other than what the judge found to be an enigmatic statement that "some white man a year or two years ago had killed two Indians."[6]

According to oral accounts of native elders, documented many decades later, the shooting was not an act of random violence. Sometime previously, an old woman at Marsh Lake found or had been given a tin of white powder which she mistakenly identified as baking powder. The powder, which was probably arsenic, was used to bake bread which caused the death of an elderly man and a boy. At the time, First Nations dealt with such deaths by well-understood rules of either retribution or compensation.

All southern Yukon First Nations people belonged to either the Crow or Wolf clan. This membership, and its responsibilities, governed all aspects of daily life. The poison

victims were Crow, as were the four Nantuck men. Normally, compensation would be sought, in either goods or an equivalent death, from the clan held responsible for the deaths. Apparently the four First Nations men held the prospectors accountable for the deaths as members of the "white" clan. When Meehan and Fox did not take the opportunity to open negotiations, the young men decided to take what they thought was appropriate revenge for the deaths of their relatives.

In this case, members of both cultures acted appropriately according to their own systems of justice but neither could understand the perspective of the other. It is only recently that the territorial and federal governments have involved First Nations people and some of their traditional practices in the justice system.

Corporal Rudd with the Nantuck brothers at Tagish. During their month-long detention at Tagish, the prisoners were something of a tourist attraction to passing travellers, many of whom stopped to photograph or sketch the men.

Special Constables

Over the winter of 1897-98, the North-West Mounted Police sent 31 special constables to the Yukon. The majority were engaged as dog drivers but were expected to work at any additional duties assigned by a superior officer.[7] Most special constables earned $1 a day and rations, with the inducement of a $10/month bonus if their services proved satisfactory after a year. Special constables with expertise in particular trades were paid more. Early in the century, there was a flurry of correspondence between

Engagement form for Stick Sam.[8]

Ottawa and Dawson over the high salary being paid to cooks, as much as $100/month. Since cooks could earn so much more in hotels and roadhouses, the officers had to pay what, for the force, seemed a princely salary.[9]

According to police records, the first Yukon native people hired as special constables worked in the Dalton Trail area. In July 1898, Inspector A.M. Jarvis, in charge of the Dalton Trail Post, hired "Doctor Scottie" as a scout and guide, declaring that, "This is a very intelligent Indian and will be well worth the money we are paying him." In the spring of 1900, Constable Pringle and Special Constable

Doctor Scottie travelled 600 miles in a month to take a census of all the First Nations people in the Dalton Trail area.

In 1899, two other men, "Paddy" and "Stick Sam," began working for the police. Stick Sam worked for the police for four years and was described as "the best and most intelligent Indian in that district." In 1903, Special Constable Stick Sam drowned while attempting to cross the Kaskawulsh River on horseback during a patrol. The party missed the ford and after swimming a few strokes, Stick Sam was swept away by the current. The 26-year-old man left behind a wife and

---

DUPLICATE TO BE FORWARDED TO THE COMPTROLLER'S OFFICE.   Form No. 72.

North-West Mounted Police.

ENGAGEMENT.

I, *Stick Sam* do hereby contract, engage, promise and agree to and with the Commissioner of the Police Force, constituted by law in and for the ~~North-West Territories~~ *Yukon Territory* of Canada, to serve in such Police Force ~~for~~ _____ ~~years~~ from *month to month at $30⁰⁰ per month with bonus of $10⁰⁰ per month if services proved satisfactory at end of one year's service from September 28th/99*, and do hereby declare myself subject to all the provisions of the Act of Parliament of Canada, 57 & 58 Vic., Cap. 27, intituled : "An Act to Amend and Consolidate the Acts respecting the North-West Mounted Police Force," and any Acts amending the same which may be passed during my term of service ; and to all rules, regulations or orders made by virtue of the said Acts, or any of them, and that I will, during the said term of service, take care of and protect all articles of public property which shall from time to time be entrusted to me, and make good all deficiencies and damages occurring to such property while in my care or possession, except through fair wear and tear or unavoidable accident. *And I do hereby declare and admit that by reason of such engagement no right accrues to me for any transport expenses returning from the* ~~North-West Territories~~ *Yukon Territory of Canada on being discharged.*

SIGNATURE *"Stick ✗ Sam"* (his mark)

DATE *September 28th 1899*

PLACE *Dalton Trail Post*

WITNESS *Am Jarvis J.P. Insp.*

500-28-2-97.

---

children. Inspector A.E. McDonell recommended that the bereft family be supplied with rations. He is the only Yukon native special constable listed on the force's official Honour Roll. At the RCMP Training Academy in Regina, local landmarks named after Honour Roll members include Stick Sam Walk.[10]

The number of special constables working in the Yukon, both native and non-native, ranged from a high of 44 in early 1906 to a low of two in 1917. For six years, from 1917 to 1923, an unnamed native special constable ran a detachment at Moosehide, the First Nations village a few miles downstream from Dawson. His enforcement work resulted in a notable decrease in alcohol-related offences.

By 1969 the RCMP were taking a new look at the role of special constables. Coincident with the last northern dog patrol, the Solicitor General's annual report for 1969 contained the following reflections:

> *The conversion from dog teams to motorized transport and the general movement of the native people to larger settlements has affected our need for Indian and Eskimo Special Constables. They are no longer required as hunters, guides and dogdrivers, however, an increasing need has been found for capable interpreters. As suitable natives become available, they will also be utilized to an increasing extent in an actual enforcement role.[11]*

The special constable program underwent a number of changes. Native special constables were hired from Yukon communities, trained and then given an enforcement role in their home community. The first person hired under this program was Roger Kay from Old Crow. Two Yukon members who got their start in this program are Corporal Doug Reti, in charge of the Carcross detachment, and Constable Debby Morris, stationed in Old Crow.[12] In recent years, special constables were given the opportunity to become regular members. As of January 1995, 21 First Nations people are members of the Yukon RCMP. [13]

Alfred Hunter served as special constable for the First Nations village of Old Mayo in the late 1920s and 1930s. His wife Maggie probably sewed his unique uniform jacket.

Mounted Police at Fort McPherson, ca. 1904. Interpreter and guide Louis Cardinal is standing on the right.

...I have never seen his equal. Tireless always alert, a good boatman, an excellent tracker, an unequalled woodman, a dead shot, a splendid axeman, a fine cook, a packer that beats anything I ever saw, good-natured and with a heart that is never discouraged. Louis Cardinal is the greatest man I have ever had with me on a hunting trip and I have hunted in all parts of the world.

— F.D. Selous, 1904[14]

Louis Cardinal was one of the force's most experienced and well-travelled special constables and guides. In January 1898, he left the prairies to work as a dog driver in the Yukon during the peak of the Klondike gold rush. He was one of the small force stationed at the Chilkoot Summit, ready to fight off a potential invasion from the infamous Soapy Smith and his gang. Cardinal later commented, "It was lucky for us Soapy didn't come because we didn't have enough bullets to ward them off."[15]

Cardinal went on to serve in Dawson and guided many patrols between Dawson and Fort McPherson. He also made a few patrols to Herschel Island from Fort McPherson, including one in the spring of 1911 to inform the detachment of Inspector Fitzgerald's tragic death. Cardinal settled in Fort McPherson where his hunting and guiding skills were in great demand.[16]

Inuvialuit elder Albert Oliver spoke of Cardinal's hunting skills:

There was lots of natives that would help them [the police] even Big Louie...Fred Cardinal's dad...

They say when he came back with them from Old Crow they had hard time travelling too because there was so much deep snow and no food too...At one time they saw moose tracks and right there they stopped and told the police to make camp there while he'd go look for that moose following the tracks. And he was very good on snowshoes. As he went not far, he shoot few times and he knew those white people were almost starving and now they had food. So he killed and started skinning the moose half way and brought just enough for meal and went to them. And there, they stayed for few days. Only when they had enough strength they went again and made it.[17]

A lthough he became better known as an Anglican missionary, in his youth John Martin was one of the first Mounted Police guides on the northern patrols between Dawson City and Fort McPherson. He also crafted snowshoes for the Mounted Police. The police used his cabin on Christmas Creek near the Blackstone River as a layover spot and, after the tragedy of the Lost Patrol in 1910-11, cached supplies here for the annual Dawson-Fort McPherson mail patrol.

John Martin was born at Fort McPherson and was a teenager at the time of the Klondike gold rush. When the Mounted Police began making patrols from Dawson to Fort McPherson, John and his older brother Richard guided the Mounties through their traditional trapping and hunting territory. Richard led the first Mountie patrol from Dawson to Fort McPherson via the Hart River-Little Wind River route in 1904, while John guided more of these patrols than anyone else. On one notable patrol over the winter of 1915-16, Martin and his party carried 100 pounds of mail, including illustrated papers and half a year of the *Dawson Daily News* to the people of Fort McPherson, Herschel Island and Kittizgazuit.[18]

John Martin married Bella Kunizzi of Fort McPherson and was ordained as an Anglican deacon at Aklavik in 1925. During his ministry, he travelled throughout the Yukon working in Moosehide, Ross River and Mayo. His son, Robert Martin, worked as a special constable at Ross River for a few years until the detachment closed in 1936.[19]

Claude Tidd, who took this portrait of John Martin in May 1930, described him as "a dogmushing Indian missionary."

Special Constable John Moses with his family in Old Crow, ca. 1930-31.

I n 1932, Special Constable John Moses took part in the great manhunt and final shoot-out with the man known as Albert Johnson, the "Mad Trapper" of Rat River. During the search, he and Constable Sid May travelled nearly 400 miles by dog team over 14 days. Moses Hill, just south of the Rat River, was named in his honour in 1973.[20]

John Moses came from Circle, Alaska but spent most of his adult life around the Rampart House and Old Crow area. He and his wife, Louise Roberts from Dawson, raised seven children. In 1929, he signed on as a guide and interpreter with the Mounted Police for a salary of $65 per month and a single ration. Since he provided his own dog team, he was also allotted an additional 400 pounds of dried salmon. According to the Commanding Officer at Dawson, this had many advantages:

This Special Constable has his own team which will be available for Police use, and as there is just the one team of dogs on charge to this Detachment, the advantage of the extra team is readily seen, as numerous small side trips from a regular patrol, are thus practicable without reducing the efficiency of the regular patrol, also in many cases where minor patrols are made, it leaves the Police team at the Detachment, where, should the necessity arise for their immediate need, the N.C.O. I/Charge of the Detachment can readily get them.[21]

During the four years Moses worked for the force, Corporal A.B. Thornthwaite characterized him as "fun and a good friend and guide to have." Moses briefly rejoined the force in 1944. After his death, the RCMP recognized his services by erecting a headstone in his memory.[22]

Andrew Tizya born 1921

Andrew Tizya, Annie Henry, Louise Profeit-LeBlanc and Sarah Abel in Old Crow, 1990. Gladys Netro, photographer.

They [the RCMP] good friend with anybody, just like now anyways…But then, they're good friends with us. Visit us even. They sit with us, they play cards with us. They eat with us too. You know, while we were hunting, make camp. They camped with us. Even they got their own tent they still eat with us, sit with us, and tell story.

…We tell them stories like how we lived long ago, that way they ask us questions, and that way they know us good, you see.

— Andrew Tizya, 1994[23]

Over the summer of 1994, two elders of the Vuntut Gwichin First Nation reminisced about their experiences working with the police in the northern Yukon. Andrew Tizya and Charlie Peter Charlie also spoke of some special constables who had worked with the RCMP at Rampart House and Old Crow: Thomas Njootli, John Moses, Lazarus Sittichinli, and Peter Benjamin.

Old Crow resident and former Mounted Police guide Andrew Tizya vividly remembers travelling to Fort McPherson and Herschel Island by dog team. The last trip he made was during construction of the DEW (Distant Early Warning) Line system. This was the onset of the Cold War in the early 1950s, when American forces were building radar stations and landing sites across the north to be alert for a potential attack from the USSR.

But I take that DEW line patrol that. So that's American and Japanese war that time. So nobody know about it. So we camp there. Ah, they treat me good. So they give me dogfeed, everything, grub and we go to Herschel Island, was across there 75 mile.

During his work with the police, he guided winter patrols, cut wood and hauled water for the detachment, cared for the police dogs, and caught and dried fish for dogfood. On winter patrols, he supplied his own sled, dog team, snowshoes, bedding, and clothing. All this for the salary of ten dollars a day:

. . Just seven dollar a day they pay. So me, I tell them, ten dollar a day. Work, hard work. They feed me, I used to eat dog feed [dried fish]. But still is, I tell them ten dollar a day, so they make it ten dollar a day, see. So that way they pay me.

At the time, the RCMP at Old Crow made frequent winter patrols to visit people on their traplines as well as making the longer annual patrol to Fort McPherson, a distance of nearly 500 miles. In summer, they took their boat to visit people at their fish camps and travelled downriver to the Yukon River to collect supplies from Dawson and to fish during the annual salmon run. Most of the fish were dried for dog food.

Although people worked hard, they also enjoyed themselves. Corporal George Kirk and his wife Minnie lived at Old Crow on two different occasions in the 1930s and 1940s and were well-liked by the community:

They danced lots with us. Them days no drink. Had a good time anyway… Corporal Kirk could really dance…his wife too. Had a good time with us.

In summation, Andrew Tizya expressed concern that people should learn of the contributions of the First Nation police guides and constables, men such as Thomas Njootli, John Moses, Lazarus Sittichinli and Peter Benjamin:

They don't know why I went to that last patrol I make, they don't know. They should write down what we did [for] them, all that, we Indians here, like Thomas, your grandfather [John Moses], Lazar and me, and Peter…I don't think they write us down.

*I used to be an interpreter for court.
When I was chief, I helped the RCMP lots,
and that's volunteer. When somebody's in
trouble, even in my sleep, they'd wake me
up. I'd go down…I'd go there…*

— Charlie Peter Charlie, 1994[24]

harlie Peter Charlie Senior is best
known for his skill playing oldtime
fiddle tunes, but in his younger years he also
did a lot of work with the police. He guided
one of the legendary patrols from Old Crow to
Herschel Island, worked as an interpreter
during court sessions, and served as a link
between his people and the justice system
during his 12 years as chief. During a recent
interview he told the story of how in the
1950s he led a police patrol to the Firth River
and incidentally went shopping at Herschel
Island. The story begins in March, sometime in
the late 1950s, when Inspector Fraser of the
Aklavik Sub-division appeared at Charlie's
camp on the Crow Flats:[25]

*Inspector Fraser come to my camp from Old
Crow, from Aklavik. Make patrol to Old Crow and
from there he hire me, so where I stay, so he
follow that trail right to my rat camp. So he talked
to me and he don't know about going to Firth
River. And where that Firth River gonna run into
this fish hole there…So he know I know that road
so he tell me to guide for him and we make it in
about two days. And now it lots of snow, deep
snow…Me, and Peter Benjamin is with me. That
time Peter Benjamin is, he always with me since
his father died. And then before we get to Firth
River it's pretty late. And we just go a little ways
and then we camp.*

When the party set up camp, Inspector
Fraser recorded the day's events in his journal.
He also read aloud from a patrol journal of
1915, when Inspector Dempster had travelled
over that same route.

*That time I remember, Inspector, when we
started camp, he just took book out and he write
down what happen today, and how long we travel
and the weather I guess. And then he got book too
for where we started set camp. He kept book out
and he read book, and pretty soon he tell
me…something. I stop working and just listen to
him and he say, nine, nineteen fifteen I guess. It's
a Inspector from Rampart House, Inspector travel
this long, this road we follow. [probably the 1915
patrol report of Sergeant, later Inspector,
Dempster] So that day he, he run it to Firth River
and camp there. That's where I got camp
now…But that time 1915, it's long ago. That
Inspector, from Dawson, he go through by
dogteam and he go to Rampart House. So when*

*he got to Rampart House, from there Peter Moses
take him with dog team right to the Herschel
Island. [still talking about 1915 Dempster
patrol]*

*So me I took Inspector from Crow Flat and go
to Firth River. And then from there just follow
Firth River right to the Herschel Island... by dog
team. Two days to Firth River then two days, three
days to Herschel Island.*

After they reached the Firth River,
Inspector Fraser persuaded Charlie and
Benjamin to go on to Herschel Island to buy
groceries at the island's store.

*And then Inspector tell me, Herschel Island
got native store there and stuff is really cheap.
Even you, you got big load to come back with, you
wouldn't even need a hundred dollar. That's why
I went to Herschel Island. [ca. late 1950s and
1960s, the police supervised a store at Herschel
Island for the Inuit.]*

*And that Inspector, Inspector got lots of
people with him. Special constable and Father
Pleine. And I think there's two constable with
him. So that's two constable, and with Inspector
that's three and Father Pleine and me and Peter
Benjamin. That many. So when we got down
there, April 10, that's all I remember is April 10,*

*we got to Herschel Island. There was wind and
there was 40 below. Felt really cold. So our dogs
can't even sleep, it's so cold for them, and Peter's
dog too. So next day we stay there and next day
we come back with big load of grocery. Flour—
100 pounds, 15 dollar and in Crow is about 50
dollar. There were lots of grub like that and all
that Inspector, what he [had] left over he give it to
me too.*

At the time, there were six or seven people
at Herschel Island as well as two RCMP
constables and a special constable. The pair
stayed one day then headed back. The trip
home was not an easy one.

*When we left Herschel Island to go back to
my camp, it was, you can't see any stick or willow
or nothing. No trail can show. So when I go back
to the Firth River and then I go up, follow where
fish spawning, I see it. So, even we're going up,
me and Peter, we go up that Firth River and think
that sometime it's maybe not Firth River. Maybe
different river I took. No stuff, tree, or anything,
nothing. We can't see trail. We were on the right
track. We go back to that camp and then we camp
there. Next day we make long day from cabin up
to that fish hole. I call it is, 84, 80 mile. We make
a long day. Then we camp there and then next
day, about four hour to my camp.*

Billy Fox 1909-1970

In the 1930s, Billy Fox worked as a special constable for the Teslin detachment for $65 a month. When he left the force, both the RCMP constables recommended his services.[26]

Former constable Derek Parkes describes Special Constable Roland Saguak's (also spelled Saȓuak) job at Herschel Island in the early 1930s:

> Special Constable Roland Saguak was kept busy in the Summer net fishing and seal hunting for dog-feed and in the Winter hauling ice from the lake in the middle of the island, cooking dog-feed, etc...The main duty of the Police was to be ready for emergencies and it was essential for each Detachment to have a good strong and well trained dog team and a reliable guide and snowhouse builder.[28]

Herschel Island detachment, 1933. "Shades of Regina." Constable "Frenchy" Chartrand, Special Constable Roland Saguak and Constable Derek Parkes had just been shingle-staining the roof of the Inspector's house and, incidentally, themselves.

Unidentified Mountie and special constable at Dawson City, ca. 1920s.

December 23rd, 1933.

To Whom It May Concern :

I have known the bearer, Billy FOX for the past eight years and in that time I have found him to be honest, trustworthy and energetic. Having employed this man periodically I have found him to be a most capable Guide and Pilot.

A. Bryde.
A. Bryde.

Facsimile of testimonial[27]

CHAPTER 6

The Mounted Police in the Yukon met with little serious crime before World War II. The few murders were easily solved, usually a crime of passion or a partnership gone awry. There were only a few routes out of the territory: down the Yukon River into Alaska, or south through the mountain passes into the Alaska panhandle. Thanks to the telegraph line, suspects could be apprehended long before they reached the border. Most were well aware of the long arm of the Mounties and few dared defy it. The majority of the Yukon's citizens were law-abiding, making the exceptions all the more notable.

In the early years, the Mounties of the Yukon achieved national renown for solving the O'Brien and Labelle-Fournier murders. In both cases, a continent-wide manhunt located a suspect or a key witness—proving the adage that "the Mounties always got their man." Skilled forensic work recreated the crimes and led to convictions.

A third murder in 1914 was less well-known, but no less challenging. The body of prospector Dominic Melis was found floating in the Yukon River near Whitehorse, trussed up with branches. Medical evidence established a probable date of death long after the most likely suspects had left town. It was a puzzle, but excellent detective work by Sergeant Lewis McLauchlin proved more than equal to the test.

In 1901, Mounties at Whitehorse, Dawson and Dalton Trail were called on to defend Canadian sovereignty. They fortified their detachments to repel a hostile invasion. Official police reports tell nothing about this. While the conspiracy of the Order of the Midnight Sun may have been mostly fantasy, this incident demonstrated police readiness to respond promptly to any type of threat.

In 1923, Herschel Island became the scene of one of the first courts held above the Arctic Circle. The trials and subsequent hangings of two convicted murderers marked a turning point in Inuit–police relations.

Judge Macaulay and court members at Old Crow with Constable Sid May at right, ca. 1930. The court party travelled from Dawson to try a man for the theft of furs from a trapline.

The Remolo Cesari case

The year 1914 marked the eruption of World War I but in the Yukon, the year was noted for the Mounties' solution of a puzzling murder case. The unlikely motive for this crime was not robbery or passion, but plans for a "perpetual motion machine."[1]

In June, the liveliest place in Whitehorse was the riverbank by the train station at the foot of Main Street. Here, incoming passengers and freight were transferred to the riverboats headed downriver to Dawson City. On June 11th, some longshoremen noticed

Convicted murderer Remolo Cesari at Whitehorse in 1915.

what seemed like a bundle of clothing floating in the water between the docks and a barge. When they spotted a blackened hand poking out from the clump, they called for the Mounted Police.

The Yukon River was the territory's main summer highway and accidental drownings were not uncommon. It was clear, however, that this was no accident. The body was trussed up in a framework of poles. The medical examiners found death was caused by numerous skull fractures from blows of a blunt instrument. Two doctors determined the body had been in the water no more than four to six weeks. This information later created a dilemma for the investigating officer, Sergeant Lewis McLauchlin, as the two prime suspects had left town nearly four months earlier.

After extensive inquiries around town, storekeeper Cap Martin identified the dead man as Dominic Melis, an Italian immigrant who had rented quarters in the Bissler House with his partner Remolo Cesari. The pair formerly worked at the Pueblo copper mines north of Whitehorse. In December 1913, they became friendly with George Ganley, after he repaired their water pump. The three went hunting together in January. Cesari and Ganley, both heavy drinkers, became increasingly friendly while relations between Cesari and Melis worsened. The two argued incessantly over rights to an invention they had been working on, a perpetual motion machine. The two began purchasing their supplies separately, claiming it was better for "each to have his own teapot."

Melis dropped out of sight early in February. Cesari later told a number of people that Melis had gone away. Ganley and Cesari travelled to Dawson together a few weeks later. When Sergeant McLauchlin examined the rooms rented by Melis and Cesari, he was shocked at the sight of blood all over the walls and floor. The back of a chair also had blood stains. This was soon explained. The bachelors had hung small game to season on nails in the walls. He did notice, however, two places where an ineffectual effort had been made to mop blood stains off the floor and the door. Why wipe up two spots in a room already awash in gore? The sergeant took some samples.

More evidence came to light in a sack Cesari had left at Martin's store. It contained an axe head, a raincoat and a pair of rubber boots—one with a suspicious dark stain on the inside.

Detective Sergeant Eion McBrayne found Ganley working for the Yukon Gold Company on Bonanza Creek. Cesari had quit some weeks before but was finally tracked down in Dawson. Despite the problem about the date of death, McLauchlin and his superior, Inspector Acland, decided to issue a warrant, charging the two men with murder. McBrayne travelled to Whitehorse with the suspects, then stayed to work on the case.

The pair collected testimony, including a few confusing statements from Ganley and Cesari. Mounting evidence pointed toward Cesari. He ended up with, then later sold, a shotgun that had been one of Melis' treasured possessions. He had removed about three inches from the end of the barrel. According to Ganley, Cesari claimed the barrel had cracked after being placed in the snow. The

shotgun, located in Dawson, was thought to be the blunt instrument used in the murder.

The poles used to tie up the body remained a problem. McLauchlin and McBrayne surmised that the body had been trussed in the basket-like structure to make it easier to move, assuming Melis had been killed in his residence. There were five sticks all about five feet long: two alders, one small pine, one willow and one "balm of Gilead" (balsam poplar). There were a number of places where similar poles could be cut along the riverbank above Whitehorse. That was the problem. Scores of fishing poles about the same size had been cut all along the riverbank. Nonetheless, McLauchlin and McBrayne continued to sift the evidence and by September were ready to present their case before a judge and jury.

The prosecutor, J.P. Smith, asked the judge and jury to travel south of town, a short distance up the old tramway around the White Horse Rapids. Twenty feet from the riverbank, he pointed out stumps matching three of the sticks wrapped around the body. Two nicks in the axe head found in Cesari's possession matched ridges in the balm of Gilead stick. A nearby bank contained clay matching that found in a head wound on the

body. Witnesses attested that, during the winter, there were caverns within the shore ice, large enough to hide and preserve a frozen body until the rising river floated it away in spring. The prosecution surmised that one of the victim's hands had been exposed to the sun causing it to decompose and blacken. Finally, Cesari's effects included a map showing the trail to that very spot. Cesari was unable to explain away this evidence and his testimony had many discrepancies.

The defence counsel, J.A.W. O'Neil, demanded to know the results of the blood tests taken from the boot and the partners' residence. The judge cautioned the lawyer against pursuing his inquiry but O'Neil insisted, convinced that they would prove to be animal blood. A telegraph was read from Dr. Charlton at Regina stating the samples were definitely human blood.

On September 30, the case ended after a six-day trial. The jury took only one hour and forty minutes to decide on their verdict—guilty. Justice Craig sentenced Cesari to death by hanging on February 5, 1915.

Longshoremen spotted Melis' corpse floating near the White Pass docks on the Whitehorse waterfront in June, 1914. The train station is at left.

Death watch

A "death watch" consists of 3 men, one of whom is always sitting in front of the condemned man's cell to see that he does not commit suicide and be responsible for his safekeeping. I was one of the party for 3 months – viz. November, December and January – my hours of duty being 12–4 am and 12–4 pm and a drearier job one can hardly imagine.

— Cst. William Kellock McKay[2]

On February 1, 1915, Remolo Cesari's death sentence was commuted to life imprisonment after he was certified insane. The death watch ended. Cesari was expected to work as part of his imprisonment, although he still wore leg irons.

On the evening of February 10th, at 6:00 p.m. Constables York and Hayes were on guard duty. York took off the irons so Cesari could remove his trousers. The prisoner suddenly stood up and swung a table at his guards, then bolted out of the jail and into the night. According to McKay, "It was very dark and snowing and blowing hard, a really bad night even for the North." The two constables followed, Hayes ringing the alarm bell on his way out.

Constable Hayes fired once in the air, then three times at Cesari, hitting him twice. When the escapee was carried back to the guard room, the members discovered Cesari had been wounded in the thigh and the abdomen. He died at 10:30 p.m.

In his report to the Commanding Officer at Dawson, Inspector Acland wrote that "Hayes was fully justified in resorting to extreme measures in order to prevent his escaping." The subsequent inquest also exonerated Hayes of any blame.[3]

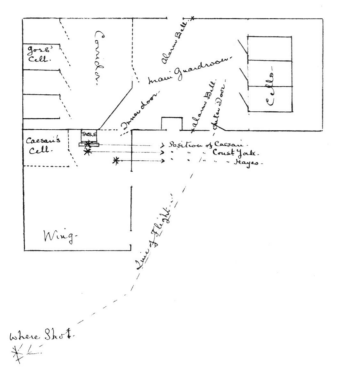

Diagram illustrating Cesari's escape attempt.

Constable W.L. Pritchett sits in the Whitehorse guard room during his shift on death watch over Remolo Cesari, 1915.

Detective William H. "Billy" Welsh

Detective Welsh has proved himself a clever man in his particular line and has done some very good work. His experience as a detective in various coast cities is of great assistance to us here, as most of our criminals come from these places.

— Ass't. Commissioner Z.T. Wood, 1905[4]

As early as 1898, the Mounted Police in the Yukon employed plainclothes detectives, years before this practice was adopted by the force elsewhere in Canada. In their undercover work, the detectives tracked the movements of known criminals. Police policy was to prevent crime by encouraging undesirables to leave the territory. Detectives also handled "insider" jobs such as theft, monitored illegal gambling games, and travelled all over the continent to seek and apprehend suspected criminals. Detectives were paid handsomely compared to the regular constable on plainclothes duty, earning between $175 and $200 per month plus expenses. The most renowned of these men was Detective "Billy" Welsh.[5]

Welsh's excellent detective work was frequently cited in annual reports. Perhaps his most important contribution to early Yukon police work was the introduction of fingerprint identification. In 1904, Welsh travelled to St. Louis, Missouri, on an extradition case. While there, he visited the World's Fair, where he saw an exhibit of fingerprinting. He brought the concept back to the Yukon. In his annual report, Assistant Commissioner Wood enthusiastically advocated the adoption of the system across Canada. The following year, Wood proudly announced the first solution of a Yukon theft using fingerprint identification.[6]

Little personal information is available about Welsh, other than that he had a talent for making political enemies. By 1905, three people had either laid charges against Welsh or threatened to do so. The accusations ranged from intimidating voters (apparently for telling the men they were not allowed to vote twice at different polls), to accepting bribes from gamblers. One of Welsh's denouncers even claimed that it was a disgrace that a "Liberal" should be charged "by a man from the slums of Portland, such as Welsh." Welsh was wholeheartedly supported by his superiors, who saw the accusers, all local Liberals, as mounting a general attack on the police. When the matter finally came to trial in 1906, Justice Craig found Welsh not guilty.[7] As Inspector T.A. Wroughton reported with great satisfaction, Craig had some nasty words for Welsh's accusers, stating that:

…the informant Joseph Andrew Clark, was moved only by animus and revenge, and that the evidence of Thomas Chisholm, the prosecuting witness, was unworthy of credence and that in his (the judge's) mind he was branded as a 'coward, a dastard and a liar.'[8]

Detective Billy Welsh, March 1902.

99

The Midnight Sun conspiracy

Ottawa, 18th November, 1901
CONFIDENTIAL
Dear Major Perry,

Wood is positive of the existence of a conspiracy to seize our Yukon Territory. Snyder has ascertained that the correspondence is in Skagway, but the U.S. authorities will not seize unless an affidavit can be made naming the conspirators, which Snyder is unable to do.

It is not likely that there will be anything further than scheming and threats, but Mr. Sifton [Canadian Minister of the Interior] feels the responsibility of the unexpected happening, and has decided to raise the strength of the Police in the Yukon to 300; or in other words, to increase White Horse district by 50 men, thus enabling Snyder to double the detachments on the Dalton Trail and to have 100 men at White Horse.

Officially of course we deny that there is anything more than the usual group of manufactured stories, and I am to ask you to send the additional men required in small numbers, as going in to replace others who have taken their discharge or have returned to the North West after completing the regulation term of service in the Yukon.

We have two Maxim guns at White Horse, and one at Dawson. Insp. McDonell can look after that at Dawson; but I shall be glad if you can send a man from Regina to White Horse.

I know that the supplying of these men will give you a lot of trouble, and temporarily deplete your strength in the Territories, but it is one of the contingencies we cannot avoid.

Yours very truly
[Frederick White, Comptroller NWMP]

Extra · The Seattle Daily Times. · **Extra**

SIXTEEN PAGES. SEATTLE, WASHINGTON, THURSDAY EVENING, NOV. 21, 1901. FIVE CENTS EVERYWHERE.

REBELLION AGAINST CANADIAN AUTHORITIES WAS PLANNED BY DESPERATE MINERS

Ex-Governor Ogilvie of the Yukon laughs at the stories about plots to capture that country. Speaking to a Journal reporter this morning Mr. Ogilvie thinks most such stories are made up by newspapermen…At the time he was in the Klondike Mr. Ogilvie says he never heard of Fenian plots or raids on the country, and he sees no reason to believe them.

— *Evening Journal*, Ottawa, Nov. 22, 1901

Suppose we did capture all the Canadian territory in the North. Have not they stolen every inch of ground from Taggish [sic] to the summit, while our soldiers laid around here eating their regular rations and hobnobing with British subjects? There should be more Americanism instilled into some of our native Americans.

— *The Guide*, Skagway, Alaska, Nov. 1901[9]

The international boundary dispute along the Alaska panhandle, which nearly led to battle on the mountain summits at the height of the Klondike gold rush, flared up again in 1901. The Canadians were fighting for ocean access, while the Americans resented the Canadians occupying territory up to the mountain passes. Many American miners, angered at having to pay duty and gold royalties to the Canadian government, were convinced that the land they mined should be U.S. territory.

In the spring of 1901, amid this heated atmosphere of nationalism and mistrust, Superintendent Primrose of Dawson heard rumours of a plot by American citizens, based in Seattle and Skagway, to forcibly seize the Yukon. The conspirators, members of the Order of the Midnight Sun, purportedly planned to rush Whitehorse, take the smaller detachments along the Yukon River, then capture the barracks at Dawson. Apparently they expected assistance from men at Circle City and Eagle, Alaska, downriver from Dawson. This fantastic report, based on stories told by one Herbert Grehl, and some papers he carried, was taken seriously by both Superintendent Snyder, commanding officer of "H" Division at Whitehorse, and Superintendent Zachary Taylor Wood, commanding officer of the Yukon.

An undercover Dominion Police Constable, R.G. Chamberlin, interviewed many former northerners in San Francisco and Seattle—"Gamblers;

Police Officers and others galore"—but learned nothing of a threatened invasion. Primrose could never confirm the rumours but, the wheels of government had been set in motion.

Clifford Sifton, the same Canadian cabinet minister who sent machine guns to the Chilkoot and White passes in 1898, ordered reinforcements and arms to be sent to the Yukon immediately. At Dawson and Whitehorse, watches were stepped up and special squads held daily drills with the Maxim machine guns. By October, word of the conspiracy and the Canadian response hit the Alaskan newspapers, most of whom ridiculed the story and derided the Canadian government for its paranoia. Some even suggested that the Canadians had made up the conspiracy themselves as a ploy to seize Skagway for Canada.[10]

The affair reached its all-time low on October 20th, when Superintendent Primrose was arrested and fined in Skagway for drunk and disorderly conduct. Some contended he had been drugged by the conspirators. Many local scribes suggested it would be poetic justice if Primrose put in some time on the woodpile.

By the spring of 1902, the story had all died down. The hated five percent gold royalty tax was replaced with a reduced gold export tax of 2.5 percent. The following year, the boundary negotiations finally reached a conclusion. Canada did not get access to an ocean port. The commission voted for the status quo, keeping the border along the mountain summits.[11]

Seattle Daily Times, November 21, 1901. Headline and illustration.

Supt. A.E. Snyder, commanding officer of "H" Division in Whitehorse.

Stamp impression of the Skagway Grand Seal.

CONFIRMATION OF SAN FRANCISCO STORY

"Order of the Midnight Sun" Was the Secret Organization Back of Movement to Overthrow the Government.

MARSHAL SHOUP

JUDGE MELVILLE C. BROWN.

ROOT A. FRIEDRICH.

The Affair Planned on Lines of the World-Famous Jameson Raid.

Inspector Howard and the detachment under his command have performed excellent service in the Arctic regions. His small detachment of six men has been divided between Fort McPherson and Herschel island, some 200 miles apart….

I attach several reports from Inspector Howard which show that the presence of the police at Herschel island was most desirable, both for the unfortunate [whaling] crews, and for the preservation of law and order.

— Commissioner A.B. Perry, 1906[12]

In July 1901, Inspector D.M. Howard led ten NWMP members to their new posting in Whitehorse. They were among the reinforcements and armaments being quietly slipped into the territory in response to the Order of the Midnight Sun conspiracy. Howard's immediate assignment was to drill a squad of men for an hour every weekday in target practice with the two Maxim machine guns. These armaments, neglected since the Klondike gold rush, took on new importance as defence against a potentially large hostile force. When the threat of invasion faded away, Howard stayed on in the Yukon for another three years. From 1905 to 1907, he ran the Herschel Island and Fort McPherson detachments.

Donald MacDonald Howard was a well-educated, seasoned soldier by the time he joined the force as an inspector in 1890. He practiced law in Toronto after graduating in Arts from Trinity College. For seven years, he served as an officer with the 10th Battalion Royal Grenadiers. He had attended both the Royal School of Infantry in London, Ontario and the Cavalry School at Québec City. Like many of his fellow officers, Howard interrupted his career with the NWMP to volunteer for the South African War, serving as captain with Lord Strathcona's Horse.

By the time he retired in 1920, after 29 years service, Inspector Howard had held posts all over the west and north. His diaries at the RCMP Museum in Regina are a legacy of his long and varied career during the expansion of the force into Canada's new territories.[13]

Inspector D.M. Howard and "Ikey" at Dawson City, 1903.

Holding court above the Arctic Circle: *Hangings at Herschel Island*

…that time, them two Quangmalik, they make them dig their own grave the day before they hang them. Made them visit the people the day before they hang them. One of them…he didn't like it when people asked him he was going to die because he figured he didn't deserve to be hanged. But the other one didn't mind because he killed enough men.

— Jimmy Jacobson, 1990[14]

The year 1923 marked the first time the Canadian government sent court parties north of the Arctic Circle—one to Pond Inlet, Northwest Territories, and the other to Herschel Island, Yukon Territory. For many Inuit, it was their first opportunity to witness the Canadian justice system in action. The court party left Edmonton on June 12th and returned September 21st. The group consisted of Judge Lucien Dubuc; I.B. Howatt, K.C., counsel for the Crown; L.T. Cory, counsel for the accused and for the Department of Indian Affairs. Three Mounties accompanied them: Sgt. F.E. Spriggs and two constables, one of whom acted as court stenographer. The police also handled all the logistical arrangements. A jury was rounded up from Fort Norman, Fort Good Hope, Aklavik, and Herschel Island.

The court was held in the police barracks at Herschel Island and five people were tried for murder. According to Commissioner Cortlandt Starnes:

A feature of the trial[s] was the careful explanation given by His Honour the Judge to the assembled Eskimos of the nature of the proceedings, the function of the several officials comprising the court and jury, and the purpose of the trials. He laid especial stress upon the pains taken to prevent the wronging of an innocent person.[15]

Of the five people tried, two were acquitted, one was found guilty of manslaughter and sentenced to one year's imprisonment at Herschel Island, and two were found guilty of murder and sentenced to death. These last two, Alikomiak and Tatamigana, were hanged at Herschel Island on February 1, 1924. Alikomiak had shot Cpl. W.A. Doak at Tree River detachment, NWT while imprisoned for another murder. This sentence caused much debate at the time. Some felt that clemency should be shown to people ignorant of Canadian law while others, particularly government officials, insisted that a stern example be set.

Before the trial, defence lawyer L.T. Cory wrote that:

"as kindness has failed in the past I strongly recommend that the law should take its course and those Eskimos found guilty of murder should be hanged in a place where the natives will see and recognize the outcome of taking another's life."

Commissioner Starnes shared his opinion, stating that:

"there is a danger of the Natives concluding that crime is a thing to be rewarded by the White man."[16]

This episode marked a turning point in police-Inuit relations. The Mounties dropped some of their paternalistic attitudes and were less inclined to treat the Inuit people as friendly innocent children. The Inuit, for their part, were much more wary of the police. Nearly 70 years later, Inuvialuit elder Dora Malegana still held this memory of the RCMP in the early days: "Every time, when people used to do something wrong, the police used to hang them."[17]

Herschel Island RCMP detachment buildings, ca. 1923. The warehouse at right was the setting for the murder trials and, six months later, the hanging of Alikomiak and Tatamigana.

CHAPTER 7

Frances Augusta Wood, wife of Inspector Supt. Zachary Taylor Wood, strikes the symbolic "Last Spike" on the Carcross to Whitehorse section of the White Pass and Yukon Railway in Whitehorse on June 8, 1900.

Despite the force's masculine image, women were essential to the early history of the Mounted Police in the Yukon. Although they received little mention in official reports, these prison matrons, gold inspectors, launderers, tailors, nurses and police wives contributed enormously to northern police work.

Often isolated by geography and gender, these women lacked the simple camaderie of their male counterparts. While their role may not have been glamourous or high-profile, they shared hardships with the police and were indispensable in getting the job done. This required a particular type of stalwartness and courage equal to the well-known tenacity of the Mounties.

Tannis Strickland hams it up with a whipsaw at Tagish Post, ca. 1898, while her son Buster looks on.

"Mesdames Constantine and Strickland"

There are many stories detailing the hardships of the Yukon's first Mounted Police detachment in 1895, their trials on the long trip north and the challenges of building the first police post, Fort Constantine. Few are aware that two women and a child travelled with the 20-man force. The two senior officers, Inspector Constantine and Inspector Strickland, were accompanied by their wives and the Constantines' son, Francis.

Unfortunately, little is known about these two valiant women or their northern experiences. Henrietta Armstrong Constantine compiled a photograph album of her Yukon days but did not include any pictures of herself. When Constantine wrote to Commissioner Herchmer, she is usually only mentioned as joining him in "sending kind regards to Mrs. and Miss Herchmer." A few telling comments do slip through, however, as in the letter of October 1895, written as the force was settling into their first Yukon winter:

> *Mesdames Constantine and Strickland are quite well, but think they would exchange the solitude of the Yukon for the gaieties of Moosomin & Prince Albert. I don't think they regret coming, but find it very lonesome.[1]*

By the following year, Constantine was coping with the excitement following the Klondike strike, food shortages, and Mounties suffering from gold fever. Young Francis had gone south, presumably to attend school, and the Constantines missed him greatly. Henrietta Constantine suffered from a bad leg. Despite her poor health and her husband's urgings to take the last steamer south in 1897, she insisted her place was by his side.

In 1896, Tannis Strickland gave birth to her first child, Roland D'Arcy or "Buster," probably attended by the detachment surgeon Dr. Willis. In an era when pregnancy and childbirth were very private matters and infant mortality was high, it is impossible to imagine her apprehensions at this time. The Stricklands left Dawson in the summer of 1897. Inspector Strickland was back in the north by the following autumn. In 1898, his wife joined him at Tagish Post where she delivered her second child, Frances Mary, on December 5, 1899.[2]

A few exceptional women did share the explorations and privations of the first members in the Yukon. These officers' wives brought a touch of civilization and family life to the wilderness detachments and the rough mining camps.

Buster Strickland and Stuart Wood (the son of Supt. Z.T. Wood) at Tagish Post.

Tannis Marie Louise Strickland holding Buster. D'Arcy is in the background.

A tender scene at Forty Mile RCMP Post, 1938. Claude Tidd, photographer

"Only the strongest and most sinewy women"

When the 203 soldiers of the Yukon Field Force began their "long march" over the Stikine Trail to the Yukon in June 1898, they were joined by six adventurous women. Lady Aberdeen, wife of the Governor General of Canada, was the founder and President of the Victoria Order of Nurses (VON). She arranged for four "fully trained nurses of great experience" to accompany the troops. Georgina Powell took charge of the small group consisting of Amy Scott, Rachel Hanna and Margaret Payson. The Toronto newspaper, *The Globe*, sent Faith Fenton, an experienced, independent and energetic correspondent, to cover the expedition. Her dispatches documented the travels of the Field Force and she later scooped other newspapers with her reports from Dawson City. The sixth woman was Marie Sicotte Starnes on her way to join her husband, Inspector Cortlandt Starnes, in Dawson City after nearly a year's separation.

All along the trail between Telegraph Creek and Teslin Lake, the nurses practised their trade. Their patients included area miners and packers as well as soldiers. As Georgina Powell later wrote, the trail was no Sunday stroll:

Through deep forest we went, where the trail was narrow and the branches of trees threatened our eyes or tore our veils disastrously, through tracts of burnt and blackened country, in some places the ashes still hot from recent burnings, and the dust rising in choking clouds under our feet; through forests of windfallen, upturned trees, whose gnarled roots and tangled branches made insecure and often painful footing; over sharp and jagged rocks, where slipping would be dangerous, we went trampling, leaping, springing and climbing, a strain that only the strongest and most sinewy women could bear …[3]

The destination of the Yukon Field Force was Fort Selkirk. They were barely ready to move into their newly-built quarters when Supt. Sam Steele appealed for 50 soldiers to reinforce his small force of overworked Mounted Police in Dawson. When the troops left on the steamer *Gold Star*, Faith Fenton and two nurses joined them. Caught in the grip of a typhoid epidemic, Dawson desperately needed experienced medical workers. Miss Scott went to work in the NWMP hospital at Fort Herchmer and her companion nursed at the Good Samaritan Hospital. Faith Fenton jumped at the opportunity to make first-hand reports from the heart of the Klondike.

The soldiers showed their appreciation for the nurses by collecting $350 to build them a log cabin. In a crowded town with little or no accommodation for single women, this was a

*En route to the Klondike, aboard the steamer **Islander**, (L-R)* **Amy Scott, Georgia Powell, Rachel Hanna, Faith Fenton, Margaret Payson.**

— The women of the Yukon Field Force

real boon. Assistant Surgeon Thompson of the NWMP praised the "invaluable services" of Amy Scott. Two of the nurses left Dawson within a year, one due to health problems and the other, Georgina Powell, on transfer to a new post. Another obtained permission from the VON to take charge of a Dawson hospital and the fourth took a job with the Dawson post office. Inspector and Mrs. Starnes remained in the Yukon until 1902. Cortlandt Starnes subsequently became Commissioner of the RCMP from 1923 to 1931. After his death, Marie Starnes entered the convent of the Sisters of the Visitation in Ottawa where she took the name Sister Marie-Louise. Faith Fenton married a local doctor and stayed on in the Yukon for a few years. When the

telegraph line was completed in 1901, linking the Yukon to the outside world, she sent the first press dispatch by telegraph from Dawson.[4]

Faith Fenton Brown in Dawson, ca. 1898.

Two female veterans of the Stikine Trail relax in Dawson City. (L-R) Supt. S.B. Steele, Amy Scott, Insp. C. Starnes and Mrs. Starnes, and Capt. Burstall (Yukon Field Force). "Photographed at Midnight, Dawson, June '99."

Courtship, marriage and detachment life

Although many detachment wives cheerfully worked as unpaid members, the Mounted Police discouraged non-commissioned officers and constables from marrying. The force's administrators felt that a wife tied a man down and discouraged mobility. Also, it was hard to support a family on the small salary paid to lower ranks. Over the years, the rules and regulations concerning marriage changed

several times. Normally a member needed several years of service, a healthy bank account and permission from his Commanding Officer—not always easily obtained. More than a few members gave up and finally purchased their discharge in order to wed.

Despite these discouragements, many Mounties met and married the women of their dreams during their Yukon service. The

Anglican missionaries running the hospital at Fort Yukon must have felt that they were running a matrimonial bureau. At least three of the hospital's nurses married Mounties from nearby Rampart House (nearby being a relative term in this case, as in winter, the Alaskan community was a five-day dogsled trip away). Other members married local First Nations women, although they usually had to resign from the force in order to do so. This was probably due more to the rigid marriage rules and regulations in general than the women's background, although mixed marriages were frowned upon. Such unions raised issues such as whether First Nations women married to non-native men should be treated as "whites" under the liquor laws. Apparently, Inspector Francis Fitzgerald of Herschel Island requested permission to officially marry his common-law Inuit wife early in the century but was turned down.[5]

The other centre of operations, the Thornthwaites' kitchen in the Old Crow detachment, ca. 1930.

A NWMP wife in front of her Whitehorse home, ca. 1902. J.E. Lee, photographer.

"Daily life was such a chore!" – Clara May, 1994 [6]

Housekeeping in a log cabin with no electricity, no running water, and no nearby grocery store involved a lot of hard work day after day. Until the first few decades of the century, rural women all over Canada kept house under these circumstances. Yukon women, however, had to cope with the added factors of long cold winters and extreme isolation. The women who thrived in this situation were those who learned to love the outdoors, and appreciated their First Nations neighbours and the simplicity and intimacy of life in the remote communities.

As well as cleaning and cooking—sometimes for a detachment of two or three men—Mountie wives often handled various police duties. They became matrons whenever the detachment housed a female prisoner. In their husband's absence, they handled paperwork, such as recording mining claims. At Fort Selkirk in the 1930s, Martha Cameron took on the contract to cut the detachment firewood for the winter. She also handled airstrip maintenance once the small Yukon River community got regular air service. A number of spouses either had a background in nursing, or quickly learned the rudiments of first aid. Minnie Kirk of Old Crow found she was expected to attend local births and later learned how to deliver babies herself.

Despite the incredibly hard work, most of these spouses later claimed that the best part of their lives were the times spent living and working in remote Yukon detachments. They remember that period as a time of great adventure, breathtaking country and close friendships.

Mary Tidd doing laundry in her Ross River home, ca. 1930.

> By the end of February we were ready for the required Police patrol to Whitehorse, the nearest headquarters. It meant three hundred miles by dog team as the crow flies across wild uninhabited country and unbroken trails…It took fifteen days. Fifteen days of glorious adventure and then seeing people—white women—tea in a living room, instead of outdoors by an open fire tasting of spruce needles and campfire smoke—and best of all—mail!
>
> — Mary Tidd, ca. 1928[7]

Mary Tidd tends her flower garden at Ross River, ca. 1930.

Ross River RCMP detachment. "In the good old summer time (the mosquitoes don't show up very well)."

Claude and Mary Tidd prepare for the weekly bath at Ross River, 1929. "We carry it indoors once a week." Clara May recalled bathing in two washtubs in Old Crow—a large one to sit in and a smaller one for the feet!

In 1924, Mary Ryder learned through her church about an understaffed Alaskan mission hospital fighting a serious influenza epidemic. Trained as a Red Cross nurse, she leapt at the chance to be of service and see the north. When her steamer stopped at Dawson on the way to Fort Yukon, she met a dashing young Mountie, Claude Tidd. Their romance flourished and they married the following year.

The pair shunned the niceties of Dawson society and were never happier than when they were snowshoeing, dogmushing or canoeing in the wilderness from their small log cabin detachment. Over eight years, the Tidds served in Rampart House, Old Crow, Mayo, Ross River, Teslin and Atlin. After Tidd's retirement from the RCMP in 1934, the pair spent another ten years working in Yukon communities, living the outdoor life they loved best.

Clara Dickinson May born 1905

When Clara "Dixie" Dickinson met Sidney May for the first time in June 1931, she was not impressed. Constable May of Rampart House had brought a sick man to the Fort Yukon hospital but was unable to tell her what was wrong with the patient. "Oh, what a dumb cop!" she thought.

May felt differently. "Met one dam fine nurse," he confided to his diary.

Eventually Sid May won Dixie over and they married in July 1932. Alas, the happy young couple had not reckoned with the RCMP marriage restrictions:

> That was our problem. He had expected that – he'd been in long enough and he had expected his papers would come through on a certain boat. Then he made all our plans and at the time there was a new Inspector in charge of Dawson…He said he had other plans for Sid. But, by that time we had made plans and Sid said "Well that's too bad." And then, we had to come back downriver under arrest.[8]

A fine way to spend one's honeymoon! The Mays stayed on in Old Crow for a few years but Sid ended up leaving the force.

During her time in Old Crow, Clara learned what it meant to live on rations. A tremendous amount of paperwork had to be completed for the annual grocery order, mostly canned or dried food. By spring, they would be running low on provisions. Clara saved her husband's cigarette butts so they could later be salvaged for leftover tobacco. Like their First Nation neighbours, they supplemented their diet with game, fish and wild berries. Mail came only a couple of times a year and there was no radio or telegraph communication. In the winter evenings, the Mays visited, read or played cribbage with a candle at the end of the crib board.

The Mays' first child, Marion, was born in Old Crow in March 1934. The local trader had saved a tin of pineapple and six "fresh" eggs from his fall order for the occasion. Clara enjoyed the pineapple but, more than 60 years later, still shuddered at the memory of the aged green eggs.

Clara May and two friends going caribou hunting, ca. early 1930s.

Clara and Sid May at Rampart House, ca. 1931.

Clara "Dixie" wearing her new parka from Old Crow, ca. 1931. The parka was a birthday gift from her husband-to-be, Sid May.

Martha Ballentine Cameron 1904–1990

She was like a man there. I'd be away a month or so at a time. She'd do all the work and I'd have to sign when I'd get home.

— **G.I. Cameron, 1993**[9]

Martha Ballentine, the daughter of a Klondike stampeder, was working in a Dawson cafe when she met her Mountie in 1925. After a three-year courtship, the couple planned to wed. Knowing the RCMP strictures against marriage, Cameron was reluctant to re-enlist. His Commanding Officer assured him there would be no problem with the marriage regulations so Cam signed up for another stint. The C.O. suddenly died and his successor forbade the marriage. Cameron purchased his discharge and they married that same night, June 16, 1928.

By 1934, the rules about marriage had been relaxed and Cameron rejoined the force. The couple and their new daughter Ione moved to the Yukon River settlement of Fort Selkirk, their home for the next 15 years. Martha led a busy, active life. There were the many housekeeping chores: laundry, baking bread, knitting and crocheting, putting up preserves. She also took on extra jobs such as cutting the detachment firewood supply, maintaining the airstrip, and acting as agent for the airline, which meant handling all the mail and freight. On behalf of Indian Affairs, she dispensed medicine and first aid to the local First Nations people. In later years, Martha even had her own radio program. Once a week she went on the air over the Camerons' two-way radio to read the Dawson newspaper to trappers in remote locales.

There was also time for fun—winter sledding down the riverbank in washpans, the Mother's Day hike up Victoria Mountain to make tea with the last snow on top, visits, card parties and boating expeditions. Throughout her life, this energetic and generous woman was an inspiration to all who knew her.[10]

Martha Cameron driving a tractor at Fort Selkirk to build a fire break. Oscar Adami sitting on plough, Pat Van Bibber and Bella Cook walking behind.

Martha and G.I. Cameron's wedding photo, June 16, 1928.

114

Minnie Young Kirk 1905–1986

It seemed life was stripped of trivial things, only the essentials mattered. Our pleasures were simple, long walks in the woods, birds to be identified in spring. The habits of wild animals, making Christmas for the Indian children, baking our Christmas cake, all of us involved, constables, George and I and perhaps an old-timer. The Christmas we made was shared by all, our pleasures overflowed into the village. Old Crow is a very small village, the friends we made there have remained friends all these years…A northern detachment is something different to every person. But it can be a very rich and rewarding experience.

— Minnie Kirk, 1975[11]

When Minnie Kirk wrote about her life as a detachment wife in Old Crow, she neglected to mention one of her most dramatic experiences. In December 1944, she happened to be standing nearby when 12-year-old Joseph Frances fell in the snow in front of the sled dogs he was leading. The pack immediately attacked the youth, tearing his clothes and biting his face. Without hesitation, Mrs. Kirk picked up a stick and charged the dogs, managing to drive them off. The boy was flown to the Fort Yukon hospital and he survived the ordeal. The following year, the Royal Canadian Humane Association presented Minnie with an award for her "heroic action and presence of mind."[12]

The Kirks served in Old Crow twice: 1935 to 1939 and 1943 to 1949. Elders of the Vuntut Gwichin First Nation still have fond memories of the Kirks. Minnie Kirk merited two mentions in the RCMP annual reports. In 1945, she joined the members in nursing Old Crow residents during a two-month-long influenza epidemic. Six years earlier, the Kirks set a unique record. During a 12-day dogsled patrol, Corporal Kirk packed along a home-made radio transmitter. Every evening he sent Morse code messages to his wife who was "quite proficient in telegraphy." The portable radio, set up in his tent, worked fine in temperatures as low as 48 degrees below zero Fahrenheit. The RCMP Commissioner noted in his annual report that the Kirks had made history. For the first time, a member had communicated from the field during a dogsled patrol.[13]

Minnie and George Kirk, well-clad for winter in Old Crow.

Minnie and Cpl. George Kirk proudly pose with their newly-adopted daughter Eloise at Old Crow, September 1948.

Matrons and gold inspectors

At the turn of the century, the Women's Christian Temperance Union lobbied for better treatment of female prisoners. In February 1900, the NWMP were instructed that a "woman special" should be hired to assist the police with female prisoners. Unfortunately, few records survive to tell us about these women and their work. In Dawson City, Selina Howard held the prison matron job from about 1901 to 1904. Supt. Z.T. Wood wrote this about her in June 1903:

> She has been our night matron for about 18 months and has proved herself trustworthy. Formerly they were changing matrons every month or so, endeavouring to get some one who would not carry messages and notes to and from the female prisoners and convicts.[14]

In Whitehorse, a Mrs. Warnes was hired as matron to look after a female prisoner in the fall of 1915. The best-known woman special, however, was "Klondike Kate" Ryan.

Gold inspector Kate Ryan on "smugglers patrol."

Katherine Ryan 1869–1932

> *To tell you the truth, I never felt at home in the civilization that obtains in our cities and towns. In fact, I hated it. While wallking along the streets of a city and gazing upon the paved streets, the concrete sidewalks and the towering buildings, I would say to myself in scorn, 'The work of man, that and nothing else.' So I gradually became more and more obsessed with the desire to live and have my being where things were made by God.*
>
> — Katherine Ryan, 1922[15]

Kate Ryan had come a long way from her hometown of Johnville, New Brunswick when she ventured north over the Stikine Trail in 1898. By 1900, she had settled in the new town of Whitehorse, where she opened a restaurant and invested in local mines. On February 5, 1900, the Whitehorse police hired her as their first woman special.[16]

Kate Ryan also doubled as a gold inspector. Two female gold inspectors worked in Whitehorse and Dawson. They took on the tricky job of searching any women passengers suspected of smuggling gold out of the territory to avoid paying the gold export tax of 2.5 percent. One woman fashioned an elaborate hairdo around a cache of nuggets—an unsuccessful stratagem. Ryan, described by Superintendent Snyder as "warmhearted, affable and efficient," managed to perform this delicate task with tact and good judgment.[17]

Ryan held both jobs until 1919 when she left the Yukon and eventually settled in Stewart, B.C. When she died in 1932, an RCMP honour guard attended her funeral.

Kate Ryan in front of her Whitehorse home.

116

Tailors

The Yukon Mounted Police soon learned that the best way to survive the harsh Yukon winters was to adopt the fur and skin clothing of the First Nations people. The parkas, mitts, pants and mukluks were lightweight, windproof and warm. All over the Yukon, First Nations women made winter clothing for the Mounted Police. Again, there are few records of these transactions or names of these artisans, although many examples of their work survive in family closets and museums.

In 1897, Superintendent Constantine complained that the many newcomers had bought all available native clothing, making it impossible for the police force to buy a new pair of native fur boots for each member.[18]

Mary Smith of Moosehide, the Han First Nation community just downriver of Dawson City, had a contract to make parkas for members in the late 1920s. About the same time, Julia Cadzow and other women of Rampart House were also making clothing for the police. Derek Parkes, a retired member, remembered the arrangements for purchasing winter clothing on Herschel Island:

> Our skin clothing was made by local women. No cash was used. We gave the woman a note to the H B C manager "Please give Aveadluk trade for four foxes and charge to the Police account." A fox was about ten dollars.[19]

Agnes Gruben White, an Inuvialuit woman, was married to an RCMP member in the early 1960s. She recalled her work at Herschel Island:

> I was never part of any of them but I sure made their clothes! Their parkas and mitts, their liners, mukluks. I used to make an awful lot of bread buns for them. There were three of them. Every year I have to do over and repair. Pretty much doing it over and over.[20]

Supt. A.B. Allard and Mrs. Allard and daughter Dorothy in Dawson City, winter 1926-27. Supt. Allard is wearing a parka made by Mary Smith. The parka is made from white canvas trimmed with blue and gold ribbon and shoulder flashes of beadwork. The hood was trimmed with wolverine fur which does not frost up with the breath of the wearer. Dorothy's parka matches her dad's.

1931 RCMP constable in winter patrol dress, parka and mukluks made of caribou hide, by the First Nations women of Moosehide.

Anna DeGraf 1839–1930

I learned later from experience that nothing too good can be said about the Canadian officials in the Yukon. The lives they saved, their kindness to travellers, their courtesy and honour have never been excelled. In Dawson, later when I worked for a fur store, I made many a fur coat for the Canadian Mounted Police, and how proud I was of those coats—and of those men! When I completed one of the outfits, and the officer came in to put it on, the whole establishment would gather around and admire. The coats were fastened with brass buckles and I can't imagine a nobler figure of a man than one of those boys in his trim, buckled furs.

— Anna DeGraf, ca. 1925[21]

Anna DeGraf was in her fifties when she first hiked the Chilkoot Pass in 1894 on a mission to find a lost son. She never did find her boy but spent the winter at Circle, Alaska. She earned her living sewing everything from tents to dresses for dance hall girls.

A few years later, when gold fever spread throughout the world, this indomitable woman decided she too would return to the Klondike to seek her fortune. Once again she hiked over the Chilkoot Pass with her sewing machine. This time there were many more fellow travellers as well as detachments of North-West Mounted Police to help them on their way. DeGraf credited the police with saving her life when she fell through the shore ice at Lindeman Lake. At Dawson, DeGraf had more sewing than she could handle, an important part of which was making fur coats for the police.

DeGraf worked until she was 90, a year before her death. Her last job was as a wardrobe lady for the Pantages Theatre in San Francisco.[22] Her published memoirs are a valuable record of an exciting time in Yukon history from the perspective of a mature woman.

Portrait of Anna DeGraf, ca. 1897. She wrapped burlap sacks around her feet after her shoes wore out.

Beading, bread and banquets

Kitty Saguak had been trained by Bishop Stringer's wife and was a good cook. She did not cook for the Police but if we were very busy we would get her to bake us some bread. Using the old Royal yeast cakes it took us about twelve hours to bake bread but if we gave Kitty the ingredients at 8 a.m. she would have a pan of rolls ready by lunch time, I don't know how she did it.

— retired member Derek Parkes, 1994[23]

Kitty Saguak (Saȓuak), the wife of Special Constable Roland Saguak, at Herschel Island, 1933.

Beaded wall hanging of the Mounted Police crest crafted by a Fort Yukon woman. The buffalo head was painted by Mary Tidd and the hanging was a wedding gift from Helen Thornthwaite to her husband. The Glenbow Museum in Calgary now has this hanging.

A festive dinner party in Old Crow, ca. 1940s. Two children in foreground: Betty and Bertha Frost. (L-R) Clara Frost, ___ , Claude Tidd, Mary Tidd, ___, Minnie Kirk, George Kirk, ___, Stephen Frost, Martha Frost Benjamin, Minnie Frost Joe with Gordon Frost just peeping over the table, Donald Frost, former member Harold "Jack" Frost, Albert Frost (baby), ___.

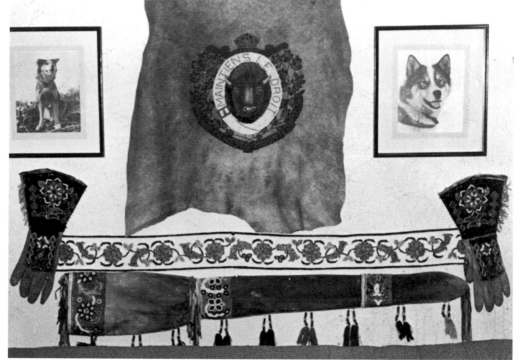

CHAPTER 8

In a land as vast as the Yukon with few people scattered over long distances, the Mounted Police relied on extensive patrols to keep track of the people and activities in their area. Patrols served a number of purposes: Mounties delivered mail, checked on the ailing and infirm, ensured isolated cabin-dwellers weren't suffering from want, and checked that woodcutters, homesteaders and prospectors had all the proper permits. From early in the century, the police were also game wardens, noting wildlife movements and enforcing game regulations.

The very presence of the Mounted Police deterred wrongdoing. For their part, the police prevented crime by checking out suspicious characters or trouble-shooting potentially tricky situations. Patrols were also social occasions. Most people welcomed the break in their isolation and gladly gave the visiting Mountie a meal and a bed in return for news of distant neighbours and the world outside.

When the Mounted Police went patrolling, this could mean anything from a brisk walk along the streets of Dawson City, with stops to check the action in the dance

halls, to a canoe or dogsled expedition of several months. In the early years, Mounties got around by foot, snowshoe, canoe, horseback and dog team. They rode the railway between Whitehorse and the Alaskan border and caught rides on steamships on the Yukon River and some of its major tributaries. In 1930, the Mounted Police of the Yukon recorded patrols of nearly 100,000 miles:

22,623 by horse, 30,278 by water, 13,406 by foot or sled dogs, 14,246 by train or stage, and 7,707 by motor car.

In 1907, Inspector A.M. Jarvis of the Herschel Island detachment patrolled over 1500 miles along the Arctic coast aboard the American whaler, *Beluga*, in an unsuccessful search for a sea captain accused of murder. After much lobbying, the police eventually obtained their own patrol boats for the Yukon River detachments and the Arctic coast. The most famous RCMP patrol boat of all was the motor schooner *St. Roch*. From 1928 to 1948, this floating detachment patrolled the Arctic coast, safeguarding Canadian sovereignty in northern waters.

On patrol near Fort Constantine, ca. 1895.

121

The northern patrols and Herschel Island

The first of the legendary northern patrols between Dawson City, Yukon, and Fort McPherson, Northwest Territories, left Dawson City on August 30, 1899. Supt. Sam Steele had instructed Corporal G.M. Skirving to learn the fate of a party of three Edmonton stampeders, missing for nearly a year. Skirving returned December 10th, after discovering that the unfortunate goldseekers had died of starvation and that their remains had been buried by local First Nations people. Corporal Skirving had left Dawson by canoe and returned by dogsled. At several points, he hired local First Nations people to guide him along sections of the trail. In his subsequent report, Skirving described the conditions of the countryside and its inhabitants. He also learned from the Hudson's Bay Company trader at Fort McPherson that American whaling boats on the north coast were trading with the local people without paying duty on their goods.[3]

Since the late 1880s, American whalers had overwintered at Herschel Island off the Yukon's north coast to gain a head start on the short whaling season. This tiny island offered one of the few protected harbours in the western Arctic. For several years, missionaries had complained of the whalers' treatment of the Inuit, who had suffered from exposure to alcohol and introduced diseases. The Hudson's Bay Company, meanwhile, was incensed at being undercut by American traders.

North-West Mounted Police at Fort McPherson, 1903. (L-R) Cst. S.S. Munroe; Sgt. F.J. Fitzgerald, Supt. C. Constantine, Csts. Forbes D. Sutherland, John Galpin and R.H. Walker. J.W. Mills, photographer.

The first detachment at Herschel Island was in a rented sod hut similar to these humble structures.

Inuit technology used to improve western construction. The snow tunnel afforded protection against the prevailing wind and acted as a vestibule. Herschel Island detachment, winter 1924-25.

Initially, the Mounted Police simply lacked the resources to investigate this new frontier. Already over-extended in the Yukon, the NWMP was further diminished in 1899 when over 250 police took leave of absence to fight in South Africa's Boer War. It took four years before the NWMP established their first Arctic detachments at Fort McPherson and Herschel Island.

Once again a small force of Mounties patrolled to a little-known northern region, this time well above the Arctic Circle, to raise the Canadian flag in an area mainly occupied by Americans. On May 26, 1903, Supt. Charles Constantine led an expedition from Athabaska Landing down the Mackenzie River to determine the policing needs for the Arctic coast. Constantine stayed only long enough to settle the men at Fort McPherson before returning south. He left Sgt. Francis J. Fitzgerald in charge with orders to travel to Herschel Island and, if warranted, to set up a police post.

In August, Fitzgerald travelled to the island in a small whaleboat, accompanied by Cst. Forbes Sutherland and an interpreter named Thompson. Although the whaling era was past its peak, Herschel was still a busy place. Fitzgerald rented a small sod hut for a

detachment, and his small force prepared for the challenges of their isolated position. They suffered from a chronic shortage of supplies, they lacked a sea-going vessel even though the detachment was on an island, and their supply and communication line was long—responses and orders from Ottawa took a year to arrive. As Constantine had advised them, they had to rely heavily on their own "discretion, tact and management."[4]

One way to bypass the long, slow overland route down the Mackenzie River from Edmonton was to send mail overland from Dawson City, a division centre with regular mail and telegraph service. From 1904 on,

the Mounted Police made a winter mail run from Dawson City to Fort McPherson and in later years, over the sea ice to Herschel Island. The route traversed 475 miles of tundra, mountains and numerous rivers and creeks. Local Gwichin people guided the patrol parties and hunted along the way. This patrol route was the scene of one of the Yukon's great tragedies and, 20 years later, the Yukon's largest manhunt.

Mounties and dog team at Herschel Island, ca. 1923.

Inuit schooners from Banks Island and Mackenzie Delta moored in Pauline Cove, Herschel Island, 1930.

123

The Lost Patrol

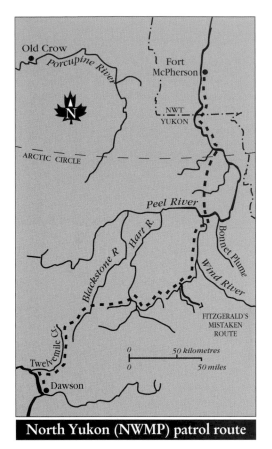

North Yukon (NWMP) patrol route

You will leave tomorrow morning for a patrol over the Fort McPherson trail, to locate the whereabouts of Inspector Fitzgerald's party…I cannot give you any specific instructions; you will have to be guided by circumstances and your own judgment, bearing in mind that nothing is to stand in your way until you have got in touch with this party.

— **Supt. A.E. Snyder to Corp. W.J.D. Dempster, February 27, 1911**[5]

In 1910, Frank Fitzgerald, now an Inspector, obtained permission to make the annual Dawson to Fort McPherson patrol

from north to south. This would allow him to personally deliver his dispatches and take a break from the isolation of Herschel Island. Fitzgerald and his party travelled the first leg of their journey, from Herschel Island to Fort McPherson, without incident. On December 10, 1910, Inspector Fitzgerald set out from Fort McPherson with Constables George Francis Kinney and Richard O'Hara Taylor, and his guide, former Constable Sam Carter. Two weeks later, they met several First Nations families and learned they were on the wrong trail. They hired Esau George to guide them across the portage to the Peel River. On New Year's Day, they paid and discharged Esau. No one ever saw them again—alive.

Cpl. W.J.D. Dempster, Ex Cst. F. Turner, Cst. J.F. Fyfe and guide Charley Stewart and their dog teams preparing to leave Dawson in search of the lost Fitzgerald patrol, February 28, 1911. J. Doody, photographer.

Cpl. Dempster (seated right) with 4 patrol members at Fort McPherson.

On February 20th, seven weeks later, Esau and a group of his people reached Dawson and were surprised to not find Fitzgerald's party already there. When Superintendent Snyder learned that Fitzgerald had not been spotted further along the trail, he ordered Corporal Dempster to organize an expedition to seek out the missing patrol. Dempster and his party, guided by Charley Stewart, left

Dawson on February 28, 1911. On March 21st, they found two bodies near the Peel River and the following day found the emaciated corpses of Carter and Fitzgerald. The party had turned back when they lost their way and ran short of supplies. Ironically, they perished within 35 miles, or a day's travel, of Fort McPherson.

Fitzgerald's patrol failed for a number of reasons: the inexperience of his guide (Carter had taken the route only once before, travelling in the opposite direction), an inadequate supply of food, little gear for living off the land, and plain bad luck in the form of excessive cold, sparse game and heavy snows. Many also suggested the party would have survived had they hired an experienced First

Nations guide and hunter. One consequence of this tragedy was that the police put up rest cabins and supply caches along the patrol route, and between Fort McPherson and Herschel Island, and all subsequent patrols included a capable guide and hunter.

In conclusion I would draw to your attention the really remarkable work done by this patrol. Corpl. Dempster and all members of his party are deserving of the highest praise. Not only did they make this patrol in record time, which was all the more remarkable as they had to search the rivers while travelling, which necessarily took them longer, but they travelled at a time when travelling is more difficult on account of soft snow, high winds, blinding snowstorms, &c.

— Supt. A.E. Snyder, April 18, 1911[6]

Cpl. Dempster shortly after his return to Dawson.

Return of Cpl. Dempster, Cst. Fyfe, Ex Cst. Turner and guide, Charley Stewart, after the successful completion of their mission. J. Doody, photographer.

Charley Stewart was the First Nations guide for Corporal Dempster's 1911 rescue patrol.

...The Inspector will be much missed here, as he was so much esteemed by all. He was an able and splendid man in every way.

— **Rev. C.E. Whittaker, 1911**[7]

From the time of his enlistment in 1888, Fitzgerald had an exceptionally adventurous career with the Mounted Police. After nine years service at various posts in western Canada, he accompanied Inspector John Douglas Moodie on a 14-month, 1200-mile patrol overland from Edmonton to the Yukon River, yet another futile attempt to locate a practical all-Canadian route to the Klondike goldfields. He was one of the many Mounties who volunteered to go to South Africa to fight in the Boer War and served under former NWMP Commissioner, L.W. Herchmer in the 2nd Canadian Rifles. In 1903, he was given command of the first two police posts above the Arctic Circle. Over the next seven years, he earned promotion to the rank of inspector.

His untimely death came as a great shock to all northern residents as well as his fellow Mounted Police. He left behind a daughter from his common-law marriage with an Inuit woman.[8]

Inspector William John Duncan "Jack" Dempster 1876–1946

...I have been over this patrol several times, but I think this trip was the hardest I ever made, and certainly it was the most disagreeable.

— Cpl. W.J.D. Dempster, 1911[9]

In 1911, Corporal Dempster passed into legend as the man who discovered the tragic fate of the "Lost Patrol," and returned with the news to Dawson during a record-breaking dogsled run from Fort McPherson. Dempster and his three companions had travelled 475 miles in 19 days. Dempster commanded more northern patrols than any other member. In 1920, he broke his own record, making the same trip in only 14 days.

Dempster came north during the Klondike gold rush, and for the next 37 years served in detachments all over the Yukon. His postings included Dalton Post, Bennett, Halfway, Bonanza, Caribou, McQuesten, Stewart River, Forty Mile, White River, Rampart House, Dawson and Mayo. In 1926, he married Sarah Catharine Smith, the matron of the Mayo hospital. When he retired to Vancouver in 1934, he had achieved the rank of inspector.

In 1959, construction of a new highway began between Dawson and Inuvik, NWT, crossing much of the territory of the northern patrols. Completed in 1978, it was named the Dempster Highway to honour the Mountie who had known this country so well. [10]

The North Yukon detachments: Rampart House

In August 1911, Superintendent Z.T. Wood was notified of a serious smallpox epidemic at Rampart House. He immediately sent Cst. James Fyfe with nurse Arthur Lee to deliver vaccine and to assist the doctor already on hand. Fyfe's immediate orders were to enforce a quarantine in the community. As the epidemic spread from eight to nearly 100 cases, Fyfe also disinfected tents and cabins, and patrolled to outlying areas, warning people to stay away from Rampart House. By the following June, most people had recovered and there had been only one fatality, an infant.[11]

Rampart House was a small community centred around a fur trade post on the Porcupine River near the Alaskan border, about 250 miles northwest of Dawson City. The year-round residents were the fur trader and his family and an Anglican missionary.

Both were there because of the large population of First Nation people in the area, who came to the post to trade and visit as part of their seasonal round.

As early as 1905, traders at Rampart House requested that a customs agent be stationed at the post to collect duty on American goods purchased at nearby Fort Yukon. The customs department in turn requested that the police be detailed for this duty. Assistant Commissioner Wood refused due to the shortage of men. When the request was repeated in 1913, supported by the Yukon's Member of Parliament, George Black, Wood reluctantly complied. Corporal Dempster was sent to open a detachment, collect customs and act as agent for the mining recorder. This detachment operated for the next 16 years.[12]

Group of First Nations people watching Bishop Stringer leaving for Dawson.

Shipment of furs, stacked in front of the trading post at Rampart House, ready to be sent to market in London, England.

Constable Charles Young, Joanne Cadzow, the fur trader's daughter, and Corporal Thornthwaite stand in front of the police post at Rampart House, ca. 1926.

128

Old Crow

The newly-built Old Crow detachment. Thornthwaite said of this photo, "Note triangle aerial poles from my radio receiving set. Instructions were received on this aerial during the Mad Trapper hunt."

Cpl. Thornthwaite, S/Cst. John Moses and two others power-sawing logs into three-foot lengths for firewood, 1929. Thornthwaite observed that it "sure beats Rampart House and ABT's cross-cut sawing."

Erecting the RCMP detachment at Old Crow.

In 1929, the Rampart House Mounted Police followed the Gwichin people to the new settlement of Old Crow, further upriver at the confluence of the Porcupine and Old Crow rivers. Corporal Arthur B. Thornthwaite, Constable Sidney May and the police carpenter, Special Constable Fox from Dawson, built a handsome new log detachment building. Unfortunately, that particular cabin stood for only four years before its destruction by fire.[13]

In the 1930s, Old Crow replaced Dawson as the departure point for the northern patrols. These winter dog team patrols to Fort McPherson and Herschel Island continued right up until the 1960s.

"The scene of many pleasant hours work." Claude Tidd in the RNWMP post at Rampart House, ca. 1919.

With the single exception perhaps of the radio set our amusements were largely those of our making…Neither of us were card players but we had a fairly good library of books of our own and read a great deal during the long winter months…We had a wide circle of friends throughout the north as well as in other parts of the continent, and our personal correspondence kept us both quite busy. During the spring and summer, a study of the northern wild birds provided me with another unending source of pleasure. Finally I was a photographic addict of the most violent type and spent many pleasant hours with my camera and what little photographic work I was able to carry out in our small home.

We had our difficulties and troubles of course—who doesn't—but on the whole

we enjoyed the life tremendously, and the memories of our experiences in Old Crow and in the Yukon generally, will, I'm sure give us much pleasure for many years.

— Claude Tidd[14]

Claude Tidd was a man of many interests. He was an outdoorsman, in love with the life of small Yukon outposts, a musician, a writer and not least, a photographer. His legacy of more than 1000 photographs and several 8 mm films document Yukon life in the 1910s, 1920s and 1930s. His inquisitive eye captured First Nations lifestyles, the housekeeping details in the detachment, life on the trail during patrols, and northern community events.

Tidd joined the Royal Northwest Mounted Police in 1914. Apart from one year in Regina and another in Vancouver, he served his 21-year career in the Yukon and northern British Columbia. He and his wife Mary lived and worked in Dawson, Rampart House, Ross River, Whitehorse, Forty Mile, Mayo and Atlin. After leaving the force in 1935, he stayed on in the north working as a fur trader at Forty Mile and Old Crow for another ten years.

The clarity and quality of Tidd's photographs are all the more remarkable when one considers the primitive conditions under which he processed film. In winter he chopped and melted ice to get water for developing film and made his prints using a battery-powered headlight.[15]

The Mad Trapper episode

One of the most notorious cases in northern Mounted Police history is the 1932 hunt for the mysterious "Mad Trapper" of Rat River. During a seven-week period, seven Mounties, three special constables, and more than 30 First Nations and non-native civilian volunteers tried to track down the man known as Albert Johnson. Additional patrols set out from Whitehorse, Dawson, Mayo and Fort Norman. The many dog teams consumed hundreds of pounds of dried fish during the various sorties to find the fugitive. Supplying the searchers became a major logistical exercise.

After wounding Constable Alfred King during a routine inquiry, Johnson withstood a 15-hour assault with dynamite and more than 700 rounds of ammunition before fleeing his trapline cabin. He travelled over 150 miles on snowshoes in bitter winter conditions and killed Constable Edgar Millen in another confrontation—all the while living off the land on whatever small game he could snare without risking a rifle shot.

The case was the first where Mounties used radio and airplanes in their search. These two new technologies were crucial in tracking Johnson. Orders and reports between Old Crow, Aklavik and Edmonton helped coordinate the massive manhunt. Meanwhile, all over North America, listeners breathlessly followed the chase on their home radios. The well-known northern bush pilot, Wilfred "Wop" May, helped track the trapper as well as transport supplies and people to the site of the final confrontation on the Eagle River. From the air, he was able to signal the hunting parties that the trapper had finally met his end. He then flew the Mad Trapper's final casualty, Staff Sergeant Earl Hersey of the Royal Canadian Corps of Signals, to the hospital in Aklavik.

Constable Alfred King wrote the following letter to his friend and comrade, Constable "Frenchy" Chartrand at Coppermine, NWT from the hospital in Aklavik. He relates the story from the initial Mounted Police encounter with Johnson, until just before the final shoot-out on February 17, 1932. This dramatic and eloquent letter has been reproduced on the following pages as Constable King wrote it, with a few clarifications marked by square brackets.[16]

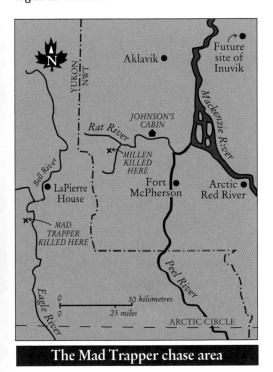

The Mad Trapper chase area

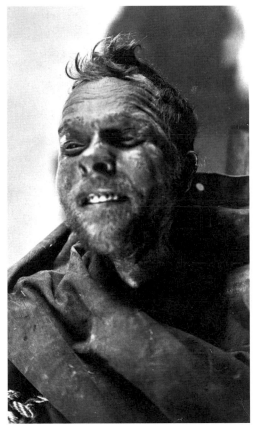

Portrait of the "Mad Trapper," taken shortly after the death of the man known as Albert Johnson.

The "Mad Trapper's" victim, Cst. Edgar Millen, at Arctic Red River, NWT.

"Gosh Frenchy it is a terrible affair"

Aklavik, N.W.T.

Feb. 4th 1932

Dear Frenchy,

Hellow old timer how goes it? Thanks for the wire old man it was darn good of you. I'm feeling fine now. Not out of the hospital yet but soon I think. Guess I'll tell you the whole story then you will be able to see what we were up against. First of all a new chap called Melville was with Newt [Constable Millen] at R. River. He cut his foot and had to come to Aklavik. I was sent up to take his place till February. Got there just before Xmas and poor Millen and I had a decent time Xmas day. The next day Dec. 26th I left [Arctic] Red River and see this fellow Johnson who was trapping without a license and bothering the Indians trap line. This fellow Johnson came down the Peel on a raft and no one knows where he came from. Millen met him, and asked him a few questions but Johnson wouldn't tell him anything. Well I got to Johnsons place with Joe Bernard and Joe was scared to death I don't know why. I spent an hour trying to get Johnson to open the door and talk but would[n't] open it at all. He looked out the window at me and thats all. I left and came in to Aklavik to get a warrant. Next day, Mac [Cst. R. C. MacDowell] and I left with Joe and Lazerous [Lazarus Sittichinli]. We got there on the 31st of Dec. I got Mac to take cover in the bush with a rifle and I walked up to the door with an axe. I called to Johnson to open the door and he fired at me through the door. I guess he was using an automatic revolver with steel jacket bullets, the slug hit me just below the nipple on the left side and went through a rib out the right side under the nipple and didnt break a rib. Well I managed to get up, and go to where Mac was and from him to the dogs and Mac brought me in. Johnson fired at Mac but didnt hit him. Well Mac got me hear in 21 hours. Some trip and I thought it was all up. The dogs did 105 miles with no stop.

On the 3rd of January the old man [Inspector Eames] and Mac & Southerland [Ernest Sutherland] & Lang[,] Gardlund & Lazerous & Joe Bernard all left and went up to Johnsons place. Well the Insp. called out to Johnson to come out and surrender but nothing doing. They used dynamite on his cabin and put 700 rounds into it. Then 2 or 3 times they rushed the cabin and smashed the door in with rifle butts each time Johnson only fired when he

Cst. Alfred King.

Peter Alexis was one of the many people who volunteered for the hunt. His party found the snowshoe tracks that led the police to Johnson.

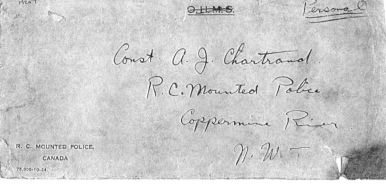

132

had something to shoot at. How it happened no one was killed I dont know. Johnson has 2 revolvers and a 30-30 rifle. Well this happened at night and the boys gave him hell for 15 hours. Then the[y] were out of grub and dog feed. So the[y] came in to Aklavik and got a bigger party to go out again. Johnson had his cabin dug out and all the rifle fire was going over his head. The dynamite wasned so hot it couldnt move the cabin though it put a big hole in the roofe. Once they put a big charge on his roofe and then rushed him, Lang got to the door and saw Johnson laying under a log bed in his eiderdown and Lang thought he was dead so looked around and called the boys. The next minute Johnson woke up and with a gun in each hand let go at Lang how Lang got away no one knows.

Well the next time Riddle and Millen and Hersy [S/ Sgt. E. F. Hersey of the Royal Canadian Corps of Signal] went along with the old crowd. But Johnson had left his cabin. The old man stayed with the party for a week searching the hills then they ran out of feed and came back leaving Millen & Riddle & Gardlund and Noal [Noel] Verville at the Rat. Not long after these four men found him in a creek bottom with open camp. Riddle and Gardlund crawled up on him and were close enough to hear him moving around and making fire. But couldnt see him. Well the other 2 boys came after Riddle & Gardlund and made a noise so Johnson heard them and ducked. Gardlund saw

Johnson and fired 3 shots and thought he hit him. Then the gang talked it over and waited 2 hours but could[n't] hear a sound or see Johnson. So they closed in. Riddle was walking along and saw something sticking out of the snow, as he looked it fired at him and missed by inches he jumped over the creek bank and called to Millen but Newt stood there and fired two shots at the place where he thought Johnson was. Johnson fired 3 shots at Newt and the last one killed poor old Millen. They couldnt get his body away though they got him over the bank and found he was dead. So they had to come away and leave his body there within 30 yards of Johnson. Riddle came hear with Lazerous and made 100 miles without a stop. The Insp. wired for a plane and has gone away with a big party. The plane will be hear to-morrow with ammunition and teer gas bombs. Gosh Frenchy it is a terrible affair. There is a rumor that Johnson trapped for 2 winters at LaPiere house and his partener dissapeared dont know for sure. The plane will stay hear till we get him and will haul supplies out to the boys in the hills. I think when the plane goes out I will be going out with it.

I hope you can read this Frenchy but I cant write worth a darn these days but I wanted to give you the story in the mail. I dont think we will be sending a man with the mail patrol this year. The Father [Catholic Priest] will carry it for us. We are all off duty hear. Mac sprained a

tendon in his knee when he brought me in and cant travel.

Every white man in the Delta has offered to go and when the plane takes this crowd out there will be near 20 out there.

Well old man I must close for this time. My best to yourself and George.

Yours Truly,
King.

Cst. Sidney May and S/Cst. John Moses led a search party east from LaPierre House. They met the party from Aklavik on February 15 and took part in the final shoot-out at Eagle River two days later. During their search patrol, May and Moses travelled more than 400 miles by dog team in 14 days.

John Moses and his children in Old Crow.

Cst. Sid May on patrol in the early 1930s.

133

rthur B. Thornthwaite celebrated his 18th birthday by enlisting in the Royal Northwest Mounted Police. After five years service in northern British Columbia, he transferred to the Yukon in 1924. On the trip north, he met his future wife Helen, on her way to work as a nurse in Fort Yukon. Two years later, he took charge of the Rampart House police post and later supervised the detachment's transfer to Old Crow. After his Yukon stint, he transferred to British Columbia where he worked until his retirement in 1947.

Corporal Thornthwaite learned of the hunt for Albert Johnson on his radio set from a message sent by the Commanding Officer at Dawson, broadcast out of Anchorage. The message was backed up by a telegram sent to Fort Yukon. The cost of the telegram was 35 cents; its subsequent delivery by dog team, $175. Thornthwaite coordinated the search from Old Crow and sent dog teams north and south to warn local people of the possible approach of Johnson. All were warned to stay away from the man but immediately notify the police of his location.

Thornthwaite was another avid photographer who has given us a vivid record of Yukon community and police life from the late 1920s and early 1930s.[17]

A.B. Thornthwaite at Rampart House.

Air patrols

By the early 1930s, the Yukon Mounted Police began to make their first patrols by commercial aircraft. Nationally, the RCMP formed their own "Air" Division in 1937. The Mad Trapper case demonstrated the usefulness of aircraft in searching and travelling over large expanses of country. During World War II, the tremendous activity generated by the construction of the Alaska Highway and the Canol pipeline also brought more aircraft to the region and opportunity for patrols by air. Later, planes were to prove invaluable in search and rescue operations. In 1948, Yukon members patrolled 10,100 miles by air. The Yukon obtained its own air division in 1962. Today, a three-member crew of two pilots and a mechanic operate the RCMP Twin Otter.[18]

RCMP sled dogs from Old Crow travelled in style to attend the dog team races at Whitehorse Rendezvous, February 1969.

During Inspector Martin's annual inspection of the Yukon and Northwest Territories in 1942, he covered 17,547 miles by land, water and air transportation. Here the RCMP Norseman CF-MPF is docked at the Whitehorse waterfront.[19]

On patrol

In 1939, Corporal J. Pearson Clemmitt was sent to apprehend John Lorrie Hill, wanted for breaking and entering. During the ensuing 1700-mile patrol, Pearson travelled by foot, canoe, steamboat and airplane in his hunt for the fugitive. Eventually, Pearson arrested Hill in Fairbanks and returned with him to the Yukon. The photographs (below and right) document three stages of this patrol, showing Clemmitt on the Yukon River filling a boat motor with fuel, aboard the steamer *Yukon*, and at Fairbanks, Alaska, shortly before his return to Dawson City.

One of the sadder patrol duties of the Mounted Police was to check on the welfare of aging miners. These independent holdovers from the Klondike era continued prospecting and trapping in remote areas, even when they became too infirm to look after themselves properly. Constables Buck Coleman and Alfred King return from a patrol up the Klondike River with a prospector's body in September, 1928. They had to carry the body more than five miles to the police buckboard and team.

Mountie leaving Forty Mile on patrol, 1938.

Patrolling by horse-drawn buckboard.

By the 1920s, the RCMP were patrolling roads near communities by car. Mayo detachment, 1932.

Patrol vessels

In 1899, the NWMP obtained two small gas-powered launches, the *Gladys* and the *Jessie*. The *Gladys* patrolled the headwater lakes and upper Yukon River until being sold in 1912. It is now beached at Atlin.

In 1902, the NWMP finally purchased their own river steamer for $3000, allowing them to travel hundreds of miles up and down the Yukon River and its tributaries without being dependent on the schedules of commercial vessels. For many years, the *Vidette* patrolled the major waterways, supplied detachments, and transported civil servants around the territory. As the Yukon force diminished, the vessel became too expensive to maintain and was replaced by a number of smaller boats.[20]

Mounties and Yukon Commissioner W.W.B. McInnes and his party pose in front of the Gladys *on the boat dock at Carcross, 1905. J. Doody, photographer.*

NWMP steamer Vidette, *ca. 1905.*

St. Roch

When the newly-built *St. Roch* left the shipyards in North Vancouver in 1928, the 80-ton motor schooner immediately headed north to begin a 20-year career patrolling Canada's Arctic coast. The 104-foot patrol vessel upheld Canadian sovereignty in Arctic waters, checked on the welfare of the people living in this remote part of the world and, in winters, was a base for patrols to the surrounding regions. Local Inuit were hired to hunt and provide dog teams and guiding services to the crew. Over the winter of 1947-48, the *St. Roch* stayed in the sheltered harbour at Herschel Island. The Herschel detachment, closed since 1933, was reopened within the Aklavik Sub-division.

This floating RCMP detachment won international fame for its remarkable achievements. The *St. Roch* was the first vessel to travel the Northwest Passage from west to east between 1940 and 1942. It then repeated the feat two years later heading westward, becoming the first vessel to navigate the passage both ways. In 1950, the *St. Roch* travelled from Vancouver to Halifax via the Panama Canal, achieving another first—the circumnavigation of North America. In 1954, the Canadian government handed the *St. Roch* over to the City of Vancouver. Later, the vessel was declared a national historic site and today can be visited at the Vancouver Maritime Museum.[21]

The St. Roch*'s nine crew members spent many Arctic winters in the boat's cramped quarters. Captain Henry Larsen, described it as "the most uncomfortable ship I have ever been in." Here, the* St. Roch *is frozen in and covered over for winter quarters, ca. early 1940s.*

The St. Roch *leaving Halifax, Nova Scotia for its second crossing through the Northwest Passage, July 22, 1944. Inset portrait shows Captain Larsen, the vessel's skipper for both Northwest Passage voyages.*

etzman-Photo-Dawson.

N.W.M.Police B

NWMP Band at Dawson City, ca. 1900.

"On the whole we enjoyed the life tremendously…" — Claude Tidd[1]

The Yukon Mounted Police led a busy life patrolling, maintaining law and order, and performing their many civil responsibilities, which ranged from enforcing wildlife laws to collecting radio licence fees. But, like the rest of us, they also welcomed the chance to relax and enjoy life. In the isolation of a dark and cold Yukon winter, Mounties needed diversion and recreation. The ones who thrived in these circumstances enjoyed socializing with their neighbours, spent time outdoors for pleasure as well as work, and entertained themselves with a variety of hobbies.

Many enjoyed fishing and hunting. An afternoon on the shooting range was considered a great treat. In Whitehorse and Dawson, Mounties formed their own hockey and curling teams. Members also snowshoed and went for winter outings by dog team and horse-drawn sleigh. In summer they swam, picnicked, played tennis, hiked to scenic spots, and took boat trips. Card games and card parties were always popular pastimes. The police also pursued a variety of personal interests, including reading, painting, music, writing and photography. In the 1930s, the introduction of wireless radio provided many hours of entertainment. Sometimes atmospheric conditions allowed a Mountie in the northern Yukon to tune into stations all over the world.

Mounties in their smart uniforms were in demand at a variety of Dawson and Whitehorse society occasions such as dances and theatrical entertainments. In the early years, the NWMP organized their own marching band, using instruments left behind by the Yukon Field Force. Members got together for all-male "smokers," elaborate meals based on the regimental dinners of an earlier time. Christmas in the north was always special, particularly in the smaller detachments. The local Mounted Police

Two members relax on bunks in their frame tent. Early police barracks were under canvas at many temporary detachments or until more permanent quarters could be built.

Corporal Wm. Shuckburgh's copy of a 1904 RNWMP Christmas menu.

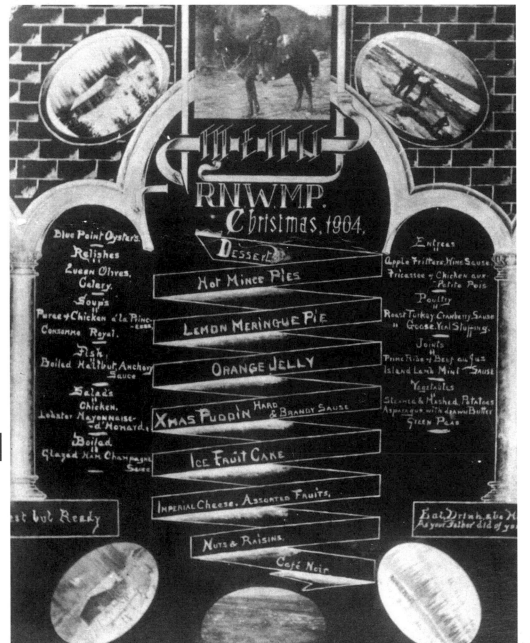

MENU

RNWMP.
Christmas, 1904.

Blue Point Oysters.
Relishes
Queen Olives.
Celery.
Soups
Puree of Chicken à la Princesse.
Consomme Royal.
Fish,
Boiled Halibut, Anchovy Sauce
Salads
Chicken.
Lobster Mayonnaise—d'Homard.
Boiled
Glazed Ham Champagne Sauce

Dessert
Hot Mince Pies

Lemon Meringue Pie

Orange Jelly

Xmas Pudding Hard & Brandy Sauce

Ice Fruit Cake

Imperial Cheese. Assorted Fruits.

Nuts & Raisins.

Café Noir

Entrees
Apple Fritters, Wine Sauce.
Fricassee of Chicken aux Petits Pois
Poultry
Roast Turkey, Cranberry Sauce
Goose, Veal Stuffing.
Joints
Prime Ribs of Beef au jus
Island Lamb Mint Sauce
Vegetables
Steamed & Mashed Potatoes
Asparagus with drawn Butter
Green Peas

wholeheartedly joined the community in the round of visits, dinners and celebrations.

Off duty time also meant relaxing in barracks and horseplay with one's comrades. Both divisional headquarters at Dawson and Whitehorse had canteens supplied with a library, newspapers, stationary, billiard tables and a piano. As well as looking after the well-being of the members, the officers hoped to keep them from the expensive and less wholesome distractions of the dance halls, gambling houses and red light district. They were not always successful, despite the many stiff punishments handed out for drunkenness and for returning to barracks after lights out.

On February 15, 1900, Dawson citizens gave a concert at the Palace Grand Theatre to aid widows and orphans of the South African War. Mounted Police and Yukon Field Force officers were on the organizing committee. This scene shows a tableau representing Great Britain and its colonies. The actors are joined by uniformed NWMP and YFF soldiers on stage and the Yukon Field Force orchestra.

Two musicians in the Dawson orchestra, members Andrew Cruickshank and Claude Tidd, sit by the piano in the Tidd's Dawson home practising their saxophones, ca. 1926.

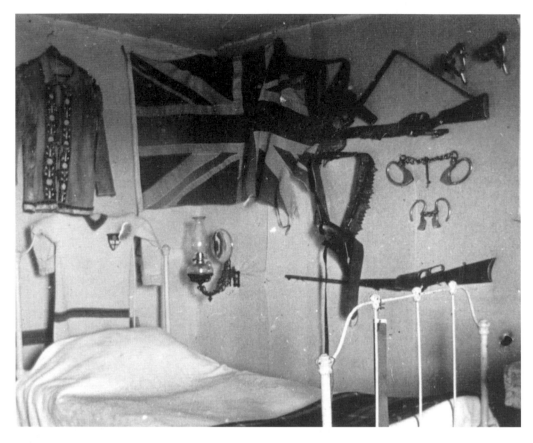

Constable Thornthwaite's bedroom in the Mounted Police detachment at Carmacks, ca. 1925.

Two Mounties painting and playing the guitar at Whitehorse, ca. 1903. Sgt. Anderson, photographer.

Strumming a mandolin in a Dawson City home at the turn of the century.

The recreation rooms are supplied with illustrated papers and magazines from Ottawa, and they are also supplied with local papers. Each division is supplied with a billiard table and various games.

…This will be a great help to the men, and will be the means of keeping a great many in barracks during the long winter evenings instead of their having to go to town, where there are so many temptations.

— Supt. Z.T. Wood, 1900[2]

NWMP constables in the reading room at Whitehorse, 1914.

To this day, Dawson City residents celebrate summer solstice by ascending the Midnight Dome behind the town to watch the sun set and rise on the longest day. In this shot, taken June 21, 1899, the townspeople are joined by a few Mounties and some soldiers of the Yukon Field Force.

Midnight on the Dome June 21st 1899

Kely Photo

145

AT EASE

Clowning around on the job. Although officers might impose fines, hard labour and imprisonment for missing lights out and for drunkenness, the punishments were never quite this severe.

The Mounted Police at Whitehorse had their own ice rink in the compound and hockey was a popular winter pastime. In 1901, the Mounties won the "Renwick Silver Cup" after defeating two other teams. This 1902 shot was probably not taken at a championship tournament.[3]

NWMP playing hockey near the riverbank at Dawson, ca. 1899.

NWMP officers and some prominent citizens of Dawson at Captain Scarth's farewell dinner, September 10, 1901.

Portrait of Officers outside of the Officers' Mess, "B" Division, Dawson, 1901.
(L-R) Front row: **Judge Walsh, Insp. C. Starnes, Supt. Z.T. Wood, Insp. A.E.C. McDonell, Mr. Sinclair;**

Back row: **Insp. T.A. Wroughton, Surgeon W.E. Thompson, Insp. D.M. Howard, A.J. MacLennan, Insp. Cosby, Richard Cowan (Canadian Bank of Commerce), Insp. W.H. Routledge.**

SEASON'S XMAS 1925 GREETINGS

from

DAWSON, Y.T. CANADA.

Portrait of Claude and Mary Tidd on their 1925 Christmas card.

Portrait of Claude and Mary Tidd on their 1925 Christmas card.

Menu cover for "B" Division Troop Mess, Fort Herchmer, Dawson, Christmas 1903.

Christmas dinner at Fort Herchmer in 1903 included: blue points; cream of chicken, à la royale; fried halibut, dutch sauce; game pie, forester style; croquettes of lobster, french peas; roast turkey, cranberry sauce; asparagus, julienne potatoes; plum pudding, brandy sauce; mince pie, jelly; blanc mangé; cheese, celery, nuts, fruits; café noir.

Helen and Arthur Thornthwaite's first Christmas at Rampart House, 1927. Note the RCMP crest done in beads on moose skin.

CHAPTER 10

Route of the Alaska Highway

WARTIME AND ALASKA HIGHWAY CONSTRUCTION

Father Charles Hamel reads the invocation at the official opening of the Alaska Highway at Kluane Lake, November 20, 1942. The thermometer read 35 degrees below zero. While everyone else wore winter parkas, the Mounties stoically froze in their scarlet tunics, breeches, and leather boots.

The friendly invasion

The Yukon's greatest period of upheaval after the Klondike gold rush came with the construction of the Alaska Highway in World War II. In what was later termed "the friendly invasion," tens of thousands of American troops and civilian workers poured into the country to work on two major defence projects—the Alaska Highway from Dawson Creek, British Columbia, to Fairbanks, Alaska; and the Canol pipeline and road project, from the oilfields of Norman Wells, Northwest Territories, 600 miles over the Mackenzie Mountains to a brand-new refinery in Whitehorse.

Existing airports were upgraded and new airstrips built for the Northwest Staging Route. Pilots ferried war planes along this system from Montana to the USSR via the Yukon and Alaska. A newly-built telephone system improved communications along the length of the highway.

The vast influx of people, machinery and supplies overwhelmed the existing transportation facilities and the Yukon's previously-isolated small communities. Crime and social problems mushroomed. First Nations people suffered through several epidemics of diseases introduced by the workers. As well as coping with a great increase in police duties, the small force of Mounties shouldered the responsibility of maintaining good international relations with the visiting American forces and workers, many of whom were unaware they were in a different country.

At the outbreak of World War II, 21 Mounties policed the Yukon's population of about 5,000 from seven detachments. Like other Mounted Police across Canada, the Yukon force took on new duties when war was declared. They identified potential enemy aliens, undertook public security duties, handled recruitment for the armed forces, and later, enforced wartime regulations.

From the spring of 1942, however, their wartime duties and challenges were unique in the country. Within a few years, the number of Yukon RCMP rose to 35, a sub-division was created at Whitehorse, staffed by 17 Mounties, and three detachments opened along the brand-new Alaska Highway.[1]

"May I please see your travel permit?" On duty at an Alaska Highway checkstop north of Whitehorse, ca. late 1940s.

WARTIME AND ALASKA HIGHWAY CONSTRUCTION

Whitehorse Sub-division

Whitehorse detachment at Front and Wood streets, ca. 1940s.

View of Whitehorse from the escarpment, ca. early 1950s. RCMP compound with U.S. army-built "H-huts" in right foreground. In 1950, a new detachment building (centre) replaced the Front Street quarters.

Mounties, led by Cpl. "Jock" Kerr, parade down Fourth Avenue in Whitehorse, ca. 1948.

In 1939, Whitehorse was a quiet community of about 300 people. The population doubled in summer when the sternwheeler crews and hotel staff came north. The focus of the town was the train station and docks at the end of Main Street on the banks of the Yukon River. Here, freight and passengers arrived on the train from Skagway to be transferred to sternwheelers bound for Dawson. The two-storey RCMP detachment was only a block away, handy for meeting train and boat traffic. Crime was rare in the close-knit community. Many oldtimers recall that no one had, or needed, locks on their doors.

After the bombing of Pearl Harbour in 1941 and the subsequent Japanese landings in the Aleutian Islands in Alaska, an invasion of mainland North America seemed imminent. The coastal shipping route, the main supply line for both the Yukon and Alaska, was vulnerable to aerial attack. The American government decided to build a highway to move armed forces and supplies to this potential front. Early in 1942, the Canadian and U.S. governments agreed to build a highway to Alaska, through northeastern British Columbia and the Yukon, using American forces. Within months, a large civilian force followed the soldiers to build the permanent road and start work on the ambitious, but ultimately unsuccessful, Canol oil supply project.

Whitehorse was the ideal site to administer the Alaska Highway project; it had ready access to air, water and rail transport. Troops and supplies began pouring into the Yukon River community in the spring of 1942. The soldiers set up their own "Tent City" near the airport but had free run of the town. There were line-ups everywhere: in stores, at the movie theatre, at the bank, and, especially at the liquor store. Hotel rooms were booked 24 hours a day. Desperate for a place to rest, people slept in hotel lobbies, on the train station floor and on any vessels tied up at the dock. Other Yukon residents flocked to new job opportunities in Whitehorse. Many settled in sprawling squatter communities along the riverbank.

153

Inspector Steinhauer in front of Whitehorse Sub-division headquarters, ca. 1950.

Suddenly the sleepy community acquired all the problems of a major city: public drunkenness, bootlegging, theft, assaults, and even murders. Women no longer felt safe walking the streets at night. It also began to feel like occupied territory—the U.S. military took over the railway, imposed travel restrictions, and often bumped other cargo to ensure their supplies received priority. Locals complained of the aggressive attitude of the U.S. Military Police. In July 1943, the MPs actually stopped a uniformed corporal and two constables to inform them they were speeding and to order them to report to MP headquarters. The indignant Mounties ignored this directive. Other incidents prompted the Yukon's member of parliament, George Black, to complain that the "U.S. Army Gestapo" conducted themselves like "thugs and gangsters." Despite these examples of soldiers overstepping their authority, the sergeant in command of the detachment asserted:

Our relations with the U.S. Army 254th Military Police Company here have been excellent, and I have found all of their men to be courteous and efficient. Very close cooperation is maintained between this Det. and the Military Police, and the system has worked very well to date.[2]

While the two enforcement agencies generally cooperated, jurisdiction often proved tricky. The RCMP could arrest a soldier off base but then had to turn him over to the U.S. military authorities, although a Canadian observer could attend any subsequent trial. If a soldier sought by the Mounties made it to barracks, the military would not release him to the Canadians. If there was sufficient criminal evidence, however, the suspect might then be arrested by the Americans and tried by court-martial. American civilian workers could be tried under either Canadian or American law. The RCMP, in their role as public administrators, often ended up disposing of the estates and property of

American civilian workers who had died or been accidentally killed.[3]

The Mounted Police were quick to assign extra men to Whitehorse. Within a year, the Yukon's Sub-division headquarters were transferred from Dawson to Whitehorse under the supervision of Inspector H.P. Mathewson. Patrols throughout town increased. Babe Richards recalled being accompanied by either a Mountie or a U.S. Military Police when she took cash deposits from her family's hotel and restaurant business to the bank two blocks away.[4]

The new roads brought an added dimension to police work. Motor vehicle infractions, previously nonexistent, rose to 23 in 1943; these included speeding, failing to stop at stop signs and illegal parking. The greatest change was the dramatic increase in patrols by vehicle. In 1942, the Yukon RCMP still patrolled more miles by dogsled than by vehicle, mushing 2,138 miles and motoring

154

Civilian workers and American soldiers line up outside the Whitehorse liquor store, October 1943.

Mountie in Whitehorse office, ca. 1950.

1,800. A year later, Yukon members drove 87,381 miles, mostly on the Alaska Highway, in ten trucks and one passenger car, four of which were assigned to Whitehorse. In late summer 1943, Corporal W.H. Hanna travelled from Edmonton to his new posting in Whitehorse over the Alaska Highway, becoming the first member to travel the highway in his own car. He made the trip in six days "without even a puncture en route."[5]

After the Americans formally turned over responsibility for the Canadian portion of the highway to Canada in 1946, the Mounted Police took over all policing of the Alaska Highway, including the operation of three traffic control gates at Blueberry, B.C. and just north and south of Whitehorse. This brought an onerous new duty:

> *At the Subdivision office in White Horse, drivers and vehicles are registered and the necessary permits issued for travel on the Highway; this duty alone entails a considerable amount of office work and interrupts our routine police office duties, owing to our cramped office space.[6]*

The highway detachments patrolled the highway between Dawson Creek, B.C. and the Yukon-Alaska border once a week during the summer, and once a month in winter.

Two years later, all travel restrictions were lifted and the Alaska Highway gradually became the main travel and freight route into the territory. Whitehorse had grown tenfold and become the economic and political centre for the territory. In 1953, the Yukon's capital was transferred from Dawson City to Whitehorse. To this day, Whitehorse remains the headquarters for Royal Canadian Mounted Police operations in the Yukon.

155

Teslin detachment

RCMP detachment at Teslin, ca. 1920s.

In 1942, the U.S. Army used sternwheelers to barge fuel down the Yukon River from Whitehorse, up the Teslin River and across Teslin Lake. In the background are the Three Aces (the Tlingit people call it Tlên'àxh T'àwê) the landmark mountains east of Teslin.

U.S. Army 302nd Engineers with dead moose, Teslin, 1942. They were fined $200 by the RCMP, acting as game wardens. Although the Yukon's Game Ordinance was amended to allow army personnel to buy hunting licenses, many did not bother, or just shot at any wildlife they spotted. In 1943, a further amendment placed a mile-wide no-shooting zone along the length of the Alaska Highway.

Until 1942, the lone Mountie at Teslin had a fairly quiet job. The small settlement on the shores of Teslin Lake was inhabited by a handful of non-natives and a large seasonal population of Tlingit First Nations people who spent most of the year out on their traplines. The busiest time was summer when First Nations people came to town to resupply, visit, and celebrate with dances, sporting events and traditional potlatches. Supplies for the local trading post arrived once a year via the Teslin River on the Taylor & Drury steamer *Thistle*.[7]

The detachment's principal duty was patrolling the area on trips lasting from a few days to two weeks. The Mountie and a special constable travelled by boat in summer and dogsled in winter. Although local First Nations entrepreneur George Johnston had bought a car in 1928 and actually built a few miles of road along the shores of Teslin Lake, there was no road link to other parts of the Yukon.

After war was declared in 1939, people followed the news and some local men enlisted, but for the most part, daily life continued much as usual. The war came a little closer to home after Pearl Harbour was

bombed and the United States became involved. Many Tlingit people had relatives on the nearby Alaska panhandle and feared for their safety.

Nothing could have prepared this peaceful community for its own wartime invasion. Over the summer of 1942, two regiments of U.S. Army soldiers poured into the area to build part of the Alaska Highway between Whitehorse and Watson Lake. Their main job was to construct bridges—one over the Teslin River at Johnson's Crossing and the other

across Nisutlin Bay, the longest span on the highway. Although rumours had been flying for months, the first sight of tractors and hundreds of strangers, including black soldiers, was still a great shock. Suddenly, police work became much more stressful. The newcomers brought diseases for which the First Nations people had limited resistance. Within a year, the small community suffered eight epidemics.

In 1942, the two Teslin RCMP constables alerted headquarters of an epidemic of red

measles. Nurse Corrine Cyr flew from Whitehorse to deal with the emergency. The RCMP quarantined the village, trying to contain the infection and protect its people from contact with the soldiers. One Mountie accompanied Cyr on her twice-daily rounds. Before it ended, 129 people out of 135 were infected and three died. Still the onslaught of diseases continued: dysentery, whooping cough, German measles, mumps, tonsillitis

and bronchial pneumonia. Four children died from meningitis.

In addition to helping the settlement try to cope with these tragedies, the Mounted Police kept an eye on the newcomers. Ignorant of wilderness living, soldiers carelessly began many forest fires and entertained themselves by shooting at anything that moved. In many native communities, soldiers also illegally provided

alcohol to the First Nations people and assaulted the women.

By the end of the war, Teslin was no longer an isolated settlement on a corner of Teslin Lake, but one in a string of communities along a brand-new artery to the north. The Mounties now made patrols by truck rather than dogsled. This also marked a time of great change for First Nations people. Many, who had taken jobs as guides and construction workers, later worked for highway survey and maintenance crews. People began living in the settlement year-round to be near wage jobs, schools, medical facilities and swifter transportation. The Alaska Highway meant many changes and adjustments for the Teslin Tlingit people and an end to an era in policing for their RCMP detachment.

Teslin residents with U.S. Army doctors in 1942.

Cpl. J. Pearson Clemmitt at Teslin in 1942. The jeep at left belongs to the American 92nd Engineers working on the Alaska Highway in the area. Apparently, it was the first jeep on the Alaska Highway between Watson Lake and Whitehorse.

Fort Selkirk – Death of a Yukon River community

I used to come through town here every day, and two or three times a day, and see everybody. We'd share out medicines, or do anything that was necessary of that kind, or whatever was to be done. We were all friendly. There was no question of it.

— Cpl. G.I. Cameron, 1984[8]

In 1932, the RCMP decided to reopen a police post at Fort Selkirk, the small settlement at the junction of the Yukon and Pelly rivers, about halfway between Whitehorse and Dawson City. The Mountie lived in a rented log cabin. The detachment office occupied a front room, with family living quarters taking up the rest of the cabin.

Although two other Mounties were posted here in the early 1930s, the one everyone remembers is Corporal G.I. "Cam" Cameron. For 14 years, Cameron was responsible for the area from Whitehorse to Dawson, over to Mayo, and sometimes down to Forty Mile. In summer, he patrolled the area by river. In winter, he travelled by dog team, visiting the trappers, prospectors and First Nations' camps to check on people's welfare, register births and deaths, deliver mail, and bring news from the outside world.

The small settlement consisted of a handful of non-natives and a large seasonal population of Northern Tutchone First Nation people. At the time, the Yukon River was still the territory's major summer highway. Many small settlements, wood camps and trading posts nestled along its banks and up the major tributaries—the Pelly, Macmillan, Teslin and Stewart rivers. The majestic sternwheelers steamed up and down the river between Whitehorse and Dawson. People needing a ride or wanting to send a parcel signalled the boats with a white flag hung out on the riverbank. Sternwheelers also freighted silver-lead ore from Mayo down the Stewart River and up the Yukon River to the railhead at Whitehorse. The major method of winter travel was still by dog team or horse-drawn sleighs. Regular air service did not come to Selkirk until the late 1930s.

Even this remote community underwent change as a result of the Alaska Highway construction boom. The sternwheelers freighted supplies down the Yukon River to Circle, Alaska to work on the northern end of the highway. Other supplies, destined for Ross River and the Canol project, were trans-shipped at Selkirk up the Pelly River. For a short time, a railway survey crew made their headquarters in the community. The railway extension never happened but local First Nations people still remember some great baseball games from that time.

Cam Cameron leaving on patrol, March 1939.

Cpl. Cameron and Hudson's Bay clerk, Jim Kirk, assist at a funeral at the First Nations cemetery, ca. 1940.

After the completion of the Alaska Highway, lobbying increased to build all-weather roads to Dawson and Mayo. Construction began in the late 1940s, with completion of the road to Mayo in 1950 and to Dawson City in 1955. With the completion of the roads north, it became uneconomic to run the sternwheelers.

Most Selkirk residents moved to Minto to get work on the new highway. The stores closed and the missionary followed the people to Minto. Cut off from supplies and transport, the Yukon River communities were gradually abandoned. Cameron's successor, Constable Len Hall, was at Fort Selkirk for only a few months before the detachment was transferred to Minto in 1949. Once again the construction of a road had irrevocably changed life for the people of a Yukon community and the constable who served them.

Railway survey crew leaving Selkirk, ca. early 1940s. This American crew was surveying a railway route for a proposed extension of the White Pass and Yukon Railway. The route was to go down the White River into Alaska all the way to Nome.

After the Minto detachment closed, the buildings were moved to Carmacks in April 1954. This truck is crossing the ice bridge over the Yukon River at Carmacks.

View of Selkirk from the Yukon River, ca. 1939. The RCMP detachment building is at the far right.

The Cameron family pose in front of the sternwheeler Klondike *at Fort Selkirk. L-R: Edith Joynt holding Annabelle Adami; Martha, Ione and Cam Cameron.*

Moving day at Selkirk, 1949. This shot, taken behind the RCMP detachment, shows George Grimstead and Dave Sheffield helping Cpl. G.I. Cameron crate his belongings.

> *We were acting for Indian Agents and mining recorders and everything else. We were doing all the territorial and federal work. Even collected the license for radios — two dollars!…Whatever was necessary, we'd do it. If there was some teeth to be pulled, we'd pull that or, well, we'd give out medicines and look them over. If they were really sick, we'd give them a number nine pill. If they got well, we were wonderful men. If they weren't, we buried them. It was very simple.*
>
> **— G.I. Cameron, 1993[9]**

160 In 1919, G.I. Cameron joined the Royal North-West Mounted Police immediately after his demobilization from the Canadian army. Within a few hours of receiving his discharge papers, he found himself on a train out of Ottawa bound for Vancouver. After three years service with the force in southern British Columbia, Cameron ran his own business and worked in the California oilfields before re-enlisting.

In 1925, Cameron was assigned a one-month plainclothes posting at Keno City in the Yukon. While working as a carpenter for the mine, he investigated infractions of the Territorial Liquor Act. He stayed on in the north and met Martha Ballentine, his future wife, in Dawson City. When his Commanding Officer refused him permission to marry, he purchased his discharge in 1928. The couple went into business back east then tried subsistence farming in the Peace River country, but this was the Great Depression and times were hard. Shortly after the birth of their daughter Ione, the Camerons moved on to Vancouver.

By this time, regulations regarding marriage had been relaxed and Cameron signed up with the RCMP once again. In 1935, he was posted to Fort Selkirk. The

Cameron family lived here for the next 15 years. Cam and Martha Cameron and their daughter Ione were respected members of the community. Their home was always open to visitors and travellers who needed a place to stay.

Corporal Cameron took a number of photographs and movies depicting life at Fort Selkirk in the late 1930s and 1940s. They are an invaluable record of life at a Yukon River settlement during the sternwheeler era.

Corporal Cameron's many honours include a long-service medal, Canadian 125th Anniversary medal, member of the Order of Canada and the Commissioner's Award.

G.I. Cameron caught during a reflective moment at the dedication of the RCMP centennial mural, July 1994.

First Nations people rafting into Selkirk in spring from their traplines up the Pelly River.

161

Andrew Cruickshank mushes a long string of dogs near the steep bank of a river, ca. 1920s. After he left the force, Cruickshank piloted the Queen of the Yukon, *sister ship to Lindberg's* Spirit of St. Louis, *for the Yukon Airways and Exploration Company.*

"If their virtues are great, their vices are many"

In every part of the world the dog is the companion and helper of man, but nowhere is he so essentially a part of the life of the people as in the northern part of this continent…the dog will hold his place as the inseparable companion of the miner, hunter and traveller for a long time to come.

— Tappan Adney, 1899

It is impossible to over-estimate their importance. They are the only animals capable of hard work in harness, for which proper food could be obtained up there… They are used for every sort of purpose for which in more favoured countries the horse or ox is usually employed, such as ploughing, sleigh-driving, and hauling in stove-wood.

But if their virtues are great, their vices are many. During the day it would be impossible to get on without them: during the night, one feels inclined to shoot every dog about the place.

— S/Sgt. M.H.E. Hayne, 1897[1]

The Yukon's first Mounted Police quickly realized the transport value of dogs in a land with no roads, little open country and few good trails. The first known police dog team was an unfortunate quartet dubbed Matthew, Mark, Luke and John, shipped to Fort Constantine on the last steamer of 1895. John jumped overboard to his death. Mark and Luke teamed up to destroy Matthew, then continued to disturb the peace at the post with their nightly battles. The police had to hire additional dogs as needed.[2]

During the Klondike gold rush, dogs were a valuable and scarce commodity, with a good sled dog fetching up to $250. By 1898, the Yukon force owned 142 dogs. By the following year, this number rose to 231. In the first few years, the Mounties brought their own dog drivers; later they hired local First Nations people. These special constables hunted and fished for dog food, taught members how to handle sled dogs, and guided patrols.[3]

Mark and Luke at Fort Constantine.

The four dogs brought in by Inspector Harper were, small, ill-conditioned and of very little use; they will not eat dog-salmon, although cooked, consequently I had to trade fish for tripe. One dog has died.

—Supt. C. Constantine, 1898.[4]

Inspector Harper's relief party with the hapless dogs leaving Vancouver on the Islander, August, 1897. Tappan Adney, photographer.

Over the years, dog use decreased. Many detachments hired drivers and teams for patrols to avoid the expense of raising and feeding their own dogs year-round. Despite the advent of airplanes and snowmobiles, Mounties continued to run dogs, particularly for northern patrols, until 1969. In the early 1960s, the force instituted their own dog breeding program but by that time, dogs were on the way out, being replaced by snow machines. The Mounted Police formally recognized the end of an era with the "Last Patrol" by dog team from Old Crow to Fort McPherson in 1969. Many descendents of police dogs still survive in small communities all across the north.

In summer, some sled dogs worked as pack dogs on overland patrols. This stalwart animal was photographed at Dawson in 1931.

Dog team in Yukon collars climbing a steep slope at Rampart House, ca. 1926-28. A.B. Thornthwaite, photographer.

To climb the steep bank of a river, which may be anything from twenty-five to fifty feet high is another strenuous job. With a heavy load the dogs cannot make such a pull unaided, so the driver will have to lend a hand; lug, push, and heave and a 'Mush on boys' a few feet at a time to the top.

— **Sgt. Claude Tidd[5]**

From Labrador to the Yukon

During the frenzied days of the Klondike gold rush, not only two-footed creatures scrambled over the mountain passes into the Yukon. Many stampeders also brought along pack animals. Horses, dogs, oxen and goats were all pressed into service but few survived the treacherous mountain trails. One Mountie commented that the variety of beasts on board their northbound vessel made him feel he was on "a miniature Noah's ark."[6] All northerners agreed, however, that dogs were the best animals for travelling in the Yukon.

As a result, there was a great shortage of dogs in western Canada and northwestern United States. The increasing number of Mounties required ever more dogs to haul their supplies over the long distances between posts. The need for several teams of strong and sturdy dogs became more urgent over the winter of 1898-99, when the Mounted Police took on the mail service between Dawson and Skagway.

The ever-resourceful Frederick White, the Ottawa-based comptroller of the Mounted Police, looked to the east coast. Which animals should be better able to withstand bitter northern conditions than the large, strong, black dogs of Newfoundland and Labrador? He turned for help to J.U. Gregory, agent with the Marine and Fisheries Department in Québec City. Gregory enthusiastically took on the project and began arrangements to obtain 100 to 150 Labrador dogs for the Yukon. His first task was to find someone to handle purchasing who was knowledgeable about dogs and where to find them. Next, a boat was needed for transport between the remote coastal communities of Labrador and Québec City.

As it happened, Gregory knew the perfect person for the job. Ignace Hébert Jr., a dog driver and trainer, was intimately familiar with the Labrador coast and its inhabitants. For two dollars a day plus board and expenses, he agreed to seek out and purchase Labrador dogs, then take charge of them on their long voyage to the Yukon.[7]

Finding a boat proved more challenging. The trading schooners objected to a cargo of dogs "on account of the trouble they will give and the stench they will cause on board."

Gregory finally chartered a former smuggling vessel, the *Maggie H*. The expedition set off on September 1, 1898 with $400 in cash and a stock of supplies for barter.[8]

On October 24th, the *Maggie H*. returned to Québec harbour with a cargo of 142 Labrador dogs, collected along the length of the Strait of Belle Isle. Eight had been swept overboard during the stormy return. The boat had to make several stops at small islands along the way, allowing the animals to rest between bouts of seasickness and diarrhea.[9]

After a week in Québec City, Hébert and his crew spent half a day loading the animals and several barrels of food into two Canadian Pacific Railway boxcars. There they languished until the train set off October 31st, a day and half later. During a stopover in Ottawa, two teams of the dogs were paraded in front of the Houses of Parliament. Frederick White, several cabinet ministers, and some former Yukoners inspected the animals. After all declared themselves "highly pleased" with the government's new assets, the journey west continued, ending at Vancouver on November 13th.

Stampeder and his Labs pull heavily-laden sled past Stone House on Chilkoot Trail, ca. 1897.

In Vancouver, NWMP veterinary surgeon Inspector J.F. Burnett and a detachment of 30 Mounted Police met the canine caravan. Burnett found the dogs to be in fairly good health although "very tired and dirty." The six dog drivers felt much the same way after spending most of the trip cooped up with their charges.

The dogs stayed in a large warehouse on the Vancouver waterfront for four days before their final ordeal, the sea voyage up the coast from Vancouver to Skagway. The *S.S. Cutch* steamed out of Vancouver harbour November 17th. For the next five days, most passengers and the dogs suffered from seasickness. Sixteen dogs died en route, three from eating the rodent poison "Rough on Rats" in Vancouver, the remainder from "congestion of the liver and lungs."

This saga does not have a happy ending. As soon as they arrived in Skagway, the dogs began dying from pneumonia at an alarming rate. Inspector Burnett sent 60 of the healthier dogs over the summit to Bennett, hoping they would improve in the higher altitude and drier climate. Only 16 made it. Meanwhile, in

Skagway, despite the best care of Inspector Burnett and Ignace Hébert, the dogs kept dying. By January 1899, only 21 of the original 150 survived. During the ensuing investigation, it was learned that the same sad fate had befallen 400 to 500 other dogs imported from Newfoundland and Labrador. The verdict was that the outdoor dogs, unused to confinement, had suffered from overcrowding, overfeeding and the extreme changes in temperature. White had his own dark

suspicions that the dogs might have been "tampered with" in Skagway.

Ignace Hébert and his crew stayed on in the Yukon for a few years to work as dog drivers. The two remaining Labrador teams thrived and set new distance records. After this sad experience, however, the Mounted Police either bought their dogs from departing stampeders or imported them from elsewhere in the west.

Constable C.P. Constantine accompanied the Labs on the second-to-last leg of their journey to the Yukon. Here is how he remembered the party's debarkation from the *S.S. Cutch*:

Our arrival in Skagway would have been laughable, if it had not been so tragic.

There we were, wearing top boots, our moccasins in the hold, and the mile-long dock covered with ice. Our instructions were each to take two dogs on a chain and deliver them to a corral in town. The dogs were big, powerful brutes; they had been confined six weeks, and this was their first sniff of the wilds beyond.

We sailed down the docks like water-skiers. Some sat down and nearly burnt a hole in their britches. Others hung on to the railing long enough to get tangled up with the man and dogs behind them. Reaching the corral, we found it deep in snow. It looked as if an avalanche had fallen on a pack of snarling dogs and half-buried Mounties. As a climax, and this I remember well, a Salvation Army lass happened along and in the name of God begged us not to swear. Quite a few of the dogs got away and were never recovered.[10]

Somehow, this particular episode never made it into any of the official reports.

Labrador dog team hauls stampeders' sleigh on Bracketts's wagon road, White Pass Trail, ca. 1899.

Cst. Frenchy Chartrand and his lead dog at Herschel Island, ca. 1933. Chartrand is sitting on a half barrel used as a dog kennel. In the background are the Inspector's house and barracks.

Even as a youth, he had had much experience in the breeding and training of dogs—an acquirement that made him a valuable man in the North. Chartrand was a first-class dog driver and traveller, and it was said of him that he had few equals in the north as a fisherman and seal hunter.

— RCMP Quarterly, 1942[11]

168

"Frenchy" Chartrand fell under the spell of the north soon after his enlistment in 1926. Chartrand spent most of his 16-year career above the Arctic Circle,

serving at Herschel Island, Aklavik, Cambridge Bay and Coppermine detachments. An important part of his job was breeding and training sled dogs. Chartrand also set time and distance records on his dog team patrols— mushing 380 miles in six days and, on another occasion, travelling 1,100 miles in 32 days.

In 1940, he joined the crew of the famous RCMP schooner *St. Roch* during its first navigation of the Northwest Passage. During the *St. Roch's* second winter in the Arctic,

moored in the ice at Pasley Bay, Chartrand died from a sudden heart attack. As he had been the only Roman Catholic aboard, his crew mates determined to find a priest to read the burial service over him. Captain Henry Larsen and Corporal Hunt made an 800-mile return trip by dogsled to seek out the nearest Catholic priest. A few months later, Father Gustav Henry read the service over Chartrand's cairn. Chartrand was honoured posthumously with the Polar Medal (silver).[12]

Nikki, "the Hollywood dog," goes to Herschel Island

For many years, Hollywood and the Royal Canadian Mounted Police had a special relationship. The image of the stalwart red-coated Mountie held great appeal for filmmakers. The Canadian government, mindful of the tourist value of the Mountie films, encouraged the RCMP to cooperate with the movie studios. During the 1930s, several members worked on various Hollywood productions as technical advisors, trying to curb the worst excesses—not always successfully. An interesting twist on this relationship came in the 1960s when Hollywood donated several sled dogs to the Mounties for their new dog-breeding program.[13]

In 1960, the Cangary Film Company, a Walt Disney subsidiary, shot a sled dog adventure movie later titled *Nikki, Wild Dog of the North*.[14] The movie, filmed mostly in Banff, Alberta, portrayed the life of a sled dog from puppy to full-grown adult. The model for Nikki was a Malemute-Siberian husky cross from Whitehorse named Smokey. Smokey's owners, Alaskan residents Bill and Virginia Bacon, took on the formidable task of finding Smokey look-alikes for the movie. As well as seeking dogs throughout Alaska and Canada, they organized a breeding program to obtain dogs of all ages and temperaments. The adult

Nikki was played by seven females and four males including Nikki himself. By the end of the project, the movie-makers had employed 200 sled dogs, all now in need of new homes.

People in the Banff and Calgary area adopted dozens of the dogs. Others went to Canadian park employees. Bill Bacon approached the RCMP through member Gordon Whitehouse to offer the force some of his breeding stock. The proposal couldn't have been more timely. At the time, northern detachments were losing many dogs to epidemics and other causes. Superintendent Fraser of "G" Division, encompassing the Yukon and Northwest Territories, determined that "the breeding was running out" and that the Mounted Police should start their own breeding program using "pure-bred" Siberian huskies.[15] The hitch was that very few of the 19 Disney dogs donated to the RCMP were pure-bred, having been bred for appearance rather than bloodline.

In 1960, the RCMP set up a dog breeding program at Fort Norman in the Northwest Territories, its goal being to provide Siberian huskies to all northern detachments as needed. Less than two years later, 25 percent of all Division dogs came from the Fort Norman program. The dog breeding station was transferred to Herschel Island in the

spring of 1962. The Herschel Island detachment, located on a small island in the Beaufort Sea, was the Yukon's most northerly, and isolated, detachment. From here, progeny of the Nikki dogs were flown to detachments all over the Yukon and Northwest Territories.

Agnes Gruben White, an Inuvialuit woman married to an RCMP member at Herschel Island, helped tend the dogs:

> We had about 70 dogs. They come in from Norman Wells. They were breeding the dogs. They were Siberian Huskies… Around middle November, they flew in Nikki the famous dog from California. He used to be in movies. That dog was here. We had to take care of him carefully so that nothing would happen to the dog. They wanted to use the dog to breed. They were real tiny small dogs. I didn't think too much of them.[16]

In 1964, the Herschel Island detachment closed and the dog breeding program ended, the plan being that individual detachments would continue to breed their own stock. By that time, however, the era of the Mountie dogsled patrol was nearly at an end. Although the RCMP terminated their long relationship with sled dogs in 1969, descendents of the Disney dogs still inhabit northern settlements from Spence Bay to Old Crow.

Descendents of the Nikki dogs at Old Crow, 1969.

The end of an era—the Last Patrol

By 1969, only four northern detachments still used dogs for winter patrols: Old Crow in the Yukon; Arctic Red River, Sachs Harbour, and Spence Bay in the Northwest Territories. The force was converting to snow machines and the detachments were ordered to dispose of their dogs, many of whom were pups and grand-pups of the Disney dogs.[17]

On March 11, 1969, Constable Warren Townsend and Special Constable Peter Benjamin left Old Crow driving 21 dogs on the last RCMP dog team patrol to Fort McPherson and Arctic Red River and back—a

Minnie Kirk and friend at Old Crow, ca. 1940s.

Cst. Warren Townsend and team on Last Patrol.

distance of 500 miles. The members of the Old Crow detachment decided that this historic trip deserved recognition. They prepared special commemorative envelopes to be stamped at the Old Crow and Fort McPherson post offices. For the first two days, a writer and photographer from *Canadian Magazine* travelled with the patrol by snowmobile, guided by Old Crow residents Johnny Abel and Alfred Charlie. Two members from the RCMP Colour and Movie Section recorded the patrol departure, then flew to other points further down the trail to shoot more footage. Even a *National Geographic* photographer spent a day or two with the patrol at Fort McPherson.[18]

Despite the hoopla, this patrol bore many resemblances to other police patrols that had travelled through this area since 1899. In his diary, Townsend noted weather and trail conditions, information about game in the area, and the names of local residents met en route. There were close calls over rough stretches of trail, halts due to bad weather, a bit of caribou hunting, and breaks to care for the dogs. S/Cst. Peter Benjamin continued the tradition of Gwichin people guiding members through their traditional territory. Townsend and Benjamin returned to Old Crow on April 5th, 26 days after their departure.

The following excerpts from the patrol diary give a flavour of their experiences.[19]

23-26 Mar 69

13. This time was spent resting the dogs and caring for them as some of the younger dogs had badly cut and bruised feet. The three members of the Ident. section colour and movie unit met us at Fort McPherson and more photographs of the patrol were taken. Also present was a freelance photographer representing the National Geographic Magazine.

Miles – 0.

2 Apr 69

19. Weather – Wind nil, clear, temp. 4 F.

Broke camp at 8:30 am and Cst. EVANS returned to Fort McPherson while we continued on with FIRTH and TURNBULL [Fort McPherson guide and National Geographic photographer] to the top of the Big Chute pass. We had been advised to use this pass as the weather was good and it was shorter by five miles. After we entered the pass we found our way blocked by a drop of approx. 30 feet which had been formed by a creek backing up. We then turned north to go over one of the mountains skirting the creek. When we reached the top of the mountain we found that the only way down was on a water run off. Once again the dogs had to be turned loose to go down on their own. The toboggans were then wrapped with chains and allowed to slide down

turned on the side. We then made our way back to the Chute Creek only to find it covered with overflow. As that is the only way out of the mountains the dogs were driven through the water. We continued on past the big glacier approximately five miles and made camp. Our feet, toboggans and dogs were well coated with ice by this time. We stopped for the night at 7:00 pm. During the day many places were passed over which large herds of caribou had travelled.

Miles - 40.

5 Apr 69

22. Weather - Wind nil, clear, temp. -4 F.

We departed from the Police Cabin at 8:00 am and found that it was necessary to snowshoe after driving the dogs about two miles. We snowshoed to the mouth of the Driftwood River and found that it was possible to drive dogs on the Portage trail. Approximately one-half way across the portage it was found that the Old Crow people had been in the area recently hunting caribou and the trail was well-packed. We stopped at a group of tents for lunch but, the occupants of the tents had returned to town. We met Bill SMITH and his wife (white trapper) along the trail and they advised that a large herd of caribou

was in the area. We were met by Cpl. WHEELER, Stephen FROST, and Maynard ELLINGSON of Old Crow fourteen miles from town. We had tea and continued on to Old Crow arriving at 10:00 pm.

Miles - 50.

Within a year after the Last Patrol, northern dog mushers began making commemorative dogsled runs, following the traditional police patrol routes. This particular expedition has just arrived in Dawson City from Fort McPherson. Andrew Kunizzi (right), their chief guide and a former police guide, was 78 years old when these two photos were taken, ca. 1970. John Gould, photographer.

Special Constable Peter Benjamin during Last Patrol, 1969.

CHAPTER 12

RCMP detachments: 1932, 1995

POLICING TODAY

In 1962, the RCMP opened Whitehorse "Air," as part of the "Air" Division. The first aircraft assigned to the Yukon was a Beaver. Airplanes are used to patrol distant and isolated areas and to transport personnel, their families and supplies. Pilots S/Sgt. Gerry Anderson and Sgt. Rick Aberson pose by the force's 18-seat Twin Otter in Haines Junction, 1994.

The modern era

Construction of the Alaska Highway marked the beginning of modern police work in the Yukon. Soon other roads were built—to Mayo, Dawson and Atlin—and the romantic sternwheeler era came to an end. Many river settlements were deserted while other communities, such as Watson Lake, Pelly Crossing and Beaver Creek, grew up along the new highways. Road traffic increased dramatically and highway patrols became more important, all but replacing dog team, foot and horse patrols.

Communications improved steadily. By 1957, all Alaska Highway detachments and some patrol cars were linked by radio. All patrol cars outside Whitehorse were equipped with radios by 1974. Telephones, fax machines, computers and satellites have further reduced the isolation of the Yukon's remote posts.

As post-war Yukon grew, so did the Mounted Police force. Since 1938, the Yukon had been a part of "G" Division, a huge administrative area—run from Ottawa—which included the Northwest Territories. As the Yukon force expanded, it took on more specialized functions, and became more autonomous. The Whitehorse force grew out of the cozy detachment building by the waterfront into a series of ever-larger quarters.

The creation of "M" Division in 1974 recognized the maturity and independence of the Yukon force. Soon after, the headquarters moved into a sleek new building, seemingly a world away from the one-room log cabin detachments of yesteryear.

The RCMP of the Yukon joined the rest of the force in updating its image. Since 1974, women have worn the red serge. Native special constables assumed more responsibilities and most became regular members. The RCMP work closely with local governments, First Nations and community agencies to prevent crime and determine policing priorities. Mounted Police continue to be valued members of the community, active in volunteer work.

The majestic land attracts and inspires a special type of Mountie. Despite the modernization of the force, Yukon police work retains the flavour of its rich history. Cases such as dramatic search and rescue operations, and the hunt for a modern-day "Mad Trapper" hark back to an earlier era. The centennial of the Royal Canadian Mounted Police in the Yukon is a time to reflect on this stirring past.

Constables Terry Johnson and Karen Olito in Dawson City, 1994.

Yukon member visits Otter Falls, ca. 1969. This scenic spot was once portrayed on the back of the Canadian five dollar bill.

"M" Division: Yukon headquarters

Until after World War II, the Whitehorse RCMP detachment occupied a two-storey frame building on First Avenue. After sub-division headquarters were transferred from Dawson to Whitehorse in 1943, the three-member detachment increased to 17 and new quarters were required. For a time, the force took over the flimsily-constructed U.S. Army quarters built on the old police compound in downtown Whitehorse. These temporary structures, or H-huts, were dilapidated, hard to heat and a fire hazard. Former member Len Hall recalls that prisoners stayed in one wing, single members in

another, with both using the same central washrooms. In 1949, the Department of National Defense awarded Poole Construction of Edmonton the contract to build a two-storey combination barracks and guardroom. The Whitehorse detachment building, completed in 1950, cost about $120,000. A few years later, sub-division headquarters moved into the second floor of the new Federal Building erected on the corner of Main Street and Fourth Avenue, half a block from the detachment.[1]

Alaska Highway traffic increased dramatically, bringing new problems. Criminal code work rose, particularly theft and break-and-enters. In 1960, the annual report claimed that police work in the southern Yukon resembled that of any other sub-division. Criminal activity increased sharply by the mid-1970s. This was ascribed to the construction of the Alaskan North Slope gas pipeline, causing much more traffic through the Yukon. It was also a boom period in the

territory, with the opening of three important mines at Faro, Whitehorse and near Dawson; and several large construction projects including a large power plant at Aishihik Lake, the Dempster Highway to Inuvik and the Skagway Road between Carcross and Skagway. All these enterprises brought more transient workers and an increase in offences such as the recreational use of illegal drugs. The Yukon force had nearly tripled since 1950, from 33 to 91 personnel. The Mounted Police had outgrown both of their buildings.

On July 1, 1974, RCMP Commissioner Maurice Nadon presided at a ceremony proclaiming the Yukon "M" Division, with headquarters at the capital city of Whitehorse.[2] This move coincided with a

175

Yukon artist Jim Robb portrayed a fanciful view of the detachment building long after the structure had been demolished.

RCMP detachment building in Whitehorse, ca. 1963-64.

political climate that favoured giving the northern territories more responsibility for their own affairs. About the same time, "G" Division headquarters moved from Ottawa to Yellowknife. With the establishment of "M" Division, the Yukon got a new commanding officer, Supt. Harry Nixon, and additional responsibilities. The division needed its own financial section, staffing section and records management. The first records clerk recalls sitting in a tiny office, surrounded by truckloads of file boxes shipped in from Yellowknife, frustrated at having no place to unpack and sort them.[3] "M" Division desperately needed a larger facility to house the extra staff and functions.

The old detachment building came down and a large, modern structure took its place. The Honourable Warren Allmand, Minister for Indian Affairs and Northern Development, officially opened the "M" Division/detachment complex on September 17, 1976.

As of January 1995, "M" Division has grown to include 13 detachments and 159 employees, 38 of whom are either civilian members or public servants. Of these, 114 are stationed in Whitehorse with the remaining 45 in rural detachments. Women make up 25 percent of the total and 21 of the 79 regular members are First Nations people.[4]

It's been a long time since Mounties patrolled the Yukon by horseback and dog team. Members now travel in a variety of modern vehicles. The Division fleet includes a total of 27 cars, 24 suburbans, three trucks, six vans, four ATVs, 26 snowmobiles, 16 boats of various sizes for inland water transport, four bicycles and one Twin Otter aircraft.

The RCMP provide police service to the Yukon at a cost of approximately $17 million per year. The Yukon government pays approximately 70 percent of this amount, the remainder being federally funded.[5]

176

The RCMP operated the territorial jail at Whitehorse. By the early 1960s, they were lobbying to replace the small overcrowded guardroom with a larger facility run by civilians. Construction of the Whitehorse Correctional Centre in 1967 relieved the police of the job of looking after time-serving prisoners.[6]

The cell block in the basement of the Whitehorse detachment was not the most secure or safe facility. It was also a potential fire trap:

This shows the wooden construction of the ceiling of the cell room (downstairs), the wooden cells and the wooden double bunks. All of this construction is tinder dry and therefore

creates a great fire hazard. When these cells are full, other prisoners must be placed in single beds, in the space in front of these cells, this happens at least 50% of the year.[7]

Constable Majorie McLeod by the Whitehorse detachment lock-up, November 1992.

A NEW ERA

The RCMP in the Yukon, M Division, have entered a new era in appearances with the opening of their brand new building. Gone is the old white building with worn floor that sat back from Fourth Avenue with a cannon out in front; gone is the mood of yesterday it created. The old building now is fronted by the metallic, grey face of the new and the cannon is tucked in beside the new headquarters.

With the change goes some of the old image and not just the Sergeant Preston myth that RCMP Commissioner Maurice Nadon jokingly referred to Friday. There is more room now—along with modern architecture and an appearance of big-city efficiency in the building. We will have to resist feeling differently, though. The Mounties have not changed and their brave and colourful history in the North remains the same, with another chapter added.

— *The Whitehorse Star*, 20 Sept. 1976

Members of the Whitehorse detachment and Whitehorse Sub-division, 1969
(L-R) Front row: **Supt. Al Huget, C.O. "G" Division, Insp. Bob Wood, O.C. Whitehorse Sub-division;**

2nd row: **S/Sgt. Ray Johnson, Sgt. John Hayes, Cpl. Cec Gilmour, Cpl. John Hodgson, Csts. Brian Smith, Leon MacAllister, Ralph Falkingham, Andy Anderson, Don Mosicki, Chester MacDonald, S/Sgt. Art Deer;**

3rd row: L-R: **Csts. Roy Soluk, Bruce Hamilton, Cpl. Bob Gilholme, Sgt. Bill Pringle, S/Sgt. Rueben Fendrick, Sgt. Al MacLeod, Cst. Joe Godwalt;**

Back row: L-R: **Cpl. Bob MacEachern, Csts. Pete Jacques, Gilles Parent, Jim Sytnick, Ken Gabb, Nick Veres.**

"M" Division building, 1994.

"Just looking for the bad guys" [8]

Teslin Mountie puts cold war criminal on ice

In 1987, Corporal Dan Fudge made international headlines when he arrested an American fugitive in Teslin, an Alaska Highway community of 350 people, a two-hour drive from Whitehorse. Robert McVey fled the United States in 1983 after being indicted for diverting $15 million U.S. worth of technology to the Soviet Union and other Eastern Bloc countries. He held the number four spot on the U.S. government's list of "ten most wanted" arms and technology smugglers.[9]

One summer day, Fudge stepped into the Yukon Motel restaurant and thought the six-foot-two, 300-pound stranger looked familiar. He recognized McVey from a photocopy of a passport photo sent to his office the previous year. After a few quick phone calls, Fudge arranged for a warrant with U.S. authorities. The successful arrest brought an abrupt end to McVey's fishing holiday.

Later that year, the American government awarded Dan Fudge the Outstanding Public Service Medal at a ceremony in Washington, D.C., as well as a special certificate from the Commissioner of U.S. Customs. Corporal Fudge shrugged off the fuss.

"I was just doing a job we're expected to do and it was a pleasure to do it," Fudge told reporters.

Cpl. Dan Fudge, 1987.

Cpl. Phil Warren in the forensics lab, 1994.

1972 murder suspect is arrested in Florida

Whitehorse Star *headline, March 12, 1992*

Getting their man — twenty years later

The computerization of the national fingerprint system in 1982 has made an enormous difference to forensic work around the country. The RCMP lab in Ottawa used to take two weeks to handle a fingerprint identification request. Now requests can be processed in less than a day.

This new technology played a key role in solving a 20-year-old murder case. In September 1972, police discovered the decomposing body of Allyn Giswold in his Whitehorse residence. The elderly man had died from a savage beating three months before. The chief suspect, Walter Roderick Code, had disappeared. Despite the lack of clues to Code's whereabouts, the RCMP persisted in their search. When they transmitted the fingerprints around North America, they finally found a match in Louisiana. With the assistance of the FBI and Florida State Police, the RCMP tracked Code down in Naples, Florida in 1992. Living under an alias, Code had been running a construction business. After his arrest, Code pled guilty to manslaughter and was sentenced to six years in jail.[10]

Teslin Lake RCMP killing:
Trapper planned to kill, diary says

Whitehorse Star *headline.*

"Shesley Mike"—a modern-day Mad Trapper

Somehow, I got…country to explore and gold to dig and then I will have had the fun in my life that will make it fulfilled enough to give it all up and go out 100 per cent to kill these bastards, since it is obvious the laws are crooked.

The pigs are owned by the gangsters in power and will not punish one another for doing this stuff to me. They'll just consider they failed so far to beat me and will try more with each new batch of recruits they drum up.

— Michael Eugene Oros, February 1985[11]

Michael Oros penned these words a month before he killed Constable Michael Buday, then died himself during a shoot-out on the shores of Teslin Lake just south of the Yukon-British Columbia border.[12] The reclusive 33-year-old Oros had a history of violence and instability. He was a suspect in the 1981 disappearance of his former friend, trapper Gunter Lischy, and was known to have raided wilderness cabins.

In March 1985, a Whitehorse family discovered their cabin at the southwest end of Teslin Lake had been damaged and robbed. After spotting Mike Oros in the area, they reported the incident to Teslin RCMP. When the police flew to the cabin site in a chartered plane, Oros fired at the aircraft.

Since both the cabin break-in and shooting happened in B.C., Prince Rupert Subdivision was notified. On March 18th, a 13-member emergency response team flew to Whitehorse. The next day, three groups of RCMP travelled to the area by helicopter and small plane. When they spotted Oros, they landed some distance away. Instead of attempting to elude his pursuers, Oros stalked one party, then killed 27-year-old dog handler Constable Michael Buday with a single shot.

Constable Allan Rodgers immediately returned fire, killing Oros. Dennis Dennison, owner of Coyote Air Services of Teslin, piloted the command plane for the operation. He confirmed Oros' death by flying over the body after the shooting.

A week later, over 700 RCMP travelled to Brooks, Alberta—the home of Michael Buday—to say goodbye to their comrade. Constable Buday's police dog Trooper led the funeral procession from the church to the cemetery. Buday's name joined the Honour Roll of nearly 200 RCMP who have died in the line of duty.

Inevitably, journalists made comparisons to the Mad Trapper case of over 50 years before. In 1932, the mysterious man known as Albert Johnson killed one Mountie and wounded two other pursuers during a dramatic midwinter chase across the northern Yukon.

After the Oros shoot-out, Atlin RCMP Corporal Barry Erickson discovered the bones of Gunter Lischy while searching the area near Oros' cabin with Constable Jack Warner of Teslin. A forensic pathologist examined the bones and determined Lischy died from a bullet in the back. A coroner's jury deliberated for just over an hour before concluding that Michael Oros had killed Gunter Lischy.

Working with Yukoners

Law enforcement work has evolved in response to changes in society and new types of crime. The force today provides specialized training allowing members to keep up with new technology and the sophistication of many modern-day criminals. The Mounted Police have attempted to interact with the public in a proactive rather than a strictly reactive way. Now the RCMP emphasizes crime prevention and good community relations. Programs such as Neighbourhood Watch, Operation Gold Watch and the Safety Bear encourage citizens to take more responsibility for safeguarding themselves and their property. Under a new auxiliary police program, volunteers are trained to work with members on a variety of activities.

> *There has always been a notable tendency on the part of the drivers in the Yukon to disregard the provisions of the Yukon Motor Vehicles Ordinance, particularly in respect to exceeding the speed limit...[13]*

The quote above was written in 1952 but many Mounties on highway patrol would probably agree that little has changed. Long empty stretches of roadway between the Yukon's communities make speeding a very tempting violation. Traffic duty is complicated by the many tourists that travel Yukon roads every summer. A unique feature of Yukon police work is monitoring the high number of wilderness travellers. Members are often called on to coordinate search-and-rescue operations for missing aircraft, hunters,

The national Safety Bear program originated in the Yukon. Based on a similar program run by the Alaska State Troopers, the Safety Bear works with children. S/Sgt. Dennis Schneider poses with some fans in 1986.

Over the summer of 1994, 11 college and university students patrolled the streets of Whitehorse by bicycle, foot and car. Often, student police experience can be a springboard to future careers in law enforcement. Students on bicycle patrol in Rotary Peace Park in Whitehorse, 1994.

180

canoeists, etc. On the other hand, global shrinking has brought big-city problems such as illegal drugs and counterfeiting.

Despite the advent of computerization and international communications, many crimes are still solved by old-fashioned hard work, persistence and some luck. In this respect, police work has not changed much from the days of the dogsled patrols. Tragedies still occur and members can die in the performance of their duty.

In his spare time, veterinarian Jim Kenyon volunteers as an auxiliary constable.

Kelly Shopland joined the auxiliary police to better serve her community.

Transfer of Command Parade, 1992
(L-R) Front row: Inspector Russ Juby,
Rev. Des Carroll, retired Cpl. G.I. Cameron,
Whitehorse Mayor Bill Weigand, new Commanding Officer, Chief Superintendent E. Henderson, former Commanding Officer, Chief Superintendent J.R. Gilholme, Yukon Justice Minister Margaret Commodore, Yukon Commissioner Ken McKinnon, Bishop Thomas Lobsinger;
2nd row: Csts. Mike Nelson, Steve McLeod, Mike LeBlanc, Sgt. Al O'Donnell, Steven Poolachoff, Peter Purchase, Sgt. Frank Smith;
3rd row: Cpl. Greg Lyslo, Cpl. Brian Boleen, S/Sgt. Dennis Schneider, Mike Griffin, Cpl. Everett Parker, Cst. Pat Maloney, Cst. Harlan Inkster;
4th row: Cpl. Chris Moran, Cst. Helmer Hermanson, Sgt. Rob Nason, Cpl. Rick Noack, Sgt. Jim Herman, Sgt. Phil Humphries, Cst. Patrick Egan, Sgt. Rick Aberson;
Back row: Sgt. Brian Huddle, Cst. Dave Conrod, S/Sgt. Jim Cairns, Sgt. Rick Michael, Cpl. Andy Latham, Cpl. Doug Harris, Cpl. J. Powell, Cpl. Ron Allen, Cst. Lindsay Brine, Cpl. Jim Lamberton, S/Sgt. Gary Williams.

Policing today

Cpl. Everett Parker, Cst. Chuck Bertrand, Cpl. Sandy Irvine conduct an arson investigation on Bennett Lake, B.C. in a chartered Single Otter, 1988.

Sgt. Chris Olson, piloting RCMP Twin Otter, in 1992.

Cst. Patrick Egan on highway patrol in Whitehorse, 1989.

Constable Doug Aird and friends in Ross River, 1994.

Commemorating a centennial

The RCMP has been part of the Yukon's history for a hundred years. Since Inspector Constantine led the first Yukon detachment to Forty Mile in 1895, the Mounted Police have represented Canada and upheld Canadian law in this remote corner of the country. Thanks largely to the Mounties, the Yukon was spared the violent frontier experience of the American Wild West. During the quieter period following the Klondike gold rush, the Mounties fulfilled a host of government functions—everything from income tax assistance to hunting licences was available at the local detachment.

As well as serving the community, the Mounties of the Yukon are also in touch with the world scene, nabbing international criminals who thought they were safe in this seemingly remote backwater. The RCMP have evolved with the times. Increasingly, women, First Nations people and the community at large have become more involved in law enforcement. The centennial motto, "Working With Yukon People," reflects a fascinating past and shows optimism for the future.

Sgt. Doug Harris and Cst. Pat Maloney prepare to celebrate the centennial by travelling the northern patrol route, from Dawson City to Fort McPherson and back, in a party of nine snowmobilers and three dog teams.

Aboard the S.S. Klondike. L-R: George Rogers, Cpl. Andy Latham, Cst. Brenda Butterworth-Carr, Teslin Tlingit elder Sam Johnston and Walter Rogers. The men in helmets are visiting members of Steele's Scouts, a commemorative troop association based in Alberta.

Most members who served in the Yukon eventually moved on, taking with them vivid memories and colourful anecdotes. A smaller number fell under the spell of the Yukon and chose to remain in the north after leaving the force. They became trappers, big game guides, civil servants, miners and entrepreneurs. Often they married and raised families; their descendants are now third and fourth generation Yukoners.

There were some, however, who met an untimely end during their service. They succumbed to fatal illnesses, swift, icy rivers, a "mad trapper's" bullet, and the hardships of the trail. The advent of aviation brought new hazards as evidenced by the 1964 crash of an RCMP plane at Carmacks, killing four members.

There were many fatalities due to illness and accident which are not recorded below. Here we acknowledge and pay tribute to the members and special constables who are officially recognized by the force as having died while on duty.[1]

Ceremony to mark the official unveiling of the monument honouring the members of the Lost Patrol, September 1915.

Close-up of the plaque on the Fitzgerald monument in Dawson City.

Funeral parade for Cst. M.J. Fitzgerald at Dawson City, 1913.

ANNAND, Cst. William John David 19206
Killed on July 13, 1963, in an RCMP aircraft which crashed and burned when attempting to land at Carmacks, Yukon.

ASBIL, Cpl. Robert William 19626
Killed on July 13, 1963, in an RCMP aircraft which crashed and burned when attempting to land at Carmacks, Yukon.

BUDAY, Cst. Michael J. 33631
Killed at Teslin Lake, British Columbia on March 19, 1985 while attempting to apprehend fugitive Michael Oros.

CAMPBELL, Cst. Norman M. 2972
Drowned in the Stikine River, Alaska, while on patrol from northern British Columbia, on December 26, 1901.

CARTER, S/Cst. Samuel
Died with the McPherson-Dawson patrol in February, 1911.

FITZGERALD, Insp. Francis Joseph
Died from starvation, exposure and exhaustion while a member of the McPherson-Dawson patrol in February, 1911.

FITZGERALD, Cst. Michael J. 3617
Drowned in the White River, Yukon, on August 27, 1913.

HADDOCK, Cpl. Alexander G. 2836
Drowned in the Yukon River near Ogilvie, Yukon, while on patrol June 14, 1906.

HEATHCOTE, Cst. Spencer G. 3463
Drowned in the Stikine River, Alaska, while on patrol from northern British Columbia, on December 26, 1901.

KINNEY, Cst. George Francis 4582
Died with the Dawson-McPherson patrol in February 1911.

LAMONT, Cst. Alexander 5548
Died at Herschel Island, Yukon, on February 16, 1918, from typhoid fever contracted while nursing Vilhjalmur Stefansson, the Arctic explorer.

Funeral parade inspection in Dawson City, May 20, 1910.

RCMP cemetery in Dawson City, ca. 1948.

LAUGHLAND, Sgt. Kenneth Morley 17368
Killed on July 13, 1963, in an RCMP aircraft which crashed and burned when attempting to land at Carmacks, Yukon.

MALCOLM, Cst. Proctor Lawrence Anthony 18570
Killed on July 13, 1963, in an RCMP aircraft which crashed and burned when attempting to land at Carmacks, Yukon.

McLACHLAN, Cst. Mark 31962
Killed in a vehicle collision on February 2, 1979 on the Klondike Highway while returning to Pelly Crossing detachment from court duties at Whitehorse.

MILLEN, Cst. Edgar 9669
Killed near Rat River, NWT, on January 30, 1932, while attempting to apprehend Albert Johnson, a fugitive from justice.

SAM, S/Cst. Stick
Drowned when fording Kaskawulsh River, Yukon, while on patrol, on July 29, 1903.

SUNDELL, Cst. C.L. 18165
Accidentally shot on July 14, 1958, at Herschel Island, Yukon, while on duty.

TAYLOR, Cst. Richard O.H. 4346
Died in February, 1911, with the McPherson-Dawson patrol.

Endnotes

Introduction

1. Quoted in S.W. Horrall, *The Pictorial History of the Royal Canadian Mounted Police* (Toronto: McGraw-Hill-Ryerson Ltd.), p. 20.

2. Ibid., pp.10-21.

3. Morris Zaslow, *The Opening of the Canadian North, 1870–1914* (Toronto: McClelland and Stewart, 1971), p. 17.

4 Zaslow, pp. 22-23; Wm. R. Morrison, *Showing the Flag* (Vancouver: UBC Press, 1985), pp. 2-3.

5. Horrall, p. 22.

6. This is the term preferred by the Yukon's native people. Today there are 14 recognized Yukon First Nations distinguished by language and traditional territory.

7. I have adopted Mike Gates' usage from his book, *Gold at Fortymile Creek*. Fortymile spelled as one word refers to the river and its drainage, which includes the mining area. Forty Mile written as two words refers to the settlement at the confluence of the Yukon and Fortymile rivers.

8. Allen A. Wright, *Prelude to Bonanza* (Sidney, B.C.: Gray's Publishing Ltd., 1976), pp. 161-162, 247.

9. Michael Gates, *Gold at Fortymile Creek* (Vancouver: UBC Press, 1994), pp. 69-70, 120; A.K. Mathews, "The History of the North West Mounted Police in the Yukon Territory, 1894-1912" (unpl. ms., prepared for the retirement of Supt. Nixon, Whitehorse, 1984), pp. 4-5.

10. During his 1883 expedition, Schwatka erroneously indicated that Alaskan territory extended 12 miles into Canada, east of the actual U.S./Canada border. Zaslow, p. 87.

11. Mathews, pp. 4-5; Wright, pp. 251-258.

12. National Archives of Canada (NAC), RG 18, vol. 135, f. 262-1897.

13. NWMP, *1894 Annual Report*, Report of Supt. Constantine, p. 81.

14. Mathews, p. 16. It should be noted that the force underwent a few name changes over the years—becoming the Royal Northwest Mounted Police in 1904, and the Royal Canadian Mounted Police in 1919.

15. Mathews, pp. 6-8.

1. The first post—Fort Constantine

1. NWMP, *1894 Annual Report*, Constantine, p. 81.

2. M.H.E. Hayne & H. West Taylor, *The Pioneers of the Klondyke* (London: Sampson Low, Marston and Co. Ltd., 1897), pp. 31-32.

3. Ibid., p. 64.

4. NAC, RG 18, Series F1, vol. 2182, f. 4, 4 October 1895, Constantine to Comm. Herchmer.

5. NWMP, *1895 Annual Report*, Constantine, p. 7. The title quote comes from Insp. Strickland's report, p. 16: "The conduct of the non-commissioned officers and men of my party was very satisfactory throughout the whole trip, and they stood the hard work well."

6. Ibid., p. 7.

7. A "cord" of firewood is a stack of logs measuring 4x4x8 feet.

8. NWMP, *1895 Annual Report*, p. 13; *1896 Annual Report*, p. 235.

9. A lay was a type of lease arrangement. A claim owner allowed another miner to work the property in return for a percentage of the gold recovered.

10. Gates, pp. 113-114.

11. NAC, vol. RG 18, Series F1, vol. 2182 f4;. 12 Sept. 1896, Constantine to Herchmer. The title quote also comes from this letter.

12. Ibid., 30 Dec. 1896, Constantine to Herchmer.

13. Ibid., 2 Sept. 1896, Constantine to Herchmer.

14. The recently-developed machine guns were on the cutting edge of military technology. With these powerful weapons, a relatively small force could control a large mob. David Neufeld, *Chilkoot Trail—Yukon Gateway* (Parks Canada, 1993), p. 13.

15. RNWMP, *1912 Annual Report*, p. 35.

16. Zaslow, p. 108.

17. Wright, pp. 257-258, 298-299.

18. Hayne & Taylor, p. 175.

19. Ibid., pp. 28-29, 34.

20. *RCMP Quarterly*, July 1966, p. 47.

2. The Klondike gold rush

1. NWMP, *1898 Annual Report*, Report of Supt. Steele, p. 4.

2. NAC, RG 18, vol. 139, f. 442-97: 10 Sept. 1897, Ass't. Comm. J.H. McIlree to Herchmer and 18 Dec. 1897, Wood to Comptroller White.

3. *1898 Annual Report*, Steele, p. 21.

4. This section draws on two excellent sources that discuss the border issue and sovereignty in much greater detail. These are: A.K. Mathews, "The History of the North West Mounted Police in the Yukon Territory, 1894-1912" (unpl. ms., prepared for the retirement of Supt. Nixon, Whitehorse, 1984), and David Neufeld, *Chilkoot Trail—Yukon Gateway* (Parks Canada, 1993).

5. The treaty stated that the boundary would follow "the summit of the mountains situated parallel to the coast to the 141st longitude." If the mountain summits were more than 10 marine leagues (35 miles or 56 km) distant from the coast, the boundary would then follow "the windings of the coast" 10 leagues inland. The mountains did not parallel the coast and interpretations varied as to whether the strip should follow the general outline of the coast or bend inland along every one of the long narrow inlets that penetrated this stretch of coastline. This latter interpretation would mean that the Americans would claim all the territory from Dyea inland to Lake Bennett. The former supported Canadian claims to Skagway. Mathews, pp. 9-10; Dave Neufeld, pers. comm., 12 October 1994.

6. Neufeld, pp. 10-15.

7. *1898 Annual Report*, Steele, p. 4.

8. Telephone conversation with meteorologist, Herb Wahl, 23 Sept. 1994.

9. NWMP, *1898 Annual Report*, Report of Insp. Cartwright, p. 111.

10. According to one NWMP officer:

As points for the collection of duty they are practically useless, as no one with a spark of humanity would keep people waiting in those dreadful places, with the danger of perishing from cold, while their goods, exposed to the inclement weather + blowing snow, spoiled before their eyes.

Quoted in Neufeld, p. 14.

11. *1898 Annual Report*, Report of Insp. Belcher, pp. 89-94.

12. Ibid., p. 91.

13. S.B. Steele, *Forty Years in Canada* (Toronto: McClelland, Goodchild, Stewart, Ltd., 1918), p. 335.

14. NWMP, *1897 Annual Report*, Constantine, p. 307.

15. Steele, p. 324.

16. "General Sam Steele, Famous Yukoner, is Dead," *Dawson Daily News*, 31 Jan. 1919; S.W. Horrall, p. 134; S.B. Steele, *Forty Years in Canada*.

17. NAC, RG 18, vol. 154, f. 445-98. 6 May 1898, Steele to Comptroller.

18. NWMP, *1898 Annual Report*, Strickland, pp. 81-83.

19. Insp. Z.T. Wood's *Tagish Post Diary/Account Book*, Sept. 1898 to Jan. 1899. RCMP Museum, Regina, Sask., 972.55.70A.

20. NAC, RG 18, vol. 154, f. 445-98. 5 Jan 1899, Wood to White.

21. NWMP, *1899 Annual Report*, Report of Insp. Perry, p. 5.

22. RCMP, Public Affairs Information Directorate (PAID), f. 0.99; NWMP, *1898 and 1899 Annual Reports*.

23. *1899 Annual Report*, Report of Supt. Primrose, p. 49.

24. NWMP, *1899 Annual Report*, pp. 5, 28; Matthews, p. 50; Jeffrey Dinsdale, "Those Disney Dogs and the RCMP," typescript, May 1979, RCMP, PAID.

25. NAC, RG 18, vol. 154, f. 445-98; NWMP, *1898 Annual Report*, Steele, p. 11.

26. NWMP, *1899 Annual Report*, Report of Ass't. Surgeon Paré, pp. 66-69.

27. NAC, RG 18, vol. 153-98, f. 367; RG 18, vol. 154, f. 445-98; RCMP, PAID, f. 0-86.

28. RNWMP, *1915 Annual Report*, p. 17.

29. Most of the information from this section came from the following sources: NWMP, *1898 Annual Report*; S.W. Horrall, p. 230; and Delores Smith, "Wood: a testament to police toughness," *Whse. Star*, 10 Aug. 1994.

30. NAC, RG 18, vol. 154, f. 445-98: Steele to Comm. Walsh, 10 June 1898.

31. Ibid.

32. Much of the information in this section came from H. Dobrowolsky, "Miles Canyon Tramways" in *Study Tour of the Yukon and Alaska* (Ottawa: Society for Industrial Archaeology, 1990), and H. Dobrowolsky & R. Ingram, *Edge of the River, Heart of the City—A History of the Whitehorse Waterfront* (Whse.: Lost Moose Publishing, 1994), pp. 5-8.

33. NAC, RG 18, vol. 169, f. 321-98: 27 Aug. 1898, Sgt. H.G. Joyce to O.C., NWMP, Bennett.

34. In an attempt to avoid confusion, the second community of Whitehorse, located at the railway terminus, will be referred to using the present one word usage.

35. NWMP, *1898 Annual Report*, p. 18.

36. H. Dobrowolsky & R. Ingram, *A History of the Whitehorse Copper Belt* (Indian and Northern Affairs Canada, Open File 1993-1), p. 13; *RCMP Quarterly* (July 1955, vol. 21, no. 1), p. 84.

3. Reinforcements meets the great stampede

1. NWMP, *1897 Annual Report*, p. 307.

2. NAC, RG 18, vol. 139, f. 442-97, pts. 1 and 2.

3. NWMP, *1897 Annual Report*, Constantine, pp. 307-310; *1898 Annual Report*, Report of Insp. F. Harper, p. 67.

4. NWMP, *1898 Annual Report*, Report of Ass't. Surgeon W.E. Thompson, p. 116.

5. Ibid., Steele, p. 14-16

6. *1898 Annual Report*, p. 73.

7. *Ibid.*, p. 8.

8. NWMP, *1899 Annual Report*, Report of Insp. P.C.H. Primrose, p. 49.

9. NWMP, *1904 Annual Report*, Report of Ass't. Comm. Wood, p. 16.

10. *1897 Annual Report*, Constantine, p. 309; *1898 Annual Report*, Steele, p. 29; Mathews, pp. 30-32.

11. *1898 Annual Report*, pp. 29, 129-131; Mathews, p. 38; NAC, RG 18, vol. 219, f. 905-01.

12. Hayne & West, p. 172.

13. Ibid., p. 171.

14. Ibid., p. 174.

15. Most of this information comes from A.L. Discher, "The Long March of the Yukon Field Force," in *The Beaver*, Autumn 1962, and "Yukon Field Force Honoured" in *North/Nord*, Jul./Aug. 1972.

16. The role of these women will be examined in more detail in Ch. 7—Women and the force.

17. YA, 82/437, John A. Tinck Collection, mss 061.

18. While Tinck's unique spelling and capitalization has been kept, a little punctuation has been added and some clarifications inserted in square brackets.

19. According to a census taken 10 Feb. 1899, the population of Selkirk was, exclusive of the NWMP and Yukon Field Force, 48 Americans, 37 British subjects and about 100 Indians. NAC, RG 18, vol. 164, f. 183-99; Dawson District, periodical reports, Feb. 1899; Dobrowolsky, Ingram et al, *Fort Selkirk Interpretive Manual* (Whitehorse, Government of the Yukon, Heritage Branch, 1994), pp. 79-81.

20. NWMP, *1898 Annual Report*, Steele, p. 33.

21. Government of the Yukon, Heritage Branch, YFF research file; Tinck diary.

4. After the rush

1. NWMP, *1902 Annual Report*, p. 4.

2. Ibid., *1904 Annual Report*, p. 36.

3. Ibid., *1903 Annual Report*, p. 4.

4. Ibid., *1898 Annual Report,* Harper, p. 67.

5. YA: Search File - Grand Forks, 78/69 Dave Gairns, March 1978; Norman Bolotin, *A Klondike Scrapbook - Ordinary People, Extraordinary Times* (San Francisco: Chronicle Books, 1987), p. 10.

6. NAC, RG 18, vol. 206, f. 316-01; NWMP, *1902 Annual Report,* p. 16.

7. This amounted to $43,071.08 in royalty out of a total amount of $59,410.74. NAC, RG 18, vol. 211, file 316-01; Dawson - Periodical Reports from, 1901.

8. NWMP, *1902 Annual Report,* p. 5.

9. RNWMP, *1906 Annual Report,* p. 4.

10. NAC, RG 18, vol. 413, f. 385-11.

11. RNWMP, *1911 Annual Report,* Report of Insp. F.J. Horrigan, p. 207; RG 18, vol. 415, f. 499-11.

12. NWMP, *1900 Annual Report,* p. 148.

13. The eight buildings cost just under $17,000. Ibid., pp. 17-19.

14. NWMP, *1902 Annual Report,* p. 36.

15. Ibid., Wood, p. 5; H. Dobrowolsky & R. Ingram, *Edge of the River, Heart of the City,* pp. 12-13.

16. Ibid., Wood, p. 5.

17. Gordon Bennett, *Yukon Transportation: A History* (Ottawa: Can. Hist. Sites, Occasional Papers in Archaeology and History, no. 19, 1978), pp. 94-95.

18. The current spelling for the lake is "Laberge." Historically, the spelling for both the lake and the detachments was "Labarge." In this section, I use the current spelling for the lake and historic spelling for the detachment.

19. Glenbow Archives, McKay Collection, M753.

20. RCMP, PAID; telephone conversation with Mrs. Margaret Browning Aug., 1994.

21. Glenbow Archives, M753.

22. RNWMP, *1917-1918 Annual Report,* pp. 7-8.

23. NWMP, *1902 Annual Report,* p. 32; *RCMP Quarterly,* vol. 18, no. 1; RCMP Archives Unit; Richard A. Dickson family papers; Louise Profeit-LeBlanc, personal communication, Jan. 1995.

5. First Nations people and the police

1. NWMP, *1894 Annual Report,* p. 78.

2. Ibid., p. 70.

3. Mathews, p. 13.

4. Zaslow, pp. 144-146. In 1902, Superintendent Wood wrote that:

The Indians in the Territory will sooner or later have to be taken charge by the Dominion Government, as the game, their principal means of subsistence, is being driven further and further back every year, and it is becoming more difficult for them to obtain sufficient food.

NWMP, *1902 Annual Report,* Wood, p. 18.

5. The Mounted Police hired special constables to perform specialized jobs such as dog driving, blacksmithing or carpentry. They were hired for a shorter term and their terms of service were less rigorous.

6. Julie Cruikshank, "Oral Traditions and Written Accounts: An Incident from the Klondike Gold Rush," in *Culture,* IX (2), 1989. pp. 25-34. This article is the main source for this section.

7. On 10 Oct. 1898, Comptroller White briskly reminded Supt. Wood that:

The fact that a man is engaged as dog driver, packer or in any other special capacity, should not be held to exempt him from any other duty upon which it may be considered advisable to employ him, and the rate of his regular pay should cover all services rendered by him.

NAC, RG 18, vol. 162, f. 115-99.

8. NAC, RG 18, vol. 1445, f. 181, pt. 5, 1899.

9. NAC, RG 18, vol. 392, f. 329-10.

10. NAC, RG 18, vol. 162, f. 115-9; NWMP, *1900 Annual Report,* p. 57; RG 18, vol. 1445, f. 181; vol. 272, f. 286-04; NWMP, *1903 Annual Report,* pp. 20, 69; S.W. Horrall, p. 252; Robert Knuckle, *In the Line of Duty* (Burnstown, Ont.: General Store Publishing), p. 9.

11. Solicitor General, *1968/69 Annual Report,* p. 23.

12. These postings are as of Jan. 1995.

13. Conversation with retired member Dennis Levy, 4 Oct. 1994; letter from Sgt. Bob MacAdam, Whse., 14 Dec. 1994.

14. The *Yukon World,* 16 Dec. 1905.

15. The *Whitehorse Star,* 23 Sept. 1971.

16. Ibid., NAC, RG 18, vol. 162, f. 115-99; *RNWMP Annual Reports: 1907, 1911, 1912.*

17. Murielle Ida Nagy, *ed., Yukon North Slope Inuvialuit Oral History* (Whitehorse, Government of the Yukon, Heritage Branch, Occasional Papers in Yukon History No. 1), p. 46.

18. Dick North, *The Lost Patrol,* (Edmonds, Wash.: Alaska Northwest Publishing Co., 1988), p. 44; RNWMP, *1916 Annual Report,* p. 326.

19. Information for this profile came from: Mayo Historical Society, *Gold and Galena,* (Mayo, Yukon: Mayo Historical Society, 1990), p. 412; MacBride Museum, *People of the Transition Years* exhibit research files; and North, *The Lost Patrol,* pp. 44, 126.

20. Sid May diaries, courtesy of Nancy Pope, Tagish, Yukon; Coutts, *Yukon Places and Names,* (Sidney, B.C.: Gray's Publishing Ltd, 1980), p. 191.

21. RCMP, PAID, 31 Jan. 1930, Supt. R. Field, O.C. Yukon District, to Commissioner, RCMP, Ottawa.

22. Sources for this section include: Sidney May patrol diary, 1932; MacBride Museum research file, *People of the Transition Years* exhibit; R.C. Coutts, *Yukon Places and Names,* p. 191; YA, Thornthwaite Coll. and RCMP, PAID.

23. Andrew Tizya interview, recorded by Adeline Charlie in Old Crow, 3 August 1994. All the information for this section came from this source. Adeline is the granddaughter of one of the best-known special constables, John Moses.

24. Charlie Peter Charlie interview, recorded by Adeline Charlie in Old Crow, 6 July 1994. The information for this section came from this source.

25. From about 1958 until 1965, the Old Crow and Herschel Island detachments were under the Aklavik, rather than the Yukon, Sub-division.

26. RCMP, PAID.

27. Ibid.

28. Letter from Derek Parkes, Kamloops, 13 July 1994.

6. Crime, conspiracy and court

1. W.K. McKay Coll., Glenbow Archives, M 753.; NAC, RG 18, vol. 3253, f. 1914-HQ-681-G-1.

2. Undated account of Remolio Cesari case, W.M. McKay Coll., Glenbow Archives, M 753.

3. Ibid., NAC, RG 18, vol. 3253, f. 1914-HQ-681-G-1; RNWMP, *1915 Annual Report,* Report of Insp. Bell, p. 248.

4. RNWMP, *1905 Annual Report,* p. 16.

5. Mathews, pp. 41-42; NAC, RG 18, vol. 176, f. 3-00.

6. *Yukon World,* 18 April 1905; RNWMP, *1904 Annual Report,* pp. 14, 47; *1905 Annual Report,* pp. 7-8.

7. NAC, RG 18, vol. 299, f. 447-05; RG 18, vol. 316, f. 241-06.

8. RNWMP, *1906 Annual Report,* p. 30.

9. NAC, RG 18, vol. 229, f. 149-02.

10. *Alaska-Yukon Mining Journal,* Skagway, Dec. 1901; *Skagway Morning Alaskan,* 5 Jan. 1902; in RG 18, vol. 229, f. 149-02.

11. Ibid., *1902 Annual Report,* p. 5.

12. RNWMP, *1906 Annual Report,* p. 4.

13. RCMP, PAID; RCMP Museum, Regina, Sask.; Rob Ingram & Helene Dobrowolsky, *Waves Upon the Shore—an Historical Profile of Herschel Island* (Whse., Government of the Yukon, Heritage Branch, 1989), pp. 140-141.

14. Nagy, ed., p. 47.

15. RCMP, *1923 Annual Report,* Report of Comm. Starnes, p. 32. This was the source of most of the information in this section.

16. Morrison, pp. 160-161.

17. Nagy, p. 48.

7. Women and the force

1. NAC, RG 18, Series F1, vol. 2182, f. 4, 4 Oct. 1895, Constantine to Herchmer.

2. Ibid.

3. Disher, pp. 7 and 9.

4. Disher, pp. 14-15; NWMP, *1898 Annual Report,* p. 115; Government of the Yukon, Heritage Branch, YFF Research File.

5. NAC, RG 18, vol. 369, f. 133-09; North, *The Lost Patrol,* p. 28.

6. Clara May, personal communication, 30 August 1994.

7. Mark & Myra Ryder, *Life in the Yukon, A Royal Canadian Mounted Police Officer and His Wife, a Nurse. To honour their memory we present their descriptive writings,* (privately printed booklet, ca. 1993), p. 20.

8. Clara May interview, 30 Aug. 1994 at Tagish, Yukon, recorded by Robin Armour & H. Dobrowolsky.

9. G.I. Cameron Interview, 13 Apr. 1993, recorded in Whse. by Bill Beahen.

10. Martha Cameron, "A Mountie's Wife in the North," in *The Way It Was—50 Years of RCMP Memories* (Vancouver: Victoria Division RCMP Veterans Association, 1990), pp. 121-24; H. Dobrowolsky, ed., *Fort Selkirk Oral History Project 1984* (Whse.: Government of the Yukon, Heritage Branch, 1985) Martha Cameron Interview transcript, pp. 1-69.

11. Minnie Kirk, "Old Crow," in *Scarlet and Gold,* 57th Edition, 1975, p. 94.

12. "Saves Boy From Dogs," *RCMP Quarterly,* 1946.

13. RCMP, *1939 Annual Report,* p. 103; *1945 Annual Report,* p. 60.

14. NAC, RG 18, vol. 257, 510-03, 9 June 1903, Wood to White; RG 18, vol. 283, f. 850-04.

15. T. Ann Brennan, *The Real Klondike Kate* (Fredericton, N.B.: Goose Lane Editions, 1990), pp. 195, 206.

16. Glenbow Archives, Diary of Wm. Kellock McKay, M 753; T. Ann Brennan, *The Real Klondike Kate;* YRG I, Series 2, vol. 1855, f. 8766, 1903-07: Ryan, Miss K.M. – Royalty Export Clerk.

17. Brennan, p. 138.

18. NWMP, *1897 Annual Report,* p. 313.

19. Derek Parkes, letter to H. Dobrowolsky, 13 July 1994. Mr. Parkes asked me to excuse his typing "but I am 92 and my fingers wont do what I want."

20. Nagy, p. 48.

21. Anna DeGraf, *Pioneering on the Yukon* (New Haven, Conn.: Archon Books, 1992), p. 63.

22. Ibid. pp. vii-ix.

23. Derek Parkes, op. cit.

8. Patrolling the Yukon

1. RNWMP, *1906 Annual Report,* p. 4.

2. *1911 Annual Report,* p. 131.

3. NAC, RG 18, vol. 164, f. 183-99.

4. Morrison, p. 81.

5. quoted in North, *The Lost Patrol,* p. 1.

6. *1911 Annual Report,* Reports of McPherson-Dawson Police Patrol, p. 293.

7. *1912 Annual Report,* Rev. C.E. Whittaker to Bishop Stringer, pp. 303-304.

8. North, pp. 10-28.

9. *1911-12 Annual Report,* p. 302.

10. Mayo Historical Society, pp. 264-265; North, p. 130; Coutts, pp. 80-81.

11. NAC, RG 18, vol. 532, f. 206-11.

12. NAC, RG 18, vol. 304, f. 19-06; YA, YRG I, Series 1, vol. 43, f. 29236; YRG I, Series 1, vol. 35, f. 24271; Ken Coates, *The Northern Yukon: a History,* (Winnipeg: Parks Canada, Manuscript Report No. 403).

13. RCMP, *1929 Annual Report,* p. 55; Minnie Kirk, "Old Crow," in *Scarlet and Gold,* 57th Edition, 1975, p. 85.

14. Mark & Mary Ryder, p. 67.

15. Ibid. pp. 1-3; *RCMP Quarterly,* p. 249, 1949, vol. # unavailable; YA, Tidd Collection.

16. Letter from Cst. W. King to Cst. A.J. Chartrand, Albert Joseph Chartrand Collection, Glenbow Archives, Calgary, M207. Additional information from: Dick North, *The Mad Trapper of Rat River* (Toronto: Macmillan of Canada, 1972) and RCMP, *1931/32 Annual Report.*

17. YA, 83/22 A.B. Thornthwaite Coll., collection description notes.

18. RCMP: *1948-49 Annual Report,* p. 58; *1961-62 Annual Report,* p. 29.

19. *Annual Reports: 1942-43,* p. 48; *1943-44,* p. 50.

20. *Annual Reports: 1903,* p. 14; *1904,* p. 22; *1905,* p. 49.

21. Horrall, pp. 220-225; *1948/49 Annual Report,* pp. 58-59.

9. At ease

1. Mark & Mary Ryder, p. 67.

2. NWMP, *1900 Annual Report,* pp. 9-10.

3. NAC, RG 18, vol. 212, f. 355-01.

10. Wartime and Alaska Highway construction

1. RCMP, *Annual Reports: 1939, 1940, 1943.*

2. Coates and Morrison, *The Alaska Highway in World War II—The U.S. Army of Occupation in Canada's Northwest* (Toronto: University of Toronto Press, 1992), pp. 114-117.

3. Ibid., p. 112; RCMP, *1943 Annual Report,* p. 50.

4. Babe Richardson interview, 7 January 1990, recorded by H. Dobrowolsky for Whitehorse 50th Anniversary Society Oral History Project.

5. RCMP, *1944 Annual Report,* pp. 50-51, 53, 55, 72.

6. *1945-46 Annual Report,* p. 63.

7. Information for this section came from the following sources: Joanne MacDonald, "Fighting a measles epidemic in Teslin, 1942," (interview with Corinne Cyr) and Patti Flather, "Memories of a Tlingit Elder," (interview with Pearl Keenan) in *Women and the Alaska Highway,* special edition of the *Optimist,* vol. 18, June 1992, no. 2, pp. 5, 8-9; K.S. Coates & W.R. Morrison, *The Alaska Highway in World War II,* pp. 47-48, 77-78, 103; YA, Mathew Thom interview, recorded by Rob Ingram in Teslin, 19 Sept. 1991.

8. Helene Dobrowolsky, ed., *Fort Selkirk Oral History Project 1984* (Government of the Yukon, Heritage Branch, 1985), G.I. Cameron interview transcript, p. 137.

9. G.I. Cameron Interview, 13 April 1993, recorded in Whse. by Bill Beahen.

11. Dog stories

1. Tappan Adney, *The Klondike Stampede* (originally published by New York: Harper, 1899; reprinted by Vancouver: UBC Press, 1994), p. 208; Hayne, pp. 103-104.

2. Hayne, pp. 104-105.

3. NWMP, *1897 Annual Report,* Constantine, p. 307; Jeffrey Dinsdale, "Those Disney Dogs and the RCMP," typescript.

4. NWMP, *1897 Annual Report,* Constantine, p. 307-308.

5. Mark & Myra Ryder, p. 34.

6. Bill Jealouse, "The Vicissitudes of 1897," in *The Scarlet and Gold,* 29th Edition, 1947, p. 27.

7. The information for this section came from the following NAC files: RG 18, vol. 152, f. 296-98; RG 18, vol. 158, f. 16-99 and RG 18, vol. 163, f. 137-99.

8. During the informal transactions that followed, Hebert also swapped his own watches, some clothing and even an accordion—thereby creating accounting difficulties for the Auditor General's office.

9. White sent Supt. Charles Constantine, recently returned from his three-year Yukon stint, to Québec to inspect the dogs and determine their suitability for northern service. Constantine pronounced the canines "a good lot" although a bit thin and was impressed by the competence of the dog drivers, op. cit.

10. C.P. Constantine, *I Was A Mountie* (New York: Esposition Press, 1958), pp. 40-41.

11. *RCMP Quarterly,* Apr. 1942, vol. 9, no. 4.

12. RCMP, PAID; Sgt. Henry Larsen, *The North-West Passage: The Famous Voyages of the Royal Canadian Mounted Police Schooner "St. Roch,"* booklet issued by Vancouver City Archives, pp. 29-34; Knuckle, pp. 263-266.

13. Horrall, pp. 122-123; Dinsdale, "Those Disney Dogs and the RCMP," typescript. The latter source, obtained from the RCMP, PAID, provided most of the information for this section.

14. The film was based on a book by James Oliver Curwood titled *Nomads of the North.* Patty Howlett, Publicity Officer, Tourism Yukon, telephone conversation 24 Oct. 1994.

15. Supt. Fraser had strong prejudices against native dogs, evident in the following excerpt from the 1961/62 Annual Report:

Although it is too early to make final judgment...the reports we have on hand indicate that this dog is superior to the old arctic sled dog in several ways. He displays none of the viciousness which is common to the sled dog now in use, is very tractable, easily trained, has a friendly disposition and appears to have greater strength and stamina.

(*1961/62 Annual Report,* pp. 29-30.)

16. Nagy, p. 48.

17. Dinsdale, p. 11.

18. The information in this section comes from the following files provided by the RCMP, PAID: File G-567-65, Patrol Report: Old Crow, YT to Fort McPherson and Arctic Red River, NWT and Return; Y567-1, Cpl. Wheeler, Old Crow to O.C. Whitehorse, 13 Mar. '69; G567-65, Wheeler to Commissioner, 10 Mar. '69.

19. The RCMP Museum in Regina has a display featuring several artifacts from this patrol including a toboggan, harnesses, parkas, supplies and mounts of two dogs.

12. Policing today

1. Coates & Morrison, *The Alaska Highway in World War II,* p. 103; Len Hall, personal communication, Dec. 1994; NAC, RG 85, vol. 1154, f. 311-200 B.

2. RCMP, *1949-50 Annual Report,* p. 13; *Solicitor General's Annual Report, 1974-75,* pp. 27-28; Dennis Levy, personal communication, 4 Oct. 1994. On Mar. 31, 1975, the Yukon force consisted of 69 regular members, 11 special constables, 4 civilian members and 7 public servants.

3. Dennis Levy, Oct. 1994; Corrie Baumel, personal communication, 2 Jan. 1995.

4. The 41 female personnel includes 10 regular members, 9 civilian members and 22 public servants. Sgt. Bob MacAdam, RCMP, FSS Branch, Whitehorse, 12 Dec. 1994.

5. Ibid. The details of the actual funding arrangements are too complex to break down in this overview.

6. RCMP: *1958-59 Annual Report,* p. 28; *1960-61 Annual Report,* p. 27; *1967-68 Annual Report,* p. 42.

7. From typed caption on rear of photo, source unknown, although this may have accompanied an RCMP facility report.

8. Dave Neufeld passed on this quote made by an unidentified constable during a highway checkstop at Whse., Dec. 1994.

9. *Whse. Star,* 21 Aug. 1987, Whse. Star research file.

10. *Yukon News,* 12 Oct. 1994; *Whse. Star,* 12 Mar., 16 Apr. 1992.

11. Diary entry quoted in *Whse. Star,* 1985.

12. This account is taken from *Whse. Star* files including the following issues: 20, 22, 27 March; 28 June 1985; 15 Aug. 1986.

13. RCMP, *1952/53 Annual Report,* p. 21.

Honour Roll

1. From: Horrall, pp. 250-253, with additional information from RCMP, PAID; Knuckle, p. 439-440.

Selected bibliography

Adney, Tappan
1900   *The Klondike Stampede.* New York: Harper, 1900. (Reprinted by University of British Columbia Press, Vancouver: 1994.)

Bennett, Gordon
1978   *Yukon Transportation: A History.* Canadian Historic Sites: Occasional Papers in Archaeology and History, no. 19. Ottawa: National Historic Parks.

Coates, Ken
1993   *Best Left as Indians: Native-White Relations in the Yukon Territory, 1840 – 1973.* Montreal and Kingston: McGill-Queen's University Press.

Coates, Ken and Wm. R. Morrison
1988   *Land of the Midnight Sun.* Edmonton: Hurtig Publishers.

1992   *The Alaska Highway in World War II: The U. S. Army of Occupation in Canada's Northwest.* Toronto: University of Toronto Press.

Constantine, C.P.
1958   *I Was a Mountie.* New York: Exposition Press.

Coutts, R.
1980   *Yukon Places and Names.* Sidney, B.C.: Gray's Publishing Ltd.

Cruikshank, Julie
1989   "Oral Traditions and Written Accounts: An Incident from the Klondike Gold Rush," in *Culture,* IX (2).

1991   Dän Dhá Ts'edenintth'é – *Reading Voices.* Vancouver: Douglas & McIntyre.

Dawson, G. M.
1888   *Report on an Exploration in the Yukon District, NWT and Adjacent Portion of Northern British Columbia, 1887.* Ottawa: King's Printer. (Reprinted by Yukon Historical & Museums Association, Whitehorse: 1987.)

DeGraf, Anna
1992   *Pioneering on the Yukon, 1892 – 1917.* New Haven, Conn.: Archon Books.

Dobrowolsky, Helene and Rob Ingram
1994   *Edge of the River, Heart of the City.* Yukon Historical & Museums Association, Whitehorse: Lost Moose Publishing.

Gates, Michael
1994   *Gold at Fortymile Creek.* Vancouver: University of British Columbia Press.

Hayne, M.H.E.
1897   *The Pioneers of the Klondike, being an account of two years police service on the Yukon,* narrated by M.H.E. Hayne and recorded by H. West Taylor. London: Sampson Low, Marston & Co.

Horrall, S.W.
1973   *The Pictorial History of the Royal Canadian Mounted Police.* Toronto: McGraw-Hill-Ryerson Ltd.

Kelly, Nora and William
1973   *The Royal Canadian Mounted Police, A Century of History.* Edmonton: Hurtig Publishers.

Knuckle, Robert
1994   *In the Line of Duty.* Burnstown, Ont.: General Store Publishing House.

Lotz, Jim
1984   *The Mounties.* Greenwich, Conn.: Bison Books Corp.

Morrison, William R.
1985   *Showing the Flag: The Mounted Police and Canadian Sovereignty in the North, 1894-1925.* Vancouver: UBC Press .

Nagy, Murielle
1994   *Yukon North Slope Inuvialuit Oral History.* Whitehorse: Government of the Yukon, Heritage Branch, Occasional Papers in Yukon History No. 1.

Neufeld, David
1993   *Chilkoot Trail: Yukon Gateway.* Whitehorse: Yukon National Historic Site.

North, Dick
1972   *The Mad Trapper of Rat River.* Toronto: Macmillan of Canada.

1978   *The Lost Patrol.* Anchorage, Ak.: Alaska Northwest Publishing Co.

RCMP
1975   *RCMP "Air Division: 1937 – 1973, A History of the Royal Canadian Mounted Police Aviation Section.* Ottawa: Information Canada.

Steele, S.B.
1918   *Forty Years in Canada.* Toronto: McClelland, Goodchild, Stewart Ltd.

Watson, Jack and Gray Campbell
1993   *Yukon Memories.* Vancouver/ Toronto: Whitecap Books.

Wright, Allen A.
1976   *Prelude to Bonanza.* Sidney, B.C.: Gray's Publishing Ltd.

Zaslow, Morris
1971   *The Opening of the Canadian North, 1870-1914.* Toronto, McClelland & Stewart Ltd.

1988   *The Northward Expansion of Canada, 1914-1967.* Toronto, McClelland & Stewart Ltd.

Illustrations

MMCH/NPA—McCORD MUSEUM OF CANADIAN HISTORY, NOTMAN PHOTOGRAPHIC ARCHIVES
NAC—NATIONAL ARCHIVES OF CANADA
PAA—PROVINCIAL ARCHIVES OF ALBERTA
VPL—VANCOUVER PUBLIC LIBRARY
YA—YUKON ARCHIVES
YHMA—YUKON HISTORICAL & MUSEUMS ASSOCIATION

Front cover

Major General Sam Steele.
RCMP MUSEUM, REGINA, SASK.

Andrew Kunizzi, former police guide.
YA/ANGLICAN CHURCH COLL., 86/61-2, C9.

"Klondike Kate" Ryan.
KATHARINE MCKERNAN COLL.

Cst. A.J. Chartrand at Herschel Is., ca. 1933.
DEREK PARKES COLL.

Transfer of Command Parade, Whse., 1992.
RCMP/"M" DIVISION.

Cst. Karen Olito.
YUKON GOVERNMENT PHOTO

Sgt. Engel and members at Fort Constantine, ca. 1896.
RCMP MUSEUM, REGINA, SASK., 212/026

S/Cst. John Moses and his son Roy.
YA/THORNTHWAITE COLL., 83/22, PHO 219, ALBUM 4, P. 10, 1388

Back cover

Cst. Joe Kessler at Forty Mile.
YA 8445/TIDD COLL.

Front pages

Mounties and IODE members.
PARKS CANADA, KNHS.

Glenora on the Stikine River, B.C.
YA/TINCK COLL., 82/437, PHO 7.

Centennial Patrol.
CHRIS CALDWELL PAINTING, RCMP, "M" DIVISION.

The Officers' and Sergeants' mess of A Battery.
YA/TINCK COLL., 82/437, PHO 7.

Paul Gross as Cst. Benton Fraser.
COURTESY DUE SOUTH, ALLIANCE COMMUNICATIONS, MONTY BRINTAN PHOTO.

Sgt. Preston.
FILM FAVOURITES.

Drilling on horseback in NWMP compound.
PAA/B2093.

Introduction

12. First Nations people near Fort Selkirk.
SCHWATKA, A SUMMER IN ALASKA, P. 221.

13. Placer mining on Miller Creek, 1894.
RCMP MUSEUM, REGINA, SASK.

14. Forty Mile and Fort Cudahy.
NAC/C3954.

15. Insp. Charles Constantine.
RCMP MUSEUM, REGINA, SASK., 212/081.

1. The first post—Fort Constantine

16. Off to the Yukon aboard the steamer Excelsior.
RCMP MUSEUM/ 212/003.

18. The first Yukon contingent.
PAA/B2230.

19. The square at Fort Constantine.
RCMP MUSEUM, REGINA, SASK./34.15.21

19. Part of Yukon detachment at Regina.
YA/SCHOONOVER COLL., 79/39, PHO 98

20. Insp. Strickland at the sawmill.
YA 9407/STRICKLAND COLL.

20. Mounties on the Yukon River ice.
YA/STRICKLAND COLL., 88/139, 14.

20. Fort Constantine.
YA 9388/STRICKLAND COLL.

21. First Nations fishing camp.
YA/COUTTS COLL., 78/69, PHO 95.

22. Insp. Charles Constantine.
RCMP MUSEUM, REGINA, SASK., 212/077.

23. Sgt. M.H.E. Hayne.
YA 9404/STRICKLAND COLL.

2. The Klondike gold rush

24. Climbers struggle up the Chilkoot Pass.
YA 3626/MACBRIDE MUSEUM COLL.

26. Sam Steele's order.
YA PAMPHLET 1978-1C

26. Climbing the White Pass.
YA 2266/VPL COLL.

27. NWMP checking stampeders supplies.
YA 1338/UNIV. OF WASH. COLL.

27. Customs house at Chilkoot Summit.
YA 2004/VPL COLL.

28. Members drill with machine guns.
YA 6130/HARBOTTLE COLL.

29. On the White Pass Summit.
YA 2749/UNIV. OF WASH. COLL.

30. Crater Lake on the Chilkoot Pass.
PARKS CANADA, YUKON NATIONAL HISTORIC SITES.

31. Chilkoot tent detachment.
GLENBOW ARCHIVES, NA-1052-3.

32. Inside Lindeman NWMP/customs post.
YA/SANGUINETTI COLL., 79/87, 2.

32. Lindeman detachment and customs post.
YA 132/VOGEE COLL.

33. Tent detachment at Lake Bennett.
NAC/PA16083.

33. Bennett detachment.
YA/COUTTS COLL., 78/69-2, PHO 95.

34. S.B. Steele
RCMP MUSEUM, REGINA, SASK.

35. Mount Steele, Yukon.
CST. PATRICK EGAN, HAINES JUNCTION, YUKON.

36. Raising the flag at Tagish Post.
YA/COUTTS COLL., 78/69-2, PHO 95.

37. View of Tagish Post, 1900.
YA 175D/VOGEE COLL.

37. Tagish Post, ca. 1898.
YA 4066/MACBRIDE MUSEUM COLL.

38. Tannis, Roland and D'Arcy Edward Strickland.
YA/STRICKLAND COLL., 88/139, 5.

39. Collecting customs at Tagish.
YA, GREENBANK COLL., 89/19, 9.

40. Surgeon L. A. Paré.
RCMP MUSEUM, REGINA, SASK.

41. Ass't Comm. Z.T. Wood.
RCMP MUSEUM, REGINA, SASK.

42. Canyon City.
YA/FINNIE COLL., 81/21, PHO 141, 75TL.

43. Shooting Miles Canyon.
YA/FORREST COLL., 80/60, PHO 131.

44. White Horse.
YA 4114/MACBRIDE MUSEUM COLL.

45. Edward A. Dixon.
YA/WADDINGTON COLL., 82/331, PHO 32, 6.

46. Flotilla of stampeders.
YA/GREENBANK COLL., 89/12, PHO 371, 12.

3. Reinforcements meet the great stampede

48. NWMP firing a cannon.
YA 1313/ UNIV. OF WASH. COLL.

50. The Islander leaving Vancouver.
MMCH/NPA, TAPPAN ADNEY COLLECTION, MP 114/79 (7).

51. Front Street, Dawson City.
YA 2517/HEGG COLL.

52. Fort Herchmer during the spring flood.
YA 2046/VPL COLL.

53. Officers of "B" Division.
© RCMP-GRC 418.

53. Relaxing in barracks.
YA/JONES COLL., 78/16, PHO 81.

53. Fort Herchmer.
YA/JONES COLL., 78/16, PHO 81

54. NWMP band.
YA 6346/DAWSON CITY MUSEUM COLL.

54. The Dawson town station detachment.
YA 689 /NATIONAL MUSEUM COLL., J6183.

55. Prostitutes in Lousetown.
YA/GREENBANK COLL., 89/19, 25.

55. Last public game at Dawson.
YA/GREENBANK COLL., 89/19, 27.

56. Relaxing in barracks at Fort Herchmer.
YA/JONES COLL., 78/16, PHO 81

56. The Portus B. Weare.
RCMP MUSEUM, REGINA, SASK., 212/007

57. Shipment of gold dust.
GLENBOW ARCHIVES/NA-964-13

57. Officer at desk in Dawson.
YA, SENKLER COLL., 86/87, 80.

58. The Stikine Chief.
MACBRIDE MUSEUM.

58. Lt. Col. T. D. B. Evans.
MACBRIDE MUSEUM.

59. YFF soldiers camping on Stikine Trail.
MACBRIDE MUSEUM.

60. Soldiers haul logs at Fort Selkirk.
MACBRIDE MUSEUM.

60. Building the Yukon Field Force compound.
MACBRIDE MUSEUM.

61. Canadian Bank of Commerce fire.
GLENBOW ARCHIVES/NA-964-11.

62. Yukon Field Force Band.
RCMP MUSEUM, REGINA, SASK., 86.104.16

62. Christmas dinner.
YA 2415/GLENBOW ARCHIVES COLL.

63. Yukon Field Force, Christmas 1899.
RCMP MUSEUM, REGINA, SASK., 934.22.18

63. Yukon Field Force in Dawson.
YA/PARKS CANADA COLL., 78/80, 2.

4. After the rush

64. Mountie on the job at Forty Mile.
YA 8744/TIDD COLL.

65. A Mountie chauffeurs Martha Black.
YA 3254/MARTHA LOUISE BLACK COLL.

66. Panorama of Grand Forks.
YA 2553/ UNIV. OF WASHINGTON COLL.

66. The first Grand Forks detachment.
RCMP MUSEUM, REGINA, SASK./34.22.16

67. Grand Forks detachment, 1904.
YA/ KINSEY & KINSEY COLL., 82/318, 290.

67. The second detachment building.
YA/KINSEY & KINSEY COLL., 82/318, 138.

68. Grand Forks detachment, 1904.
YA, KINSEY & KINSEY COLL., 82/318, 292.

68. Interior of NWMP detachment.
YA/ KINSEY & KINSEY COLL., 82/318, 268.

69. Invitation to "The Dewey" opening.
YA/TINCK COLL., 83/437-2, MSS 61.

69. "Warrant to Search."
RCMP MUSEUM, REGINA, SASK.

69. Grand Forks.
YA 4756/BARLEY COLL.

70. NWMP quarters at Whitehorse.
MMCH/NPA 2024 (21)

70. Town of Whitehorse.
YA 4073/MACBRIDE MUSEUM COLL.

71. Night guard and picket.
PAA/B2076

71. The Whitehorse canteen.
PAA/B2078

72. Moving a building.
PAA/B2097

72. Whitehorse NWMP office.
PAA/B2073

73. The Mounties' best friend.
PAA/B2089

73. The "H" Division office.
PAA/B2072

74. Lower Labarge detachment.
YA/COUTTS COLL., 78/69, PHO 95.

75. Lower Labarge detachment interior.
YA/COUTTS COLL., 78/69, PHO 95.

76. Cst. Acland at Dalton Post.
YA 4685/BARLEY COLL.

77. Cst. William K. MacKay.
GLENBOW ARCHIVES/NA-1663-3.

78. RNWMP members in Skagway.
YA/MACDONALD COLL., 78/115, PHO 98.

79. "Gagoff Hanged This Morning."
THE WHITEHORSE STAR, 90TH ANNIVERSARY EDITION, 16 JUNE 1990.

79. Cst. York guards two prisoners of war.
GLENBOW ARCHIVES/NA 1663-22.

80. Constable Tom Dickson.
RICHARD A. DICKSON COLL.

80. Louise Dickson and children.
RICHARD A. DICKSON COLL.

81. Hootalinqua.
© RCMP-GRC 7425

81. Big Salmon NWMP Post.
YA/PARKS CANADA, 82/269, 16.

81. Claude Tidd at Ross River detachment.
YA 7548/TIDD COLL.

81. The Five Finger detachment.
GLENBOW ARCHIVES/NA-2595-2.

5. First Nations people and the police

82. On patrol near Rampart House.
YA/FYFE COLL., 86/42, 65.

84. A social evening.
YA/THORNTHWAITE COLL., 83/22-1, PHO 219, ALBUM 1, P. 38, 237.

85. Cpl. Rudd with the Nantuck brothers.
YA 807/NATIONAL MUSEUM COLL., J6186.

87. Alfred and Maggie Hunter.
YA 6859/HARE COLL.

88. Louis Cardinal at Fort McPherson.
HUDSON'S BAY COMPANY ARCHIVES/ PROVINCIAL ARCHIVES OF MANITOBA, 1987/ 363-R-34/3.

89. John Martin.
YA 7387/TIDD COLL.

90. John Moses and his family.
YA/THORNTHWAITE COLL., 83/22, PHO 219, ALBUM 4, P. 10, 47.

90. John Moses with his son Roy.
YA/THORNTHWAITE COLL., 83/22, PHO 219, ALBUM 4, P. 10, 1388.

91. Andrew Tizya and friends.
GLADYS NETRO PHOTO

92. Charlie Peter Charlie.
YUKON NEWS PHOTO

93. Billy Fox.
MABEL JOHNSON COLL.

93. Herschel Island detachment.
DEREK PARKES COLL.

93. Mountie and special constable.
YA/MYERS COLL., 93/142, 145.

6. Crime, conspiracy and court

94. Judge Macaulay and court members.
YA/THORNTHWAITE COLL., 83/22, PHO 220, ALBUM 5, P. 6, 1359.

96. Remolo Cesari.
GLENBOW ARCHIVES/NA-1663-23.

97. The Whitehorse waterfront.
YA 4075/MACBRIDE MUSEUM COLL.

98. Diagram of Cesari's escape attempt.
NAC, RG 18, VOL. 3253, F. 1914-HQ681-G-1.

98. Cst. W.L. Pritchett.
GLENBOW ARCHIVES/NA-1663-24.

99. Detective Billy Welsh.
TAKEN FROM NAC/C-43235

100. Supt. A.E. Snyder, 1910.
YA 6347/DAWSON CITY MUSEUM COLL.

100, 101. Newspaper excerpts.
NAC/C100784, FROM RG 18, VOL. 229, F. 149-1902.

101. Skagway Grand Seal.
NAC/C 100783, FROM RG 18, VOL. 229, F. 149-1902.

102. Insp. D.M. Howard and "Ikey."
© RCMP-GRC 2026.

103. Herschel Island detachment, 1923.
YA 9242/PASLEY COLL.

7. Women and the force

104. Tannis Strickland and her son.
YA/STRICKLAND COLL., 88/139, 6.

104. Frances Wood hammers the "Last Spike."
YA 4116/MACBRIDE MUSEUM COLL.

106. Buster Strickland and Stuart Wood.
YA/STRICKLAND COLL., 88/139, 9.

106. Tannis Strickland holding Buster.
YA/STRICKLAND COLL., 88/139,17.

107. A tender scene at Forty Mile.
YA 7461/TIDD COLL.

108. VON nurses and Faith Fenton.
B.C. ARCHIVES AND RECORDS SERVICE, VICTORIA, B.C./G 1132.

109. Miss Scott and Mrs. Starnes.
© RCMP-GRC 2397-1.

109. Faith Fenton Brown.
GLENBOW ARCHIVES/NA-2883-28.

110. The Thornthwaite's kitchen.
YA/THORNTHWAITE COLLECTION, 83/22,
PHO 219, ALBUM 4, P. 7, 128.

110. NWMP wife.
PAA/B2194

111. Laundry day.
YA 8533/TIDD COLL.

112. Mary Tidd gardening.
YA 7959/TIDD COLL.

112. Ross River RCMP Post.
YA 7960/TIDD COLL.

112. The Tidds' weekly bath.
YA 7942/TIDD COLL.

113. Clara May going caribou hunting.
NANCY POPE COLL.

113. Clara and Sid May at Rampart House.
NANCY POPE COLL.

113. Clara "Dixie" Dickinson.
NANCY POPE COLL.

114. Martha Cameron driving tractor.
YA/VAN BIBBER COLL., 79/2,128.

114. The Camerons' wedding photo.
YA/THORNTHWAITE COLL., 83/22, PHO 219,
ALBUM 1, P. 11, 240.

115. Minnie and George Kirk.
ELOISE WATT COLL.

115. George and Minnie Kirk with daughter
Eloise.
YA 8262/TIDD COLL.

116. Gold inspector Kate Ryan.
KATHERINE MCKERNAN COLL.

116. Kate Ryan.
KATHERINE MCKERNAN COLL.

117. Supt., Mrs. and Dorothy Allard.
YA/ALLARD COLL., 82/402, 2.

117. RCMP Constable in winter patrol
clothing.
YA/ALLARD COLL., 82/402, 77.

118. Portrait of Anna DeGraf.
ROGER BROWN COLL.

119. Kitty Saguak.
DEREK PARKES COLL.

119. A festive dinner party in Old Crow.
YA/FOSTER COLL., 82/415, 278.

119. Beaded hanging.
YA/THORNTHWAITE COLL., 83/22-1, PHO
220, ALBUM 5, P. 2, 343.

8. Patrolling the Yukon

120. On dog team patrol, ca. 1895.
YA 9409/STRICKLAND COLL.

122. NWMP at Fort McPherson.
HUDSON'S BAY CO. ARCHIVES/PROVINCIAL
ARCHIVES OF MANITOBA, 1987/363-R-34/
33.

122. Sod huts at Herschel Is.
© RCMP-GRC 4071-15.

122. RCMP detachment at Herschel Island.
© RCMP-GRC 2257/CAULKIN COLL.

123. Herschel Island, ca. 1923.
YA 9243/PASLEY COLL.

123. Inuit schooners.
YA/FINNIE COLLECTION, 81/21, PHO 141,
10.

124. Dempster patrol leaving Dawson.
YA 3789/ MACBRIDE MUSEUM COLL.

124. Dempster's patrol at Fort McPherson.
YA/MYERS COLLECTION, 93/142, 161.

125. Cpl. Dempster shortly after his return.
YA/ANGLICAN CHURCH COLL., 86/81-2, PHO
383, 1979.

125. Return of Dempster.
YA/FYFE COLL., 86/42, 61.

125. RNWMP guide Charles Stewart.
YA/FYFE COLL., 86/42, 42.

126. Insp. F. J. Fitzgerald.
© RCMP-GRC 2394.

127. Insp. W. J. D. Dempster.
YA/ANGLICAN CHURCH COLL., 86/81-2, PHO
383, 1961.

128. First Nations people at Rampart House.
YA/FYFE COLLECTION, 86/42, PHO 311, 13.

128. Fur shipment.
NAC/PA44616.

128. Cst. Young, Joanne Cadzow and Cpl.
Thornthwaite.
YA/THORNTHWAITE COLL., 83/22, PHO 219,
ALBUM 3, P. 9, 244.

129. Old Crow RCMP detachment.
YA/THORNTHWAITE COLL., 83/22, PHO 220,
ALBUM 5, P. 19, 96-2.

129. Power sawing logs.
YA/THORNTHWAITE COLLECTION, 83/22,
PHO 219, ALBUM 3, P. 24, 136.

129. Building RCMP detachment.
YA/THORNTHWAITE COLL., 83/22, PHO 219,
ALBUM 4, P. 6, 311.

130. Claude Tidd.
YA 7591/TIDD COLL.

131. Portrait of a "Mad Trapper."
GLENBOW ARCHIVES

131. Cst. Edgar Millen.
GLENBOW ARCHIVES/NA-1685-3.

132. Cst. Alfred "Buns" King.
© RCMP-GRC

132. Peter Alexis.
YA/THORNTHWAITE COLL., 83/22, PHO 220,
ALBUM 5, P. 40, 1319.

133. John Moses and children.
YA/THORNTHWAITE COLL., 83/22, PHO 220,
ALBUM 6, P. 13, 1415.

133. Sid May on patrol.
NANCY POPE COLL.

134. A.B. Thornthwaite.
YA/THORNTHWAITE COLL., 83/22, PHO 219,
ALBUM 3, P. 24, 103.

135. RCMP sled dogs.
RCMP MUSEUM, REGINA, SASK./72.73.7

135. RCMP plane, Norseman CF-MPF.
YA/PEPPER COLL., 89/59, 24.

136. Filling boat motor.
GLENBOW ARCHIVES/NA-3622-26.

136. Corp. Clemmitt on the S.S. Yukon.
GLENBOW ARCHIVES/NA-3622-27.

136. Corp. Clemmitt at Fairbanks.
GLENBOW ARCHIVES/NA-3622-28.

136. Csts. Buck Coleman and Alfred R. King.
GLENBOW ARCHIVES/THORNTHWAITE
COLL., NA-4335-12.

137. Mountie leaving Forty Mile.
YA 8478/TIDD COLL.

137. Patrolling by horse-drawn buckboard.
YA 2345/HUNSTON COLL.

137. RCMP car in front of Mayo detachment.
YA 8482/ TIDD COLL.

138. The Gladys at Carcross.
YA 2431/ANCHORAGE FINE ARTS MUSEUM
COLL.

138. NWMP steamer Vidette.
© RCMP-GRC 2020.

139. St. Roch frozen in for winter.
GLENBOW ARCHIVES/NA-2821-8.

139. The St. Roch leaving Halifax.
YA/WHITEHORSE STAR COLL., 82/563-1,
PHO 203.

9. At ease

140. NWMP Band, ca. 1900.
RCMP MUSEUM, REGINA, SASK., 86.104.5

142. Two members relaxing.
YA 804/NATIONAL MUSEUM COLL., J6243.

142. 1904 RNWMP Christmas menu.
YA/ SHUCKBURGH COLL., 77/61, PHO 77.

143. Andrew Cruickshank and Claude Tidd.
YA 7611/TIDD COLL.

143. Benefit concert at Palace Grand.
GLENBOW ARCHIVES/NA-2883-6.

144. RNWMP detachment at Carmacks.
GLENBOW ARCHIVES/NA 4335-1.

144. Two Mounties relaxing.
PAA/B2063

144. Strumming a mandolin.
YA/SENKLER COLL., 86/87, 81.

145. Whitehorse reading room.
GLENBOW ARCHIVES/NA-1663-12.

145. Celebrating the solstice.
NAC/C63157, KEIR COLL.

146. Clowning around on the job.
YA/MYERS COLL., 93/142, 127.

147. Fancy dress hockey.
PAA/B2160.

147. Playing hockey in Dawson.
NAC/ C59776/KEIR COLL.

148. Scarth's farewell dinner, 1901.
YA/SENKLER COLL., 86/87, 89.

148. Outside Officers' Mess, "B" Division.
YA/SENKLER COLL., 86/87, 105.

149. The Tidds' Christmas card.
YA 7704/TIDD COLL.

149. Menu cover.
YA/JONES COLL., 78/16, PHO 81.

149. Christmas tree.
YA/THORNTHWAITE COLL., 83/22, PHO 219,
ALBUM 3, P. 16, 262.

10. Wartime and Alaska Highway construction

150. Opening of the Alaska Highway.
YA/ANGLICAN CHURCH COLL., 86/61-2, L5.

152. Alaska Highway checkstop.
© RCMP-GRC 2452.

153. Whitehorse detachment, ca. 1940s.
YA, WADDINGTON COLL., 82/331, 55.

153. View of Whitehorse.
BILL PRINGLE COLL.

153. Parading in downtown Whitehorse.
YA/HALL COLL., 81/150,14.

154. Insp. Steinhauer.
YA/HALL COLL., 81/150, 59.

155. Liquor store line-up.
YA/FINNIE COLL., 81/21, PHO 142, 290-8.

155. Mountie in Whitehorse office.
YA/HALL COLL., 81/150, 61.

156. Teslin RCMP detachment.
YA 7296/TIDD COLL.

156. Barging fuel on Teslin Lake.
YA/PEPPER COLL., 89/59, 10.

156. U.S. Army 302nd Engineers.
GLENBOW ARCHIVES/NA-3622-43.

157. Teslin residents.
YA/JOHNSON COLL., 82/428, 37.

157. Corp. J. Pearson Clemmitt.
GLENBOW ARCHIVES/NA-3622-39.

158. Cam Cameron leaving on patrol.
YA/KIRK COLL., 89/83, 7.

158. Funeral at Fort Selkirk.
YA/KIRK COLL., 89/83, 15.

159. Railway survey crew.
YA/ ANGLICAN CHURCH COLL., 89/41, PHO
380, 1329.

159. Moving Minto detachment buildings.
YA/BATES COLL., 89/40, 7.

159. View of Selkirk.
YA/KIRK COLL., 89/83, 44.

160. The Cameron family.
YA 8743/BOBILLIER COLL.

160. Moving day at Selkirk.
YA/HALL COLL., 81/150, 32.

161. G.I. Cameron, 1994.
YUKON NEWS PHOTO.

161. Rafting into Selkirk.
YA/ ANGLICAN CHURCH COLL., 89/41, PHO
381,1564.

11. Dog stories

162. Andrew Cruickshank.
YA 8377/TIDD COLL.

164. Drawing of Mark and Luke.
RCMP MUSEUM, REGINA, SASK./34.15.23.

164. Harper's party on Islander.
MMCA/NPA/MP 114/79 (8).

165. Pack dog.
YA/ALLARD COLL., 84/402, 103.

165. Dog team near Rampart House.
GLENBOW MUSEUM/NA-4335-8.

166. Stampeder and his Labs.
YA 2324/WINTER AND POND COLL.

167. Labrador dog team.
YA 261/VOGEE COLL.

168. Cst. Chartrand and his lead dog.
DEREK PARKES COLL.

169. Nikki descendents.
© RCMP-GRC 69-272 (H).

170. Minnie Kirk and friend.
ELOISE WATT COLL.

170. Cst. Warren Townsend and team.
© RCMP-GRC 69-313 (A).

171. Andrew Kunizzi.
YA/ANGLICAN CHURCH COLL., 86/61-2, C9.

171. Arrival commemorative dogsled runs.
YA/ANGLICAN CHURCH COLL., 86/61-2, C10.

171. S/Cst. Peter Benjamin.
© RCMP-GRC 69-272 (E).

12. Policing today

172. S/Sgt. G. Anderson and Sgt. R. Aberson.
RCMP/"M" DIVISION.

174. Yukon member visits Otter Falls.
© RCMP-GRC.

174. Csts. Terry Johnson and Karen Olito.
YUKON GOVERNMENT PHOTO

175. Jim Robb painting.
© JIM ROBB, 1990. NICK VERES COLL.

175. Whse. RCMP detachment building.
YHMA COLL.

176. Jail cells in the old Whse. detachment.
NICK VERES COLL.

176. Cst. Majorie McLeod.
YUKON NEWS PHOTO.

177. Whitehorse detachment and Sub-
division.
NICK VERES COLL.

177. "M" Division building.
RCMP/"M" DIVISION.

178. Cpl. Dan Fudge.
WHITEHORSE STAR PHOTO.

178. Cpl. Phil Warren in the forensics lab.
YUKON NEWS PHOTO.

179. Headlines.
WHITEHORSE STAR.

180. The Safety Bear.
RCMP/"M" DIVISION.

180. Student police in Rotary Peace Park.
RCMP/"M" DIVISION.

180. Students on bicycle patrol.
RCMP/"M" DIVISION.

181. Auxiliary constable Jim Kenyon.
YUKON NEWS PHOTO.

181. Auxiliary constable Kelly Shopland.
YUKON NEWS PHOTO.

181. Transfer of Command Parade.
RCMP/"M" DIVISION.

182. Arson investigation by plane.
RCMP/"M" DIVISION.

182. Twin Otter pilot Sgt. Chris Olson.
RCMP/"M" DIVISION.

182. Cst. Patrick Egan giving a ticket.
RCMP/"M" DIVISION.

182. Cst. Doug Aird and friends.
KAY SEXSMITH PHOTO.

183. Sgt. Doug Harris and Cst. Pat Maloney.
RCMP/"M" DIVISION.

183. Aboard the S.S. Klondike.
RCMP/"M" DIVISION.

Honour roll

184. Unveiling the Lost Patrol monument.
YA 7062/TIDD COLL.

184. Plaque on Lost Patrol monument.
YA 8358/TIDD COLL.

184. Funeral parade, Dawson City.
GLENBOW ARCHIVES/NA-1663-26.

185. Funeral parade inspection.
YA/CREARY COLL., 82/339, 14.

185. RCMP cemetery, Dawson City.
NAC/C1325.

Index

Abel, Johnny, 170
Abel, Sarah, 91
Aberdeen, Lady, 108
Aberson, Sgt. R., 172, 181
Acland, Insp. A.E., 74, 76, 97-98
Acland, Margaret, 76
Adami, Annabelle, 160
Adami, Oscar, 114
Adney, Tappan, 50, 164
air travel, 111, 114, 131, 133, 135-136, 152-153, 158, 172-173, 176, 179, 184
Aird, Cst. D., 182
Aishihik Lake, 175
Aklavik Sub-division, 92, 139
Aklavik, NWT, 89, 92, 103, 131-133, 168
Alaska, 75
Alaska, 13-14, 16, 18, 25, 28, 153
Alaska Commercial Co., 13, 52
Alaska Highway, 135, 150-161, 174-175, 178
Alaska State Troopers, 180
Albrecht, S/Cst., 39
Alexis, Peter, 132
Alikomiak, 103
Allard, Supt. A.B. and family, 117
Allen, Cpl. R., 181
Allmand, Hon. Warren, 176
Anderson, Col., 28
Anderson, Sgt., 144
Anderson, Cst. A., 177
Anderson, S/Sgt. G., 172
Anglian, 60
Annand, Cst. W.J.D., 185
Arctic Red River, NWT, 131-132, 170
Asbil, Cpl. R.W., 185
Athabasca Landing, Alta., 123
Atlin, BC, 112, 130, 138, 174, 179
automobiles, 137, 154-157, 174, 176
auxiliary police program, 180-181
Aveadluk, 117

Bacon, Bill, 169
Bacon, Virginia, 169
Bank of British North America, 61
Barley, H.C., 44, 70, 76
Beaufort Sea, 169
Beaver Creek, 150
Beaver Creek, det., 174
Belcher, Insp. R., 30-31, 33, 67
Bell, Insp. A.L., 75, 79
Bell, dog driver, 39
Bell River, 131
Beluga, 121
Benjamin, Martha Frost, 119
Benjamin, S/Cst. P., 91-92, 170-171
Bennet, Capt., 62
Bennett, 24, 28, 30, 39-40, 62, 167
Bennett Lake, 14, 24, 32, 42, 182
Bennett Lake and Klondyke Navigation Co., 44
Bennett, det., 33, 36, 127
Bernard, Joe, 132
Bertrand, Cst. C., 182
Big Chute pass, 170
Big Salmon, 75
Big Salmon, det., front, 81
Black, George, 128, 154
Black, Martha, 65
Blackstone River, 89, 124
Blueberry, BC, 155
boats, see vessels
Boer War, 23, 35, 38, 102, 123, 126, 143
Bokovitch, Tom, 79
Boleen, Cpl. B., 181
Bompas, Bishop Wm., 14, 15
Bonanza Creek (see also Rabbit Creek), 48, 50, 52, 66-67, 97
Bonanza Det., see Grand Forks det.
Bonnifield Saloon, 67
Borden, Sir Robert, 65
Brady, Gov., 28
Brimston, Sheriff Geo., 79
Brine, Cst. L., 181
Brother, Cst., 18
Brown, S/Sgt. C., 14-15
Brown, Cst., 18
Brown, E.B., 33, 36, 74-75
Bryde, A., 93
Buday, Cst. M., 179, 185
Burnett, Insp. J.F., 167
Burnett, T.C., 44
Burstall, Capt., 109
Burwash Landing, 80
Butterworth-Carr, Cst. B., 183

C.H. Hamilton, 22
Cadzow, Joanne, 128
Cadzow, Julia, 117
Cairns, S/Sgt. J., 181
Cambridge Bay, NWT, 168
Cameron, Cpl. G.I., 114, 158-161, 181
Cameron, Ione (Christensen), 114, 160
Cameron, Martha Ballentine, 111, 114, 160
Camp Victoria, 60
Campbell, Cst. N.M., 185
Canadian Bank of Commerce, 57, 61, 148
Canadian Development Co., 39
Canadian government, 12-15, 18, 21, 28, 50, 62, 65, 77-78, 84, 100-101, 103, 123, 139, 153, 169, 176, 183
Canadian Light Infantry, 78
Canadian Magazine, 170
Canadian Pacific Railway, 62, 166
Canol Pipeline Project, 135, 150, 152-153, 158
canteen, 71, 143
Canyon and Whitehorse Rapids Tramway, 42-44
Canyon City, 24, 36, 42-43, 70
Carcross, 138, 172, 175
Carcross, det., 72, 80, 87
Cardinal, Fred, 88
Cardinal, Louis, 88
Caribou, det., front, 127
Carmack, George, 21
Carmacks, front, 159, 172, 184-185
Carmacks, det., 144
Carroll, Rev. Des, 181
Carter, S/Cst. S., 124-125, 184-185
Casca, 75
Centennial, RCMP Yukon, front, 161, 174, 183
Cesari, Remolo, 96-98
Chamberlin, Cst. R.G., 100
Champagne, det., 172
Charlie, Alfred, 170
Charlie, Charlie Peter, 91-92
Charlton, Dr., 97
Charman, Frank, 32
Chartrand, Cst. A.J., cover, 93, 131-133, 168
Chilkat, 14
Chilkat First Nation, 14, 28, 84
Chilkat Pass, 28
Chilkoot (Pass, Summit, Trail), 14, 18, 24-25, 27, 28, 30-31, 33, 36, 50, 84, 88, 101, 118
Chilkoot, det., 27-28, 30-31, 36, 88
Chisholm, Thomas, 99
Christensen, Cst. V., 68
Christiansen, S/Cst., 39
Christmas Creek, 89
Churchill, Cst., 18
Chute Creek, 171
Circle, Alaska, 15, 20, 51, 61, 90, 100, 118, 158
Clark, Joseph Andrew, 99
Clarke, Dr., 79
Clemmitt, Cpl. J. P., 136, 157
clothing, 21, 84, 87, 105, 113, 117-118, 151
Code, Walter Roderick, 179
Coleman, Cst. B., 136
Commodore, Margaret, 181
Conrad, det., 76
Conrod, Cst. D., 181
Constantine, Supt. C., 14-16, 18-22, 25, 50-51, 84, 106, 117, 122-123, 164, 183
Constantine, Cst. C.P., 167
Constantine, Francis, 17-18, 106
Constantine, Henrietta Armstrong, 18, 106
Cook, Bella, 114
Coppermine, NWT, 131-132, 168
Corcoran, Gr., 61
Cory, L.T., 103
Cosby, Insp F.L., 148
Coulter, S., 79
court, 20-21, 36, 44, 84-85, 92, 95, 97, 103
Cowan, Richard, 148
Cowie, James, 44
Coyote Air Services, 179
Craig, Cst., 77
Craig, Justice, 97, 99
Crater Lake, 30-31
crime, 20, 25, 35-36, 44, 50-51, 55, 68-69, 77, 79-80, 85, 90, 95-97, 99, 103, 120-121, 131-133, 136, 152, 154, 156-157, 174-175, 178-181
Crow Flats, 92
Cruickshank, Andrew, 143, 162
Curtis, Asahel, 26
customs, 12, 14-15, 20-21, 27-28, 30-33, 36, 38-39, 41, 64-65, 122, 128
Cutch, 167
Cyr, Corinne, 157

Dalton Post, det., front, 76, 127
Dalton Trail, 28, 81, 86, 95, 100
Dalton Trail Post, 86
Davis, Marion, 75
Dawson, 75
Dawson City, front, 21-22, 24-26, 35-36, 39, 42, 44, 48-49, 50-55, 57-58, 60-63, 65-67, 71-72, 74-76, 81, 85-91, 93, 95-98, 100-102, 106, 108-109, 112-114, 116-118, 120, 122-125, 127-131, 134, 136, 140-145, 147-150, 153-155, 158-160, 165-166, 171-172, 174-175, 183-185
Dawson Creek, BC, 150, 152, 155
Dawson Daily News, 89
Dawson town station, det., 35, 54
Dawson, George, 13-14, 52
Deer, S/Sgt. A., 177
DeGraf, Anna, 118
Dempster Highway, 127, 175
Dempster, Insp. W.J.D., 92, 124-125, 127-128
Dennison, Dennis, 179
detectives, 55, 68, 99
DEW Line, 91
Dewey Hotel, 69
Dickson, Adam, 80
Dickson, Andrew, 80
Dickson, Buck, 80
Dickson, George, 80
Dickson, Grace (Chambers), 80
Dickson, Kluane (Hash), 80
Dickson, Louise, 80
Dickson, Sue (Van Bibber), 80
Dickson, Cst. Thomas A., 80, 84
Division, "Air", 135, 173
Division, "B", 36, 52, 72, 78, 81, 148-149
Division, "G", 38, 169, 174, 176-177
Division, "H", 36, 41, 70-73, 81, 100
Division, "M", 174-177
Dixon, Cst. E.A., 42-45
Doak, Cpl. W.A., 103
Doctor Scottie, 86
dog drivers, 84, 86-88,164-168
dogs, 20, 39, 41, 51, 61, 66-67, 87-88, 90-92, 110, 112, 115, 121, 123, 127, 131-135, 139, 142, 154, 156-158, 162-171, 174, 176, 179, 181, 183
Dominion Saloon, 55
Doody, J., 124, 125, 138
Driftwood River, 171
Drury, Wm., 79
Dubuc, Judge Lucien, 103
Due South, front
Dyea, Alaska, 14, 16, 24, 26, 28, 84

Eagle River, 131, 133
Eagle, Alaska, 100
Eames, Insp., 132
Earl of Aberdeen, 58
Edmonton, Alta., 103, 122-123, 126, 131, 150, 155, 175
Egan, Cst. P., 181-182
Eldorado Creek, 48, 50, 66-67
Eldorado Hotel, 67
Ellingson, Maynard, 171
Ellis, hangman, 79
Enfield, Gr., 61
Engel, Sgt., cover, 18-19
epidemics, 40, 51, 60-61, 76, 84, 108, 112, 122, 128, 152, 156-157
Erickson, Cpl. B., 179
Eskimos, see Inuit
Eureka Creek, 50
Eureka, det., front
Evans, Cst., 170
Evans, Lt. Col. T.D.B., 58
Evening Journal (Ottawa), 100
Excelsior, 17-18

Fairbanks, Alaska, 136, 150, 152
Falkingham, Cst. R., 177
Faro, 172, 175
Fawcett, Thomas, 50
Fendrick, S/Sgt. R., 177
Fenton, Faith, 58-59, 108-109
Fiftymile River, 74
fingerprinting, 99, 179
fires, 51, 54, 61, 67, 129
First Nations people (see also Chilkat First Nation, Han First Nation, Northern Tutchone First Nation, Teslin Tlingit First Nation, Selkirk First Nation, Vuntut Gwichin First Nation), 12, 14-15, 21, 28, 30, 39-40, 74-75, 80, 82-93, 110-111, 117, 122, 124-125, 128, 130, 152, 157, 164, 174, 176
Firth River, 92
Firth, Herb, 170
Fitzgerald, Insp. F.J., 84, 88, 110, 122-126, 184-185
Fitzgerald, Cst. M.J., 184-185
Five Finger Rapids, 60, 72, 81
Five Finger, det., 36, 81
Fort Constantine, 19-21, 23, 52, 106, 121, 164
Fort Cudahy, 14, 18, 20-21
Fort Good Hope, NWT, 103
Fort Herchmer, 25, 48-49, 52-53, 56, 108, 149
Fort McPherson, NWT, front, 76, 88-89, 91, 102, 122-125, 127, 129, 131, 165, 170-171, 183, 185
Fort Norman, NWT, 103, 131, 169
Fort Selkirk, see Selkirk
Fort St. John, B.C., 22, 150
Fort Yukon, Alaska, 51, 110, 112-113, 115, 119, 128, 134
Forty Mile, community, front, 13-16, 18, 21, 24, 84, 130, 137, 158, 172, 183
Forty Mile, det., 64-65, 107, 127, 130
Fortymile River, 13-14, 21, 38, 84
Fox, S/Cst., 129
Fox, Billy, 93
Fox, Christian, 85
Frances, Joseph, 115
Fraser, Supt., 92, 169
Freese, H., 44
Frost, Albert, 119
Frost, Bertha, 119
Frost, Betty, 119
Frost, Clara, 119
Frost, Donald, 119
Frost, Gordon, 119
Frost, Harold "Jack", 84, 119
Frost, Stephen, 119, 171
Fudge, Cpl. Dan, 178
Fyfe, Cst., 67
Fyfe, Cst. J.F., 124-125, 128

Gabb, Cst. K., 177
Gagoff, Alex, 79
Galpin, Cst. J., 122
Ganley, George, 96-97
Gardlund, 132-133
Geological Survey of Canada, 52
George, Esau, 124-125
Gilholme, Cpl. B., 177
Gilholme, Chief Supt. J.R., 181
Gilmour, Cpl. C., 177
Giswold, Allyn, 179
Glacier Creek, 20
Gladys, 138
Glenbow Museum, 119
Glenora, B.C., front, 58, 60
Globe (Toronto), 58, 108
Godwalt, Cst. J., 177
Goetzman, 57
Gold Bottom Creek, 48, 50
Gold Hill Hotel, 67
gold export tax, 67, 101, 116
gold inspectors, 105, 116
gold royalties, 67, 100-101
Gold Run Creek, 48, 50
gold rush, see Klondike gold rush, mining
Gold Star, 61, 108
Good Samaritan Hospital, 60, 108
Gould, John, 171
Gowler, Cst., 18-19
Grand Forks, front, 48, 66-69
Grand Forks Hotel, 67
Grand Forks, det., 66-67, 127
Gregory, J.U., 166
Grehl, Herbert, 100
Grey, Lce. Cpl., 59
Griffin, Cst. M., 181
Grimstead, George, 160
Guggenheim Bros., 67
Guide (Skagway), 100
guides, 84, 86-93, 123, 125, 139, 157, 164, 170-171
Haddock, Cpl. A.G., 185
Haines Junction, 150, 172-173
Halfway, det., front, 127
Hall, Cst. L., 159, 175
Hamacher, E.J., 70
Hamel, Father Charles, 150
Hamilton, Cst. B., 177
Hamilton, C.H., 14
Han First Nation, 117
Hanna, Rachel, 108
Hanna, Cpl. W.H., 155
Harbottle, F.E., 79
Harper, Arthur, 14
Harper, Insp. F., 50, 52, 66, 164
Harris, Sgt. D., 181, 183
Hart River, 89, 124
Hayes, Cst., 98
Hayes, Sgt. J., 177
Hayne, S/Sgt. M.H.E., 18-20, 23, 56, 164
Healy, John J., 14
Heathcote, Cst. S.G., 185
Hébert, Ignace Jr., 166-167
Hegg, E.A., 26, 27, 28, 51, 66
Henderson, Chief Supt. E., 181
Henry, Annie, 91
Henry, Father Gustav, 168
Hepburn, John, 43
Herchmer, Comm. L.W., 15, 21, 52, 56, 106, 126
Herman, Sgt. J., 181
Hermanson, Cst. H., 181
Herschel Island, front, 88-89, 91-93, 95, 102-103, 110, 117, 119, 122-125, 129, 139, 168-169, 185
Herschel Island, det., 121-123, 139, 168-169, 185
Hersey, S/Sgt. E.F., 131, 133
Hill, John Lorrie, 136
Hodgson, Cpl. J., 177
Hollywood, 169
Honour Roll, 87, 179, 184-185
Hoochi Bill, 75
Hootalinqua, community, 39, 60, 74
Hootalinqua, det., front, 60, 74, 76, 81
horses, front, 20, 26, 30, 36-37, 73, 80, 86, 102, 121, 137, 142, 164, 166, 174, 176
Howard, Insp. D.M., 102, 148
Howard, Selina, 116
Howatt, I.B., 103
Huddle, Sgt. B., 181
Hudson's Bay Co., 12, 117, 122, 158
Huget, Supt. Al, 177
Humphries, Sgt. P., 181
Hunker Creek, front, 48, 67
Hunt, Cpl., 168
Hunter, Alfred, 87
Hunter, Maggie, 87
Hurley, Pte., 61

Indians, see First Nations people
Inkster, Cst. H., 181
international boundary commission, 14, 28, 101,
interpreters, 84, 87-88, 90, 92, 123
Inuit, 87, 95, 103, 110, 117, 122, 126, 139, 169
Inuvik, NWT, 127, 131, 175
Irvine, Cpl. S., 182
Islander, 50, 164

Jacobson, Jimmy, 103
Jacques, Cst. P., 177
Jarvis, Insp. A.M., 86, 121
Jenkins, Cst., 18
Jessie, 138
Joe, Minnie Frost, 119
Johnson's Crossing, 156
Johnson, Albert, see Mad Trapper
Johnson, S/Sgt. R., 177
Johnson, Cst. T., 174
Johnston, C.H., 79
Johnston, George, 156
Johnston, Sam, 183
Joyce, Sgt. H.G., 44
Joynt, Edith, 160
Juby, Insp. R., 181
Juneau, Alaska, 14, 16, 24

Kaskawulsh River, 86, 185
Kay, Roger, 87
Keno City, 160, 172
Kenyon, Jim, 181
Kerr, Cpl. "Jock", 153
Kessler, Cst. J., back cover
King, Cst. A., 131-133, 136
Kinney, Cst. G.F., 124, 184-185
Kirk, Eloise (Watt), 115
Kirk, Cpl. G., 91, 115, 119
Kirk, Jim, 158
Kirk, Minnie Young, 91, 111, 115, 119, 170
Kittigazuit, 89
Klondike, 160, 183
Klondike City, 21, 48, 55
Klondike gold rush, 13, 15, 21-22, 25, 28, 35, 42, 45, 50-51, 56, 58-59, 65, 73, 84, 88-89, 100, 102, 106, 118, 127, 136, 152, 164, 166, 183
Klondike goldfields, 25, 28, 36, 38, 48, 50, 52, 65-68, 80, 109, 126
Klondike River, 21, 35, 48, 52, 60, 136
Kluane (area), 35, 72, 80, 84
Kluane Lake, 151
Kluane, det., 76
Kunizzi, Andrew, cover, 171
Kunizzi, Bella, 89

Labelle-Fournier, murder case, 95
Labrador, 166
Ladue, Joe, 14, 52
Lake Laberge, 46-47, 74-75
Lamberton, Cpl. J., 181
Lamont, Cst. A., 185
Lang, 132-133
Langholz, F., 79
LaPierre House, 131, 133
Larsen, Capt. H., 139, 168
Larss & Duclos, 46-47, 55, 61
Last Patrol, 165, 170-171
Latham, Cpl. A., 181, 183
Laughland, Sgt. K.M., 185
LeBlanc, Cpl. M., 181
Lee, Arthur, 128
Lee, J.E., 72, 110
Lindbladt, 44
Lindeman, 28, 30, 33
Lindeman Lake, 42, 118
Lindeman, det., 32-33
Lindston brothers, 75
liquor, 13-14, 20, 25, 43, 55, 74-75, 84, 110, 122, 143, 147, 153-155, 157, 160
Lischy, Gunther, 179
Little Wind River, 89
Livingstone Creek, det., front, 76
Lobsinger, Bishop Thos., 181
Log Cabin, 30, 33
Lost Patrol, 89, 124-127, 184-185
Loucks, S/Cst., 39
Lousetown, 48, 55
Lower Labarge, det., front, 74-75
Lyslo, Cpl. G., 181

MacAllister, Cst. L., 177
Macaulay, Judge, 68, 94
Macaulay, Norman, 42-44
MacDonald, Cst. C., 177
Macdonald, Sir John A., 12

MacDowell, Cst. R.C., 132
MacEachern, Cpl. B., 177
machine guns, 21, 28, 100-102
Mackenzie River, 16, 22, 75, 123, 131, 150
MacLennan, A.J., 148
MacLeod, Sgt. A., 177
Macmillan River, 158
Mad Trapper, 90, 129, 131-135, 174, 179, 184-185
Maggie H., 166
mail, 14, 22, 35, 37-39, 89, 109, 112-14, 120, 123, 133, 158, 166, 170
Malcolm, Cst. P.L.A., 185
Malegana, Dora, 103
Maloney, Cst. P., 181, 183
Mapley, Cst., 67
marriage, 84, 110, 113-114, 160
Marsh Lake, 24, 36, 85
Marshall, Sgt., 66
Martin, Insp., 135
Martin, Cap, 96-97
Martin, John, 89
Martin, Richard, 89
Martin, Robert, 89
Mathewson, Insp. H.P., 154
May, Clara Dickinson, 111-113
May, Marion (Doré), 113
May, Cst. S., 90, 95, 113, 129, 133
May, Wilfred "Wop", 131
Mayo, 89, 127, 130-131, 158-159, 172, 174
Mayo, det., 112, 127, 137
McArthur, J.J., 35
McBrayne, Det. Sgt. E., 97
McClintock River, 85
McDonell, Insp. A.E.C., 87, 100, 148
McGavin, James, 75
McIlree, Ass't. Comm., 26
McInnes, Comm. W.W.B., 138
McKay, Cst. Wm. K., 74-75, 77, 98
McKellar, Cst., 18
McKinnon, Comm. Ken, 181
McLachlan, Cst. M., 185
McLauchlin, Sgt. L., 95-97
McLeod, Cst. M., 176
McLeod, Cpl. S., 185
McQuesten, det., front, 127
McQuesten, Jack, 13
McVey, Robert, 178
Meehan, William, 85
Melis, Dominic, 95-97
Melville, 132
Michael, Sgt. R., 181
Midnight Dome, Dawson City, 145
Midnight Sun, see Order of the Midnight Sun
Miles Canyon, 24, 35, 42-43, 45, 70-71
Miles Canyon/White Horse Rapids, det., 42-45
Millen, Cst. E., 131-133, 185
Miller Creek front, 14, 172
Mills, J.W., 122
miners' meetings, 13, 20
mining, 14-15, 37, 50, 55-56, 65-68, 72-73, 84, 100, 106, 111, 116, 136, 160, 175, 184
Minto, 159
Minto, det., front, 159

missionaries, 12, 14, 39, 84, 89, 110, 112, 122, 128, 159
Moodie, Supt. J.D., 75, 126
Moosehide, 87, 89, 117
Moran, Cpl. C., 181
Morris, Alexander, 12
Morris, Cst. D., 87
Moses Hill, 90
Moses, John, cover, 90-91, 129, 133
Moses, Peter, 92
Moses, Roy, cover
Mosicki, Cst. D., 177
Mount Steele, 35
Mulrooney, Belinda, 66
Munroe, Cst. S.S., 122
Murray, Cst. J., 18-19

Nadon, Comm. M., 175, 177
Nantuck brothers, 85
Nantuck, Dawson, 85
Nantuck, Frank, 85
Nantuck, Jim, 85
Nantuck, Joe, 85
Nason, Sgt. R., 181
Nasutlin, 75
National Geographic, 170
Neighbourhood Watch, 180
Nelson, Cpl. M., 181
Netro, Gladys, 91
Newbrook, Cpl. E., 18-19
Nikki, 169
Nikki, Wild Dog of the North, 169
Nisutlin Bay, 156
Nixon, Supt. H., 176
Njootli, S/Cst. T., 91
Noack, Cpl. R., 181
Nome, Ak., 159
Norman Wells, NWT, 150, 152, 169
North American Trading and Transportation Co., 14, 18, 20
Northern Tutchone First Nation, 158-159, 161
Northwest Passage, 139, 168
Northwest Staging Route, 152
nursing, 40, 58, 60, 105, 108-109, 111-112, 114, 128, 134, 157, 160, 185
NWMP band, 54, 140-142

O'Brien, George, murder case, 80, 95
O'Donnell, Sgt. A., 181
O'Neil, J.A.W., 97
Ogilvie, front, 14, 24, 185
Ogilvie, William, 14-15, 52, 100
Old Crow, 84, 87-88, 90, 92, 111, 113, 115, 119, 124, 129-131, 133-135, 165, 169, 170-172
Old Crow River, 129
Old Crow, det., 110-112, 129-130, 134, 170
Old Mayo, 87
Olito, Cst. K., cover, 174
Oliver, Albert, 88
Olson, Sgt. C., 182
Operation Gold Watch, 180
Ora, 44
Order of the Midnight Sun, 95, 100-102
Oregel, W.D., 44
Oros, Michael Eugene, 179, 185

Ottawa, Ont., 12, 14, 58, 86, 109, 123, 145, 160, 166, 174, 179
Otter Falls, 174
Owen, Kid, 66

Paddy, 86
Paré, Surg. L.A., 39-40, 70
Parent, Cst. G., 177
Parker, Cpl. E., 181-182
Parkes, Cst. D., 93, 117, 119
Pasley Bay, NWT, 168
patrols, 39, 88-89, 91-92, 114, 117, 120-139, 142, 154-158, 165, 168-171, 173-174, 176, 180-181, 183
Patterson, Cst. J.R., 66
Pauline Cove, 123
Payson, Margaret, 108
Peel River, 124-125, 131-132
Pelly Crossing, 172, 174
Pelly Crossing, det., 185
Pelly River, 158, 161
Perry, Comm. A.B., 15, 22, 37, 40-41, 100, 102, 122
photography, 23, 77, 130, 134, 142, 161
Pinkerton, Cst., 18
Pleasant Camp, front, 30
Pleine, Father, 92
Pond Inlet, NWT, 103
Poolachoff, Cst. S., 181
Poole Construction, 175
Porcupine River, 124, 128, 129
Portland, 56
Portus B. Weare, 23, 56
Powell, Georgina, 108-109
Powell, Cpl. J., 181
Preston, Sgt., front, 177
Primrose, Supt. P.C.H., 39, 54, 72, 100, 101
Prince Rupert Sub-division, 179
Pringle, Cst., 86
Pringle, Sgt., 39
Pringle, Sgt. B., 177
prison matrons, 105, 111, 116
Pritchett, Cst. W.L., 98
Profeit-LeBlanc, Louise, 91
prospectors, 13, 39, 84-85, 95, 120, 158
prostitution, 25, 35, 50, 55, 67, 143
Purchase, Cst. P., 181

Queen of the Yukon, 162

Rabbit Creek (see also Bonanza Creek), 21
railway (see also White Pass and Yukon Railway), 158-159
Rampart House, 83, 90-92, 110, 112-113, 117, 128, 130, 134, 165
Rampart House, det., 127-130, 134, 149
Rat River, NWT, 90, 131, 133, 185
Regina, Sask., 16, 18-20, 45, 56, 76, 87, 97, 100, 102, 130
Reti, Cpl. D., 87
Richards, Babe, 154
Richardson, A/Ass't. Surg., 51
Richardson, Cpl., 39
Riddle, R.F., 133
roadhouses, 66, 75
Robb, Jim, 175
Roberts, Louise, 90

Robertson-Ross, Col. P., 12
Rodgers, Cst. A., 181
Rogers, George, 183
Rogers, Walt, 183
Ross River, community, 89, 111, 158, 172, 182
Ross River, det., 81, 89, 111-112, 130
Rotary Peace Park, 180
Routledge, Insp. W.H., 53, 69, 148
Royal Canadian Artillery, 58
Royal Canadian Corps of Signals, 131, 133
Royal Canadian Dragoons, 58, 76
Royal Irish Constabulary, 12
Royal Regiment of Canadian Infantry, 58
Rudd, Cpl., 85
Rupert's Land, 12
Ryan, Katherine, cover, 116

Sachs Harbour, NWT, 170
Safety Bear, 180
Saguak (Saȟuak), Kitty, 119
Saguak (Saȟuak), Roland, 93, 119
St. Michael, Alaska, 15-18, 56, 72
St. Roch, 121, 139, 168
Scarth, Insp. W.H., 50, 52-53, 56, 148
Schneider, S/Sgt. D., 180-181
Schwatka, Frederick, 13
Scott, Amy, 108-109
Seattle, 61
Seattle Daily Times, 100-101
Seattle, Wash., 16-18, 56, 77, 100
Selkirk, front, 12, 58, 60-61, 108, 111, 114, 150, 158-161, 172
Selkirk First Nation, 60
Selkirk, det., front, 158-160
Selous, F.D., 88
Sheffield, Dave, 160
Shesley Mike, see Oros, Michael Eugene
Shopland, Kelly, 181
Shuckburgh, Cpl. Wm., 142
Sifton, Clifford, 28, 50, 100-101
Sinclair, Cst., 18
Sinclair, Mr., 148
Sittichinli, S/Cst. L., 91, 132-133
Sixty Mile, 14
Skagway Road, 175
Skagway, Alaska, 24-26, 28, 37, 39-41, 60, 62, 70, 77-78, 100-101, 150, 153, 166-167, 175
Skirving, Cpl. G.M., 122
Skookum Jim, 21, 80
Smith, Cst. B., 177
Smith, Bill, 171
Smith, Sgt. F., 181
Smith, J.P., 97
Smith, Mary, 117
Smith, Sarah Catharine, 127
Smith, Soapy, 41, 88
Snyder, Supt. A.E., 71, 100, 116, 124-125
Soluk, Cst. R., 177
South Africa, see Boer War

special constables, 39, 84, 86-87, 89-91, 93, 131, 164, 174
Spence Bay, NWT, 169-170
Spirit of St. Louis, 162
Spreadbury, Cpl., 39
Spriggs, Sgt. F.E., 103
Starnes, Comm. C., 53, 103, 108-109, 148
Starnes, Marie Sicotte, 58-59, 108-109
Steele's Scouts, 183
Steele, Supt. S.B., cover, 14, 26, 28, 30, 33-36, 41-43, 45, 51, 54, 61, 108-109, 122
Stefansson, V., 185
Steinhauer, Insp., 154
Stevens, Col., 60
Stewart Crossing, det., front
Stewart River, 158
Stewart, Al, 79
Stewart, BC, 116
Stewart, Charles, 124, 125
Stewart, det., front, 127
Stick Sam, 86-87, 185
Stikine Chief, 58
Stikine River, 58-60, 185
Stikine Trail, 59, 108-109, 116
Still, Cpl., 31
Stott, Cst., 18
Stott, James, 68
Strickland, Insp. D.E., 18-20, 30, 36-39, 42, 56, 106
Strickland, Frances Mary (Shaw), 106
Strickland, Roland "Buster", 38, 105-106
Strickland, Tannis, 18, 38, 56, 105-106
Stringer, Bishop (wife of), 119
Stringer, Bishop I.O., 128
Sundell, Cst. C.L., 185
Sutherland, Ernest, 132
Sutherland, Cst. F.D., 122-123
Sytnick, Cst. J., 177

Tagish Charlie, 21
Tagish First Nation, 80
Tagish Lake, 24, 36, 39, 80
Tagish Post, 24, 26, 36-40, 44, 70, 76, 80, 85, 105-106
Tagish River, 36-37, 70
Taku River Trail, 36
Talbot, Maj., 59
Tanana, 75
Tatamigana, 103
Taylor & Drury Co., 156
Taylor, Cst. R.O., 124, 184-185
Telegraph Creek, BC, 59, 60, 108
Telford, Cst., 18-19
territorial council, 35, 45
Teslin, 150, 156-157, 172, 178-179
Teslin Lake, 58-60, 108, 156-157, 179
Teslin River, 60, 74, 156, 158
Teslin Tlingit First Nation, 28, 84, 156-157, 183
Teslin, det., 93, 112, 156-157, 178-179
Thirtymile River, 74-75
Thistle, 156
Thompson, Cpl., 59
Thompson (interpreter), 123
Thompson, Ass't. Surg. Dr. W.E., 53, 109, 148

Thornthwaite, Cpl. A.B., 90, 110, 128-129, 134, 144, 149, 165
Thornthwaite, Helen, 110, 119, 134, 149
Thornton, Cst., 18
Three Aces, 156
Tidd, Sgt. C.B., cover, 81, 89, 107, 112, 119, 130, 142-143, 149, 165
Tidd, Mary Ryder, 111-112, 119, 130, 134, 181
Tinck, Sgt. J. A., front, 58-63
Tizya, Andrew, 91
Townsend, Cst. W., 170
trading, 12-15, 18, 20, 28, 50, 52, 84, 122, 128, 130, 156
tramways, 42-44, 97
trapping, 12, 39, 80, 95, 128, 131-132, 136, 156, 158, 161, 171, 180, 182, 185
Tree River, NWT, det., 103
Turnbull, Andy, 170
Turner, F., 124-125

U.S. Army, 91, 150-157, 175
Upper Labarge, front, 74

Van Bibber, Pat, 114
Vancouver Maritime Museum, 139
Vancouver, B.C., 16, 50, 58, 62, 127, 130, 139, 150, 160, 164, 166-167
Veres, Cst. N., 177
Verville, Noel, 133
Victoria, 41
Victorian, 62
Victorian Order of Nurses (see also nursing), 58, 60, 108-109
Vidette, 138
Vuntut Gwichin First Nation, 91, 113, 115, 123, 129, 170

Walker, Cst. R.H., 122
Wallace, 44
Walsh, Judge, 148
Walsh, Comm. J., 26, 28, 41, 81
Ward, Cst., 18
Warner, Cst. J., 179
Warnes, Mrs., 116
Warr, Pte., 59
Warren, Cpl. P., 178
Watson Lake, 150, 156-157, 172, 174
Webster, Cst., 18
Weigand, Bill, 181
Welsh, Det. W.H., 99
West Dawson, 55
West, H. Taylor, 23
Wheeler, Cst., 18
White Horse (see also Whitehorse), 24, 42-44, 44
White Horse Rapids, 26, 42-45, 97
White Horse Rapids, det., see Miles Canyon/White Horse Rapids, det.,

White Pass (Summit, Trail), 24-30, 33, 36, 38, 101, 167
White Pass and Yukon Railway, 37, 62, 70, 72, 77, 79, 97, 105, 121, 153-154
White Pass, det., front, 28, 30, 33
White River, 159, 185
White River, det., 127
White, Agnes Gruben, 117, 169
White, Frederick, 100, 166-167
Whitehorse, 75
Whitehorse, front, 28, 37, 39, 44-45, 58, 60, 65, 67, 70-77, 95-98, 100-102, 105, 110, 112, 116, 121, 130-131, 135, 142-145, 147, 150, 152-158, 172-180, 182, 185
Whitehorse Correctional Centre, 176
Whitehorse Star, 79, 177-178
Whitehorse Sub-district, 72, 76-77, 79
Whitehorse Sub-division, 152-155, 175-177
Whitehorse Town Station, det., 72, 153
Whitehorse, det., 153, 174-177
Whitehouse, Gordon, 169
Whittaker, Rev. C.E., 126
Williams, S/Sgt. G., 181
Williams, Jack, 68
Williamson, Cst., 77
Willis, Dr., 18-19, 106
women, 18, 42, 55, 58, 80, 105-119, 137, 154, 157, 174, 176, 183
Wood, Ass't. Comm. Z.T., 26, 36-37, 41, 53-54, 65, 99-100, 105-106, 116, 128, 145, 148
Wood, Insp. R., 177
Wood, Frances Augusta, 105
Wood, Comm. S.T., 41, 106
World War I, 35, 45, 65, 73, 77-79, 96
World War II, 73, 135, 152-159, 175
Wrangell, Alaska, 58, 60
Wroughton, Insp. T.A., 99, 148

York, Cst., 77, 79, 98
Young, Sgt/Maj., 59
Young, Cst. C., 128
Yukon, 136
Yukon Airways and Exploration Co., 162
Yukon Crossing det., 76
Yukon Field Force, front, 51-52, 58-63, 108-109, 142-143, 145
Yukon Field Force Band, 62, 142, 164
Yukon Gold Company, 67-68, 97
Yukon Infantry Company, 45
Yukon Motel, 178
Yukon River, 12-14, 16, 18, 20-21, 23-24, 28, 30, 39, 42, 48, 51-52, 58, 60, 62, 72, 74, 81, 91, 95-96, 100, 111, 114, 121, 126, 136, 138, 150, 153, 156, 158-159, 161, 185

Zarnowsky, 79

Helene Dobrowolsky is an author and historian living in Whitehorse.

Lost Moose, the Yukon Publishers—books from the North about the North. Write or fax for a current catalogue and price list.

58 Kluane Crescent, Whitehorse, Yukon, Canada Y1A 3G7, phone (403) 668-5076, 668-3441, fax (408) 668-6223